"Expanding his earlier defense of Pope Francis from critics who consider the pope a theological and intellectual 'lightweight,' Massimo Borghesi leads us through a very readable analysis of the neoconservative, largely American, detractors of the magisterium of Francis. It is not too surprising that the first Latin American pope, who prefers the peripheries to the centers of power, would generate resistance from the defenders of capitalism and whose vision of the church as a field hospital for sinners would be rejected by traditionalists who overly identify the faith with its moral teachings. Borghesi describes how Bergoglio's insistence on discernment charts an ecclesial course which rejects both extremes of fundamentalism and relativism."

—Bishop John Stowe, OFM Conv, Diocese of Lexington

"With this splendidly researched volume, Borghesi further establishes his place in the first rank of interpreters of the Francis papacy and the challenges it faces. Building upon his previous scholarship on the thought of Pope Francis, Borghesi here analyzes the fault lines on display in the stalwart resistance by Catholic neoconservatives and traditionalist culture warriors to the ecclesiological commitments of the first Jesuit pope. Profound insights into the tensions within twenty-first-century Catholicism jump off every page. Highly recommended for anyone seeking a deeper understanding of the forces behind contemporary struggles for the renewal of church life."

—Thomas Massaro, SJ, Professor of Moral Theology
    at Fordham University

"This is an essential book as Borghesi does not write a history of the pontificate of Pope Francis, but a genealogy of a tradition: his most influential intellectual opponents on the Rome-Washington axis. Borghesi draws a picture of the ideological, 'America first', neoconservative, and turbo-capitalist deviations in the Catholic Church in the USA since the 1980s. He thus offers an indispensable contribution to understanding a broader season in the history of Catholicism that precedes Francis's pontificate and probably will continue for a long time."

—Massimo Faggioli, Professor of Historical Theology,
    Villanova University

"If you have ever wondered why opposition to Pope Francis, especially from the United States, is so intense, look no further—but bring a spare highlighter. Laying bare the ideological corruption and political ambition of the 'theocons,' Massimo Borghesi has given us a masterly account of Francis's discernment of the church's mission to the contemporary world, and the resentment of those it dethrones. Thrilling in its breadth and depth, beautifully translated, and crammed with insights, *Catholic Discordance* is the definitive analysis of the choices and tensions the church faces in a post-Christendom world."

> —Austen Ivereigh, author of *Wounded Shepherd* and co-author
> of Pope Francis's *Let Us Dream*

Catholic Discordance

Neoconservatism vs. the Field Hospital Church of Pope Francis

Massimo Borghesi

Translated by Barry Hudock

LITURGICAL PRESS
ACADEMIC

Collegeville, Minnesota
www.litpress.org

| 1 | 2 | 3 | 4 | 5 | 6 | 7 | 8 | 9 |

Library of Congress Cataloging-in-Publication Data

Names: Borghesi, Massimo, 1951– author. | Hudock, Barry, translator.
Title: Catholic discordance : neoconservatism vs. the field hospital church of
  Pope Francis / Massimo Borghesi ; translated by Barry Hudock.
Other titles: Francesco. English
Description: Collegeville, Minnesota : Liturgical Press Academic, [2021] | In-
  cludes index. | Summary: "An analysis of the origins of today's Catholic
  neoconservative movement and its clash with the church that Francis un-
  derstands as a "field hospital" for a fragmented world"— Provided by pub-
  lisher.
Identifiers: LCCN 2021027533 (print) | LCCN 2021027534 (ebook) | ISBN
  9780814667354 (hardcover) | ISBN 9780814667361 (epub) | ISBN
  9780814667361 (pdf)
Subjects: LCSH: Francis, Pope, 1936- | Church. | Catholic Church—History—
  21st century.
Classification: LCC BX1378.7 .B66713 2021 (print) | LCC BX1378.7 (ebook) |
  DDC 282—dc23
LC record available at https://lccn.loc.gov/2021027533
LC ebook record available at https://lccn.loc.gov/2021027534

To the small group of friends
with whom I've shared some great intellectual sparring in recent years:
Lucio Brunelli, Rocco Buttiglione, Guzmán Carriquiry Lecour,
Emilce Cuda, Rodrigo Guerra López, Austen Ivereigh,
Alver Metalli, Andrea Monda, Andrea Tornielli

Contents

3. A Church That Goes Forth and a Field Hospital: The Missionary Face of the Church 213

Conclusion: Theo-populism, the United States, and the Future of the Church 253

Index of Names 265

Introduction

Beyond the Theological-Political Model: Pope Francis's "Mobile" Church

On the evening of Friday, March 27, 2020, as the COVID-19 pandemic claimed dramatically higher numbers of victims with each passing day, a scene unfolded in Rome that millions of viewers around the world who watched via live broadcast will not soon forget: a pope standing by himself before an empty and rain-beaten St. Peter's Square, praying to God for all humanity.

The silence that surrounded him was surreal. Behind the pope stood the icon of Mary as the *Salus Populi Romani*—that is, the health, or salvation, of the Roman people—ordinarily housed in the great Basilica of St. Mary Major, and the wooden crucifix of San Marcello, which, according to tradition, saved the Romans during the plague of the sixteenth century. The pope implored the Lord not to abandon the world to fear. Addressing the world, he began:

> "When evening had come" (Mk 4:35). The Gospel passage we have just heard begins like this. For weeks now it has been evening. Thick darkness has gathered over our squares, our streets and our cities; it has taken over our lives, filling everything with a deafening silence and a distressing void, that stops everything as it passes by; we feel it in the air, we notice in people's gestures, their glances give them away. We find ourselves afraid and lost. Like the disciples in the Gospel we were caught off guard by an unexpected, turbulent storm. We have realized that we are on the same boat, all of us fragile and disoriented, but at the same time important and needed, all of us called to row together, each of us in need of comforting

the other. On this boat . . . are all of us. Just like those disciples, who spoke anxiously with one voice, saying "We are perishing" (v. 38), so we too have realized that we cannot go on thinking of ourselves, but only together can we do this.[1]

Images of the "lonely" pope standing in a deserted St. Peter's Square circulated immediately around the world. More than any possible description, they made clear the tragedy of humanity bent low by the epidemic. As the Italian professor of political science Alessandro Campi wrote,

Images of Pope Francis celebrating Mass alone, in a dark, desolate, and rain-battered St. Peter's Square, were broadcast everywhere. To some it seemed like the withdrawal of faith and organized religion from the world—a fact so unprecedented and grandiose as to exacerbate the universal bewilderment that held sway, and not only of believers. But in those images, which are indeed disconcerting, many have instead seen a message of hope, a powerful signal. In a world deeply touched by secularization, rendered almost spiritually sterile by it, and incapable of guaranteeing a peaceful pluralism of beliefs marked by a secular and enlightened tolerance, the solitary figure of the pontiff praying for the well-being of all has suggested more encouraging thoughts: on the one hand, the redemption of religious culture over secular culture (which, in the face of the ultimate drama of death, fails to offer any consolation); on the other, an invitation to community and sharing, addressed to the world and widely accepted by it, beyond the diversity of faiths and beliefs.[2]

The pope's gesture was powerful and is surely, in terms of symbolism, one of the most significant moments of his pontificate, destined to remain etched in memory. Nonetheless, that solitude was given a totally different meaning by some commentators. These others saw the pope's solitude in that moment as an expression of his distance from the church and from the world, the end of his pontificate, now devoid of momentum, his

---

1. Pope Francis, "Extraordinary Moment of Prayer Presided over by Pope Francis," March 27, 2020, http://www.vatican.va/content/francesco/en/homilies/2020/documents/papa-francesco_20200327_omelia-epidemia.html. All URLs provided in this book were accessed in May 2021.

2. Alessandro Campi, "Nulla sarà come prima?," introduction to Campi, ed., *Come la pandemia può cambiare la politica, l'economia, la comunicazione e le relazioni internazionali* (Soveria Mannelli: Rubbettino, 2020), 14.

utopian plan to reform the church interrupted. This was the interpretation offered with obvious satisfaction by the historian Roberto de Mattei, president of the Lepanto Foundation, managing editor of *Corrispondenza Romano,* and disciple of Plinio Corrêa de Oliveira, the Brazilian traditionalist founder of the organization Tradition, Family and Property. "St. Peter's Square," de Mattei wrote, "was empty, and neither the television images of Pope Francis nor his books and interviews attract public interest anymore. The coronavirus is the *coup de grace* to his pontificate, already in crisis. Whatever the origin of the virus, this has been one of its main consequences. To use a metaphor, Francis's pontificate seems to me clinically dead."[3]

While this judgment is unsurprising coming from de Mattei, author of a popular anti–Vatican II book, perhaps more surprising is that of Alberto Melloni, a highly regarded church historian. In an August 2020 article titled "The Beginning of the End of Francis's Pontificate," Melloni wrote,

> For Francis, the symbolic turning point was the dramatic icon of the *papa solus,* facing an empty world on the rainy evening during COVID-19. . . . With that display of his institutional solitude in March, the final phase of this papacy began, a phase that could last ten years or more; and in the eyes of history, it will make the resignation of Benedict XVI stand out even more. The final phase of a pontificate is not about the pope mattering less or losing power; it is simply the moment when the future of the church (and of the conclave) passes definitively to the invisible and global body of the church, which has not yet decided whether Francis's apostolic vigor should become a Christian style or whether it is better to rest in mediocrity and nostalgia.[4]

The significant thing about Melloni's article is that he never clearly states the reasons for the supposed decline. And yet they are intuitive, and they document the dissatisfaction of a certain progressive faction, both Catholic and secular, toward the pontificate. "A growing tension around the pontificate

---

3. Aldo Maria Valli, "'Il pontificato di Francesco? Clinicamente estinto': Intervista al professor Roberto de Mattei," September 14, 2020, Aldo Maria Valli blog, https://www .aldomariavalli.it/2020/09/14/il-pontificato-di-francesco-clinicamente-estinto-intervista -al-professor-roberto-de-mattei/.

4. Alberto Melloni, "L'inizio della fine del papato di Francesco," *Domani,* August 11, 2020.

has also surfaced," writes Melloni, "which during the pandemic fluctuated on various points, even on the part of circles that had been sympathetic and people who had praised it, as if Francis not doing what they wanted quickly enough was the problem."[5]

While the conservative and traditionalist wing has been unrelenting from the start in its opposition to Francis, the weakening of progressive support is more recent. That segment of the church has been disappointed by the limitations imposed by the pope on discussions during the meeting of the 2019 synod of bishops on the Amazon regarding the possibility of ordaining married men as priests, and on German bishops who are favorably disposed to the idea of ordaining women. Francis, in the view of some, has surrendered to traditionalists, and this is the unforgivable sin. In some way, even lay commentators like Massimo Franco and Marco Marzano lend support to this telling.

In his book *L'enigma Bergoglio: La parabola di un papato* (The Bergoglio enigma: the arc of a pontificate), Franco describes Francis as an "enigmatic pope,"[6] one who is "masterful in deconstructing a church already in crisis, probably less skilled in building another."[7] Franco, too, points to the image of "St. Peter's Square, deserted and battered by the rain in March."[8] Commenting on Franco's book, Marzano, author of *La Chiesa immobile: Francesco e la rivoluzione mancata*[9] (The immobile church: Francis and the failed revolution), calls into question his own earlier reading of the pontificate as an "immobile" church, stalled by its "Jesuitic" oscillation between tradition and reform. Marzano sees in this no strategy on the part of the pope.

> I, like others, have always imagined that all these apparently contradictory moves, the constant give and take, reflected a subtle, strategic design, an exquisitely Jesuitic political finesse to try to reconcile the irreconcilable and to establish consensus among the many factions into which the church is divided. Reading Massimo Franco's beautiful book, *L'enigma Bergoglio:*

5. Melloni, "L'inizio della fine del papato di Francesco."

6. Massimo Franco, *L'enigma Bergoglio: La parabola di un papato* (Milan: Solferino, 2020), 7.

7. Franco, *L'enigma Bergoglio*, 11.

8. Franco, *L'enigma Bergoglio*, 15.

9. Marco Marzano, *La Chiesa immobile: Francesco e la rivoluzione mancata* (Bari: Laterza, 2018).

La parabola di un papato (Solferino), prompted in me more than a few doubts about the validity of this view. By the time I finished, I had to admit to myself that that this style of proceeding, by advance and reverse, raising the hopes of the advocates of reform and then blatantly disappointing them, might be, rather than the playing out of a shrewd strategy, simply the result of total absence of a strategy, a groping forward by a man who unexpectedly became pope at almost eighty years of age, probably without any plan for the reform of the church and uncertain and stammering not only on the "great theological-political issues," but also on the way in which to manage the day to day business of the church. This is what emerges with clarity in the eleven dense chapters of Franco's book.[10]

For Marzano, then, Francis is a pope without a plan for reform, a conservative beneath the patina of progressivism imagined by the media.[11] But Marzano's fluctuations and retractions on the papal "strategy" and Franco's hesitations about the "enigmatic pope" highlight how completely both men fail to understand Bergoglio's thought and intellectual formation, which is essential in being able to grasp the "reforming" plan of this Latin American pope.

In an effort to fill in the gap, Fr. Antonio Spadaro, editor-in-chief of *La Civiltà Cattolica*, offered a long article in September 2020 titled "Francis' Government: What Is the Driving Force of His Pontificate?" Here Spadaro offered a clear answer to the questions raised by Melloni.[12] His intended audience is primarily the pope's left-wing critics, those who

10. Marco Marzano, "Il Papa resta un enigma: dopo gli annunci, dolorose retromarce," *Il Fatto Quotidiano*, November 15, 2020.

11. On the "immobile Pope" imagined by Marzano, see also the observations of Iacopo Scaramuzzi: "And even on the opposite front, that of the reformists—or progressives or conciliarists, if you prefer—the more gradualist proposals are dismissed by radical criticisms of the Jesuit pope—in Italy see the book by Marco Marzano, *La Chiesa immobile*—which, from the abolition of compulsory celibacy to the ordination of women, from the election of the parish priest to democratic synodal procedures, are inspired more by the ideas of revolution than by those of reform, ignore the prospect of a new Western schism, and devalue every step forward, small or large, made by this pope, dreaming of a Vatican Council III as if it were the storming of the Bastille." Iacopo Scaramuzzi, "Papa Francesco e l'opposizione 'americana,'" *Gli Asini*, October 20, 2019.

12. Antonio Spadaro, SJ, "Francis' Government: What is the driving force of his pontificate?," *La Civiltà Cattolica*, October 14, 2020, https://www.laciviltacattolica.com /francis-government-what-is-the-driving-force-of-his-pontificate/.

imagine an ideology of change, on the part of Francis, that does not in fact exist. Spadaro writes:

> The reform would be an ideology with a vaguely zealous character. And yes, like all ideologies it would have to be feared by those who do not support it. It would be at the mercy of the disillusionment of those who have their own agenda in mind. The reform that Francis has in mind works if "emptied" of such worldly reasoning. It is the opposite of the ideology of change. The driving force of the pontificate is not the ability to do things or to institutionalize change always and in every case, but to discern times and moments of an emptying so that the mission lets Christ be seen more clearly. It is discernment itself that is the systematic structure of reform, which takes the shape of an institutional order.[13]

Spadaro insists, "The question 'What is the program of Pope Francis?' actually makes no sense. The pope has neither pre-packaged ideas to apply to reality, nor an ideological plan of ready-to-wear reforms, but he advances on the basis of a spiritual experience and prayer that he shares step by step in dialogue, in consultation, in a concrete response to the vulnerable human situation. Francis creates the structural conditions for a real and open dialogue, not pre-packaged and strategically studied."[14] In the road followed by Francis,

> there is no theoretical road map; the path is opened by walking. Therefore, his "project" is, in reality, a lived spiritual experience, which takes shape in stages and is translated into concrete terms, into action. It is not a plan that refers to ideas and concepts that he aspires to realize, but an experience that refers to "times, places and people," to use a typical Ignatian expression; therefore, not to ideological abstractions, to a theoretical look at things. So that inner vision does not impose itself on history, trying to organize it according to its own framework, but it dialogues with reality, it is part of the history—sometimes marshy or muddy—of people and the Church, it takes place in time.[15]

The response that Fr. Spadaro, who knows Francis's thinking better than almost anyone, offers Melloni, then, is to point to the spirit of dis-

---

13. Spadaro, "Francis' Government."
14. Spadaro, "Francis' Government."
15. Spadaro, "Francis' Government."

cernment and "open thinking" that are characteristic of the pope's methodology. The mistake that Melloni and others make is to have imagined a "reforming" pontificate with a predetermined plan, something that is far from the actual reality of Pope Francis.

Spadaro's article received its own critical analysis from the *Il Foglio* Vatican correspondent Matteo Matzuzzi. "True enough," Matzuzzi wrote. "But the first person to suggest that there is a program driving this pontificate was the pope himself, in section 21 of his 2013 apostolic exhortation *Evangelii Gaudium.* . . . In short, there was and there is a program, and it is not a matter of prioritizing a sort of 'opposition between spiritual, pastoral, and structural conversion'; all of these things go hand in hand."[16] In making this point, Matzuzzi's intention is to point to the failures of the "program," as his article's title, "The Decline of a Papacy," suggests.

And he is not alone. Also in *Il Foglio,* a daily Italian paper with a left-leaning Catholic slant, Daniele Menozzi, a student of Giuseppe Alberigo, seems unpersuaded by Spadaro's arguments:

> The article by [Spadaro] fails to dispel the doubt. Doesn't the very fact that a question is being asked about the driving force of the pontificate represent the rhetorical expression of a basic uncertainty about the measures adopted by the pope? This doubt is reinforced if we look at the answer from the point of view of ecclesiastical politics. Spadaro argues that Bergoglio's reformist line allows him to avoid the pitfalls of the double demands of progressives and conservatives. It is a claim of centrality made with difficulty by someone who claims to hold confidently the bridle of innovation.[17]

And so Menozzi, Melloni, and Matzuzzi all describe a pontificate blocked by indecision and an inadequate understanding of people, one that has, in terms of ideas, reached its endpoint. We can expect nothing new from it. The same doubts are expressed by Aldo Cazzullo in a *Corriere della Sera* article titled "Is There a Cardinal in Paris? Doubts about a Pope Who Remains Great."[18]

16. Matteo Matzuzzi, "Il tramonto di un papato," *Il Foglio*, September 16, 2020.

17. Daniele Menozzi, "Il dubbio che resta dopo aver letto l'analisi di Spadaro sul governo del Papa," *Il Foglio*, September 18, 2020, https://www.ilfoglio.it/chiesa/2020/09/18/news/il-dubbio-che-resta-dopo-aver-letto-l-analisi-di-spadaro-sul-governo-del-papa-1072649/.

18. Aldo Cazzullo, "C'è un cardinale a Parigi? Dubbi su un Papa che resta grande," *Corriere della Sera*, October 9, 2020.

Between August and October 2020, then, commentators from opposing ideological sides seemed to be in agreement that Francis's pontificate had reached its end. It's a suspicious harmony that inevitably prompts the question: Why? Why now, faced with the spectacle of an empty St. Peter's Square where the pope's "solitude" proved capable of embracing the whole world, do commentators of both left and right decree the end? The reasons they offer are different and even contradictory. Where some see a slavery to tradition, others see only the hesitation of a progressive who is afraid of losing consensus. Yet these reasons are insufficient to demonstrate the decline of a pope who continues to demonstrate a sound grasp of the reality around him, clear judgment, and a determination to reform.[19]

But there is more to the question, and it had to do, in autumn 2020, with *an unacknowledged certainty of the reelection of Donald Trump as president of the United States.* His defeat by Joe Biden in the November 3 election seemed unlikely. This "intuition" probably explains the widespread perception that, with the anticipated second Trump term, Bergoglio's star was falling. In the four years of his mandate, Trump had in fact represented, in the eyes of millions of Catholics in the United States and abroad, a sort of anti-Francis. For this reason, the idea of another four years of his presidency seemed likely to mean the pope's oblivion.[20]

This was possible because many Catholics saw Trump not only as a politician, welcome or not for his ideas, but a real *defensor fidei* and an alternative to the bishop of Rome. For large sections of the American church, the man residing in the White House was a new Constantine. In this way the figure of the US president—who, even before Trump held the role, occupied a prominent place in American civil religion—had become the central figure of a theological-political model that stood in opposition to the "Latin American" Catholicism of the bishop of Rome. Trump's "investiture" in this role, during the 2020 campaign season, came not through the action of a pope but by the hands of an "antipope," Archbishop Carlo Maria Viganò, former papal nuncio to the United States

19. See Marco Politi, *Francesco: La peste, la rinascita* (Bari: Laterza, 2020).

20. This is the argument of Marco Tosatti, who in May 2020 noted the alignment of the major Italian newspapers to the Trump line and their distance from the pope. See "Elkann a Repubblica: Che significa per il Papa (e Scalfari . . .)?," Stilum Curiae blog, May 16, 2020, https://www.marcotosatti.com/2020/05/16/elkann-a-repubblica-che-significa-per -il-papa-e-scalfari/.

and Francis's main opponent on the traditionalist front, with many connections in the American church.

Viganò's two letters to President Trump—of June 7 and October 25, 2020—represent a unique and at times delusional example of the theological-political Manichaeism circulating in some segments of the church.[21] The first letter refers to two biblical alignments, "the children of light and the children of darkness," the former embodied by Trump and the latter by the "deep state" and the globalist "deep church." In the second letter, made public less than a week prior to the election and dated the Solemnity of Christ the King, the apocalyptic tone is even more intense. Trump is the Pauline *kathèkon*, the "power that restrains" the power of evil that finds its expression in the pope, whom Viganò portrays as a sort of Antichrist. The archbishop wrote,

> In Sacred Scripture, Saint Paul speaks to us of "the one who opposes" the manifestation of the *mystery of iniquity*, the *kathèkon* (2 Thess 2:6-7). In the religious sphere, this obstacle to evil is the Church, and in particular the papacy; in the political sphere, it is those who impede the establishment of the New World Order.
>
> As is now clear, the one who occupies the Chair of Peter has betrayed his role from the very beginning in order to defend and promote the globalist ideology, supporting the agenda of the deep church, who chose him from its ranks.
>
> Mr. President, you have clearly stated that you want to defend the nation—*One Nation under God*, fundamental liberties, and non-negotiable values that are denied and fought against today. It is you, dear President, who are "the one who opposes" the deep state, the final assault of the children of darkness.
>
> For this reason, it is necessary that all people of good will be persuaded of the epochal importance of the imminent election: not so much for the sake of this or that political program, but because of the general inspiration of your action that best embodies—in this particular historical context—

21. Carlo Maria Viganò, "Archbishop Viganò's powerful letter to President Trump: Eternal struggle between good and evil playing out right now," LifeSite, June 6, 2020, https://www.lifesitenews.com/opinion/archbishop-viganos-powerful-letter-to-president-trump-eternal-struggle-between-good-and-evil-playing-out-right-now; Viganò, "Viganò warns Trump about 'Great Reset' plot to 'subdue humanity,' destroy freedom," LifeSite, October 30, 2020, https://www.lifesitenews.com/news/abp-vigano-warns-trump-about-great-reset-plot-to-subdue-humanity-destroy-freedom.

that world, our world, which they want to cancel by means of the lockdown. Your adversary is also our adversary: it is the Enemy of the human race, He who is "a murderer from the beginning" (Jn 8:44).

Around you are gathered with faith and courage those who consider you the final garrison against the world dictatorship. The alternative is to vote for a person who is manipulated by the deep state, gravely compromised by scandals and corruption, who will do to the United States what Jorge Mario Bergoglio is doing to the Church.[22]

Viganò, an antiglobalization reactionary and apocalyptic figure of the counterrevolution, is an extreme figure, like a character out of the novels of Umberto Eco and Dan Brown. With his public repudiation of the Second Vatican Council and his criticisms of Benedict XVI, he became another Archbishop Lefebvre, to the point of being useless even to the anti-Francis front.[23] But for two years—beginning in August 2018, when

---

22. Viganò, "Viganò warns Trump about 'Great Reset' plot."
23. As Sandro Magister wrote in his blog:

Benedict XVI promoted him to apostolic nuncio in the United States in 2011. The meek theologian pope certainly could not have imagined, nine years ago, that Archbishop Carlo Maria Viganò—who returned to private life in 2016 but has been anything but hidden—would today be blaming him for having "deceived" the whole Church into believing that the Second Vatican Council was immune to heresies and moreover should be interpreted in perfect continuity with true perennial doctrine.

But this is just the length to which Viganò has gone in recent days, capping off a relentless barrage of denunciations of Church heresies over the last few decades, with the root of it all being the Council, most recently in an exchange with Phil Lawler, editor of CatholicCulture.org.

Attention: not the Council interpreted badly, but the Council as such and en bloc. In his latest public statements, in fact, Viganò has rejected as too timid and vacuous even the claim of some to "correct" Vatican II here and there, in its texts which in his judgment are more blatantly heretical, such as the declaration *Dignitatis Humanae* on religious freedom. Because what must be done once and for all—he has demanded— is "to drop it 'in toto' and forget it," naturally with the concomitant "expulsion from the sacred precinct" of all those Church authorities who, identified as guilty of the deception and "invited to amend," have not changed their ways.

According to Viganò, what has distorted the Church ever since the Council is a sort of "universal religion whose first theoretician was Freemasonry" and whose political arm is that "completely out-of-control world government" pursued by the "nameless and faceless" powers that are now bending to their own interests even the coronavirus pandemic.

he published a dossier on the sex scandals of Cardinal Theodore McCarrick that accused Francis and other church leaders of covering up the affair—he adopted the role, incredibly, as the church's powerful moral reformer, to the point of calling for the resignation of the pope.[24] The attention and respect that he has received from many American clergy and laity can be understood only within the ideological framework that permeates so much of American Catholicism, one of culture wars, end-time struggle—children of light versus children of darkness—and religious and political Manichaeism. Like any political-theological model, this one, too, receives its full strength and meaning only in the context of a debacle, a defeat—in this case, Trump's. There is no doubt, in fact, that what French journalist Nicolas Senèze has called "the American schism" found in Trump a point of reference.[25] The defeat of the Republican president coincides, from this point of view, not with the advent of a new savior, the Democrat Joe Biden, but with the end of the illusion of the anti-Roman Constantine.

Melloni wrote in the aftermath of the November 2020 election:

> There was a historically unprecedented dimension of Trumpism, and it was his attempt to divide the Catholic Church, to produce within Catholicism the schism that has long divided the Protestant world, where "evangelical"

Last May 8, Cardinals Gerhard Müller and Joseph Zen Zekiun also carelessly affixed their signatures to an appeal by Viganò against this looming "New World Order."

And to a subsequent open letter from Viganò to Donald Trump—whom he invoked as a warrior of light against the power of darkness that acts both in the "deep state" and in the "deep Church"—the president of the United States replied enthusiastically, with a tweet that went viral. (Sandro Magister, "Archbishop Viganò on the Brink of Schism: The Unheeded Lesson of Benedict XVI," Settimo Cielo blog, *L'Espresso*, June 29, 2020, http://magister.blogautore.espresso.repubblica.it/2020/06/29/archbishop-vigano-on-the-brink-of-schism-the-unheeded-lesson-of-benedict-xvi/, English translation corrected slightly)

24. On Viganò, see Andrea Tornielli and Gianni Valente, *Il giorno del giudizio: Conflitti, guerre di potere, abusi e scandali: Cosa sta davvero succedendo nella Chiesa* (Milan: Piemme, 2018). The Vatican Secretariat of State responded to the accusations of Archbishop Viganò with the *Report on the Holy See's Institutional Knowledge and Decision-making Related to Former Cardinal Theodore Edgar McCarrick (1930 to 2017)*, published November 10, 2020, http://www.vatican.va/resources/resources_rapporto-card-mccarrick_20201110_en.pdf.

25. Nicolas Senèze, *Comment l'Amerique veut changer de pape* (Paris: Bayard, 2019).

churches are distinguished from the mainline churches of Lutheran tradition. The Trump administration wanted to create "Catholical" Catholicism in three ways: first by exploiting the resentment against Francis held by integralist traditionalists who welcomed the irresponsible and crazed pronouncements of Archbishop Carlo Maria Viganò; secondly, by financing a web of mercenary internet journalists, miserable self-styled Ratzingerians (though Ratzinger would have incinerated them with two citations), to create a digital white noise that in 0.57 seconds would provide 163 thousand hits on Google to anyone who searches "Pope Francis heretic"; and thirdly, by sending Steve Bannon to Rome as Trump's apocrisiary, to establish a study center for admirers of nationalism and racism.[26]

Given all of this, the results of the 2020 election bear a significance that transcends the primary political meaning. This is a fact that did not escape the most attentive commentators. Among them, the journalist Maria Antonietta Calabrò rightly pointed out:

Over the weeks, the "Catholic" question for the Dems has remained under wraps. But it is not only because of Biden's personal faith that his victory "frees" Pope Francis from a possible checkmate in the event of Trump's victory.

For geopolitical reasons and for reasons "internal" to the Catholic Church, Biden's win restores the Throne of the world to be in some way in sync with the Altar. This will in some ways avoid the strong tensions that arose at the end of Ratzinger's pontificate with the election of Obama and in the years of Trump's presidency with Francis.

Who can forget Steve Bannon's nationalist initiatives [here in Italy]? His alliance with "conservative" cardinals (starting with Cardinal Burke) that gradually dissolved after he left the White House until his recent arrest for financial crimes related to the construction of the anti-immigrant wall with Mexico? His alliance in Italy with Matteo Salvini, the politician with the "My Pope Is Benedict" t-shirt?

The Catholic vote (twenty-six percent of the population) was decisive for Obama's victories, but in recent years in the United States it has become increasingly polarized, because "moving" to the right for an American Catholic has also meant distancing oneself from the Francis pontificate.

For over two years, since August 2018, former nuncio Archbishop Carlo Maria Viganò's propaganda has hammered against the pope, whose res-

---

26. Alberto Melloni, "Così papa Francesco ha vinto le sue prime presidenziali Usa," *Corriere della Sera*, November 14, 2020.

ignation he has repeatedly called for. Viganò has called for prayers for Trump's re-election and won public support from Trump himself. Meanwhile, at the end of September, in an unprecedented move, Secretary of State Mike Pompeo accused the Vatican of immorality for its diplomatic agreements with China regarding the choice of bishops.

With Biden's victory, this process is interrupted.[27]

This American "turning point" frees the pope from the weight of the emperor and indirectly creates more breathing space for his program, which appeared uncertain when the fate of the ballot boxes seemed to play in Trump's favor. However, it does not solve the problem of that conservative Catholic bloc, in many cases traditionalist, which has responded to the reality of an increasingly insecure world by entrenching itself in a defensive posture. As Massimo Faggioli writes:

> The story of American Catholicism today is inseparable from the polarization of political identities, and the intense division within the American church is destined to continue. Biden's election buys valuable time while Francis is still pope, but the subversive dissent of Catholics funded by financial elites against Francis's evangelical radicalism and Biden's Catholicism will not disappear on inauguration day. The role of Archbishop Viganò, former apostolic nuncio to Washington, as the bard of Catholic Trumpism (publicly recognized by Trump himself) will at some point be assumed by someone else.[28]

The dissent, though weakened, remains. Removing it will require a variety of conditions, including an understanding of its nature and origins. In 2017, Fr. Spadaro and Marcelo Figueroa tried to describe the phenomenon, pointing out its affinities with Protestant fundamentalism.[29] The reactions, including that of George Weigel, a leader of Catholic neoconservative

---

27. Maria Antonietta Calabrò, "Biden, cattolico adulto, libererà il Papa dalla morsa di Viganò e dei conservatori," *Huffington Post*, November 7, 2020.

28. Massimo Faggioli, "Il cattolico Biden non potrà sanare lo scisma morbido in atto negli Usa," *Huffington Post*, November 17, 2020. For the possible scenarios of the American church and President Biden, see Faggioli, *Joe Biden and Catholicism in the United States* (New York: Bayard, 2021).

29. Antonio Spadaro and Marcelo Figueroa, "Evangelical Fundamentalism and Catholic Integralism," *La Civiltà Cattolica*, July 15, 2017, https://www.laciviltacattolica .it/articolo/evangelical-fundamentalism-and-catholic-integralism-in-the-usa-a -surprising-ecumenism/.

thought, came quickly.[30] American Catholicism is distinctive and exists on a different wavelength from the Francis pontificate; indeed, it does not seem to have the antennas necessary to receive and understand it. *La Stampa* Vatican correspondent Iacopo Scaramuzzi has written,

> The United States, once the chosen home for Italian, Irish, and Polish Catholic emigrants, has over time become the cradle of a peculiar brand of Catholicism, a faith that accentuates the moral dimension of Christianity at the expense of the prophetic dimension. It is intertwined with the capitalism that permeates the nation's culture, alongside a nationalist, racist, proselytist, homophobic, evangelical Protestantism. It is no coincidence that *La Civiltà Cattolica*, a Jesuit journal very close to Pope Francis, warned of an "ecumenism of hatred"—almost a Christian jihadism—that unites the most traditionalist fringes of Catholicism and Protestantism. In the long years of John Paul II, then, with the glue of anti-communism, many bishops shifted to the right, embracing a relentless culture war, identifying the Catholic faith with the "pro-life" ideology or the rejection of gay marriage, and leaving in the background Vatican II's opening to society and modernity. Finally, in recent years, in parallel with the election of Donald Trump and the rebirth of old nationalist and racist impulses, a new extremism has gained strength. It is "a new medievalist fundamentalism" in conflict with the "old neoconservative school" for "supremacy within conservative American Catholicism," according to Massimo Faggioli, an Italian historian of Christianity transplanted to the United States. In short, an almost separate Catholicism has taken shape. Tolerated before Jorge Mario Bergoglio was elected, it now exists in the odor of heresy. And it is ready for schism.[31]

According to Scaramuzzi,

> Pope Francis did not provoke this clash within Catholicism; he simply brought it to light. Before him, the Second Vatican Council (1962–1965) had instigated the detachment, on the right, of the Lefebvrian fault. The earthquake has now resumed because the Argentine pontiff returns to that

---

30. George Weigel, "Spadaro, Figueroa, and Questions of Competence," *Catholic World Report*, August 2, 2017. See also Samuel Gregg, "On That Strange, Disturbing, and Anti-American 'Civiltà Cattolica' Article," *Catholic World Report*, July 14, 2017. Gregg is research director of the Acton Institute.

31. Scaramuzzi, "Papa Francesco e l'opposizione 'americana.'"

council somewhat neglected by his predecessors, because he proclaims a Catholicism that is not understood primarily as a message about morality, that does not primarily aim at making proselytes among nonbelievers, at scolding the faithful about their sexual mores, at making political alliances in defense of "nonnegotiable values," but opens the doors of the church to the irregular, to the distant. It dialogues with people of other faiths. It does not embrace modernity uncritically, but it does call the church to an attitude of nonbelligerence, and even porosity, toward it. It has allowed Christianity to evolve and, at the same time, to remain relevant, to fertilize the culture of its time without submitting to it. Jorge Mario Bergoglio tries to translate the Christian message into the cultural terms of humanity today, as the Jesuit missionaries of the seventeenth and eighteenth centuries did when they spread Catholicism in Latin America or in Japan and China.[32]

Why is the pope's perspective not understood? Why is he dismissed as a modernist, a progressive, even a "heretic"? What has happened to contemporary Catholic thought that renders it no longer able to translate the message of the council in the present hour? In the case of US Catholicism, to understand the *coupure*, the "rupture," one must start from the historic *Roe v. Wade* ruling, with which the Supreme Court of the United States, in 1973, legitimized the right to abortion, move from there to the reactions and transformations of American Catholicism during the presidency of Ronald Reagan (1980–1989),[33] and, finally, understand the current of neoconservatism promoted by Catholic intellectuals such as Michael Novak, George Weigel, Richard Neuhaus, and Robert Sirico. The latter movement, starting from the 1990s, became hegemonic in the American Catholic world, to the point of defining the two pillars of a new *Weltanschauung*: full reconciliation between Catholicism and capitalism,

32. Scaramuzzi, "Papa Francesco e l'opposizione 'americana.'"

33. On the changes in the American church in the period from the 1960s through the Obama presidency, see the series of articles published by *Il Regno* in 2010 under the title "USA: dal 'common ground' al Tea Party" (pp. 559–75) with the contributions of James M. O'Toole ("Riforma e reazione: le strade dei cattolici americani," pp. 559–63), John T. McGreevy ("I cattolici nella vita politica: Un ruolo ridotto," pp. 564–69), Kathleen Sprows Cummings ("Stati Uniti, Chiesa e società: Le donne sono cambiate," pp. 569–73), Massimo Faggioli ("Dall'America del 'common ground' a quella del Tea Party: Andata e ritorno," pp. 574–75). A similar and more detailed account is offered in English in Steven P. Millies, *Good Intentions: A History of Catholic Voters' Road from Roe to Trump* (Collegeville, MN: Liturgical Press, 2018).

and culture wars that take morality as their battleground. The result was a strident Catho-capitalism, a new form of "Catholic Americanism" that sought a full interpenetration of faith and the American ethos.[34] To a degree rarely seen, politics shaped religion. As theologian and historian Jean-François Colosimo has written,

> This political change is also theological. On a foundation of Thomist-naturalism translated into the terms of contemporary bioethics, morality increasingly conditions the dogmatic and spiritual discourse of Catholicism in the United States. At the same time, due to the influence that American cardinals have exercised in the Vatican since the election of John Paul II, Catholic social teaching has been given an undeniable liberal slant, thanks in large part to the human rights philosopher and pro-life militant George Weigel.[35]

This shift became more radicalized, in the form of a militant Manichaeism, after the attacks of September 11, 2001 and the subsequent wars of the West against Islamic countries, which were aggressively supported by leading Catholic neoconservative thinkers despite the strong objections of Pope John Paul II himself. Questions of war and economy divide

---

34. "What happened in the last couple of decades is a certain degree of 'Americanization' of world Catholicism: in a sense, 9/11 and what happened since then made us (including non-American Catholics) all neo-Durkheimian, whether we like it or not. But there also undeniably appeared a new, early twenty-first-century Catholic Americanism. . . . What emerges after the 1980s is a new Catholic Americanism different from the one condemned by Leo XIII in 1899, especially considering that a liberal-progressive Catholic Americanism exists side-by-side with and yet opposed to a traditionalist-conservative Catholic Americanism." Massimo Faggioli, *Catholicism and Citizenship: Political Cultures of the Church in the Twenty-First Century* (Collegeville, MN: Liturgical Press, 2017), 64, 113.

35. Jean-François Colosimo, *Dieu est américain: De la théodémocratie aux Etats-Unis* (Paris: Librairie Arthème Fayard, 2006). [Translator's note: American readers should note that the word *liberal* is used here and frequently throughout this book—and throughout the Western world outside the United States—with a meaning that is rather different than the way it is commonly used in the context of contemporary US politics. Since the root of the word's meaning is freedom (Latin: *liber* = "free"), free market capitalism is often referred to as "liberalism" and its advocates as "liberals." Thus the word *liberal* is not at all, in this context, the opposite of *conservative*, and a person or idea that would often be called "conservative" in the United States would in certain ways be considered "liberal" in Europe. *Leftist* is the word often used in Europe to describe what Americans often mean when they use *liberal*.]

the popes from the Catholic neoconservatives (sometimes referred to with the shorthand term "theocons"), though the former have maintained with the latter a general sense of cooperation. The neoconservatives have succeeded in bringing about a real metamorphosis of Catholic culture, moving it from a sense of mission and openness to dialogue to antagonistic and preoccupied with identity, from socially conscious to efficient and entrepreneurial, from communitarian to individualistic and bureaucratic, from seeking peace to supporting war, from catholic and universalist to Westernist.

This transformation, which became starkly clear after September 11, is described well by the astute Vatican analyst Lucio Brunelli:

> A new kind of Christian is wandering around Europe. They are the *Christianists*. There are various versions, some wearing a cassock, others a jacket and tie. There is the aristocratic version and the disheveled one. But all Christianists have in common a combative sense of their Catholicism. Enough ecumenical chatter, they say; a strong identity is needed. They feel like they are a minority. In politics they are with the center-right. In economics they are ultra-liberal. Internationally, fervent Americanists. And so far, none of this is very remarkable. But the real novelty of the Christianists is not the sides they choose. It is the *pathos* they bring. The spirit of militancy. And above all, the strong ideological-religious motivation. A belligerent attitude toward Islam undoubtedly derives from the theology of the uniqueness of Christ the Savior. From the orthodox critique of Pelagianism comes the contemptuous accusation against Christians who dedicate themselves mainly to social initiatives that seek to protect and support "the least ones." From the denunciation of theological irenicism, we arrive at the enthusiasm—not merely approval, but *enthusiasm*—for the allied military expeditions. All these characteristics are the essence of the perfect Christianist. A new phenomenon, no doubt, at least in recent years. In the minority, but not to the extent they suggest, because their positions are reflected in the doctrinal and political tendencies of some sectors of the ecclesiastical hierarchy. The real point of distinction of the Christianists is not their differing political views; it is their use of Christianity as an ideological banner.[36]

36. Lucio Brunelli, "Cattolici e guerra: una nuova seta: Ecco i cristianisti," *Vita*, October 26, 2001. Already in 1992 Brunelli had referred to "the stars-and-stripes trinity," the Catholic neoconservative trio of the "Father" (Michael Novak), "Son" (George Weigel), and "Holy Spirit" (Richard John Neuhaus) ("La Trinità a Stelle e Strisce," *Il Sabato*, June 13, 1992).

Brunelli cleverly adopted the distinction between Christians and "Christianists" that the French philosopher Rémi Brague had introduced in his 1992 book *Eccentric Culture: A Theory of Western Civilization*. There Brague wrote:

In the religious domain, faith does not produce its effects except where it remains faith, and not calculation. The civilization of Christian Europe has been constructed by people for whom the end was not at all to construct a "Christian civilization," but to make the most of the consequences of their faith in Christ. We owe it to people who believe in Christ, not to people who believe in Christianity. These people were Christians, and not what one might call "Christianists." A good example of this is furnished by Pope Gregory the Great. His reform laid the foundations for the European Middle Ages. Now, he believed that the end of the world was very near, an end that to his mind would remove the space in which any "Christian civilization" might establish itself. What he constructed, and what would last a good millennium, was in his eyes only an entirely provisional marching order, a way of setting in order a house one was soon going to leave. Inversely, those who propose as the primary end of their actions the 'saving of the Christian West' have to be careful not to deploy practices that, as we have had examples of, are located outside of what Christian ethics, not to mention the most elementary common moral order, authorizes.[37]

With the category of "Christianist," Brague brought into focus the new version of "Western" Christianity that was taking hold in America and Europe. The Christianist embraced the religious neoconservatism imported from the United States—a Christian who was self-conscious of Christian identity, self-referential, Westernist, preoccupied with morality, politicized.

In an important 2004 interview with the magazine *30 Days*, Brague returned to the distinction between "Christians" and "Christianists."[38] He clarified the difference by noting several distinctive points of the religious neoconservative position.

37. Rémi Brague, *Eccentric Culture: A Theory of Western Civilization*, trans. Samuel Lester (South Bend, IN: St. Augustine's Press, 2002), 143–44 [English translation slightly corrected]. On the thought of Brague, see Serena Meattini, *L'Europa e la crisi del modern: Il pensiero di Rémi Brague* (Rome: Studium, 2019).

38. Gianni Valente, "Christians and Christianists" (interview with Rémi Brague), *30 Days* 10 (October 2004), http://www.30giorni.it/articoli_id_5332_l3.htm.

The first was the distinction between ideology and faith. For a French Catholic, Christianist ideology sounds a lot like *Action française* of Charles Maurras, who was excommunicated by Pope Pius XI on December 29, 1926.

> Only I would like to remind them that Christianity is not interested in itself. It's interested in Christ. And Christ also is not interested in His own self: He is interested in God, whom He calls in a unique way, "Father." And in man, to whom He proposes a new access to God. . . .
>
> *Action française,* after the First World War, may have attracted genuine and intelligent Christians: Bernanos, for example. But the ultimate inspiration of the movement was merely nationalist. France was shaped by the Church. Because of this they called themselves Catholics, because they wanted to be a hundred per cent French. Their principal thinker, Charles Maurras, was a disciple of Auguste Comte; he admired Greek clarity and Roman order. He declared himself an atheist, but Catholic. The Church for him was a guarantee against "the Jewish poison of the Gospel." Basically, it was an idolatry in its worst aspect: to place God at the service of the cult of themselves. Whether you are dealing with the individual or the nation, the substance does not change. And something live must always be sacrificed to idols, such as European youth, massacred at Verdun and elsewhere. . . .
>
> For these people, the Church must "defend certain values," and not compromise on the moral laws. But do they themselves follow them? Not always. . . . They want an organization with a firm line, with a "number one" well established. In the end, I ask myself if they don't dream of a Church in the mold of the Communist Party of the Soviet Union.[39]

With far-sightedness, Brague grasped the "ethical" preoccupation of this Christianist "church," its subordination to "devout atheists" such as Maurras, its nationalist preoccupation with identity—all characteristics that are clearly reflected in the Catholic neoconservative movement in Italy.

A second point of difference that Brague noted between the simple believer and the "new" believer is its understanding of the "Christian roots" of Europe. Brague was writing at a time when French president Valéry Giscard d'Estaing had controversially proposed to insert into the

---

39. Valente, "Christians and Christianists."

European constitution an explicit reference to the Christian origins of the continent. Brague criticized the proposal and, at the same time, shone a stark light upon the problem of a Christian preoccupation with identity fixed on tradition and on the past.

> In the debate on the alleged Christian roots of Europe, I'd be tempted to say that neither the "christianists" nor their adversaries are right. Let's begin with their adversaries. I'd say to them: if you want to be historians you need to call things by their proper names, and to say that the two religions that marked Europe are Judaism and Christianity, and no other. Why limit yourself to talking about religious and humanist inheritance? A professor of history wouldn't be satisfied with such a definition and would write in red, on the margin: "Too vague, be precise!" What annoys me is the state of mind manifested in this, and therefore the typically ideological impulse of denying reality and rewriting the past. And denying reality leads necessarily to destroying it. At the same time, I'd say to the "christianists": it's not because the past was what it was that the future must necessarily resemble it. The right question to ask is whether our civilization still has the will to live and act. And whether, instead of hedging it with barriers of all kinds, it wouldn't be better to give it back the will again. And for that you have to draw on the source of life itself, on Eternal Life.[40]

This is, clearly, an original approach, critical of the rise of secularism and at the same time of the political stance of those who insist on pushing preoccupation with identity to the bitter end. It is an approach similar to that of Pope Francis who, when asked in a May 2016 *La Croix* interview about the "Christian roots of Europe," said,

> We need to speak of roots in the plural because there are so many. In this sense, when I hear talk of the Christian roots of Europe, I sometimes dread the tone, which can seem triumphalist or even vengeful. It then takes on colonialist overtones. John Paul II, however, spoke about it in a tranquil manner.
>
> Yes, Europe has Christian roots and it is Christianity's responsibility to water those roots. But this must be done in a spirit of service as in the washing of the feet. Christianity's duty to Europe is one of service. As Erich Przywara, the great master of Romano Guardini and Hans Urs von Balthasar, teaches us, Christianity's contribution to a culture is that of Christ in the

---

40. Valente, "Christians and Christianists."

washing of the feet. In other words, service and the gift of life. It must not become a colonial enterprise.[41]

A third aspect of Christianist belief noted by Brague was "Westernism." Christianity, after September 11, 2001, became increasingly "Western." It is an Atlantic, American-European creed, defined by its identity in opposition to its eternal rival: Islam. This identity is dialectical—it exists solely in its contrast to its opponent. On this point, too, Brague's judgment is sound and understood best in reference to the tradition of French Catholicism, which, thanks to Jacques Maritain and Étienne Gilson, has a history of rejecting the colonialist identification of Christianity with the West.[42] Brague said,

> Christianity has nothing of the West. It came from the East. Our ancestors *became* Christians. They adhered to a religion which was foreign to them in the beginning. The roots? What a strange image. . . . Why consider oneself a plant? In French slang, "to plant oneself " means to get things wrong, to make an error. . . . If they want roots at any cost, then let's say it with Plato: we are trees planted the other way around, our roots are not on earth, but in the sky. We are rooted in what, like the sky, can't be grasped, it escapes all possession. You can't plant flags on a cloud. And we are also mobile animals. Christianity is not reserved to Europeans. It's missionary. It believes that everyone has the right of knowing the Christian message, that everyone deserves to become Christian.[43]

Here, too, the similarity of Brague's perspective in 2004 with that of Pope Francis more recently is clear. Brague sheds light on the misunderstanding that is at the foundation of the Catholic neoconservative, or Christianist, position: *the identification of faith with Western civilization.* This was denounced by Jacques Maritain in 1936, in his book *Integral Humanism.* There Maritain recognized that elevating the Middle Ages as a model of "Christian civilization" lent support to a pro-fascist antimodernism. In the early

---

41. Guillaume Goubet and Sébastien Maillard, "Interview with Pope Francis by La Croix," December 26, 2016, *La Croix*, https://international.la-croix.com/news/religion /interview-with-pope-francis-by-la-croix/3184.

42. See Massimo Borghesi, *Ateismo e modernità: Il dibattito nel pensiero cattolico ital-ofrancese* (Milan: Jaca Book, 2019), 152, 166–71.

43. Valente, "Christians and Christianists."

2000s, it was "Westernism" rather than medievalism that became the equivocal identification of faith with the ethos of American modernity. Neoconservative Christianity no longer perceived the difference between eschatology and history, faith and politics, the city of God and the city of man. Such distinctions are affirmed formally, but the hope of change is left entirely to worldly means. Such means become the power that determines the form of the *civitas Dei*. Grace arrives too late, when the banquet guests are full. As Brague beautifully stated at the end of his 2004 interview:

> Let's not fool ourselves about what the God of Jesus Christ wants. It is not what *we*, we want. What he wants is not to crush His enemies. But to free them of what makes them His enemies, that is a false image of Him, that of a tyrant to whom one must submit. He, being free, is only interested in our freedom. He tries to heal it. His problem is to set up a device that allows the wounded freedom of men to be seen as healed, so as to freely choose life over all the temptations to death that are carried within. Theologians call this device the "economy of salvation." The Covenants, the Church, the sacraments, and so on, form part of it. The role of civilizations is indispensable, but it's not the same. And their means are also different. They have to exert a certain coercion, physical or social. Whereas faith can only exert an attraction on freedom, because of the majesty of its object. Perhaps there could be a return to what the popes used to say to the Western emperors, about the Gregorian reform, in the 11th century: the salvation of souls is not your business, content yourselves with doing your job as well as possible. Make peace reign.[44]

The salvation of the world does not belong to Caesar. Nor does it belong to America. The economy of faith is different from that of "civilizations." The latter need strength, compulsion, armies. The capitalist model, so praised by the Catholic neoconservatives, needs victims. Faith, on the other hand, is mild; it "can only exert an attraction on freedom."

Brague's distinctions allow us to understand the problem that lies at the heart of Catholic Americanism, the stumbling block that currently opposes the church of Pope Francis. *This is the theological-political question.* In their article "Evangelical Fundamentalism and Catholic Integralism," Fr. Spadaro and Marcelo Figueroa write that in Pope Francis,

---

44. Valente, "Christians and Christianists."

The religious element should never be confused with the political one. Confusing spiritual power with temporal power means subjecting one to the other. An evident aspect of Pope Francis' geopolitics rests in not giving theological room to the power to impose oneself or to find an internal or external enemy to fight. There is a need to flee the temptation to project divinity on political power that then uses it for its own ends. Francis empties from within the narrative of sectarian millenarianism and dominionism that is preparing the apocalypse and the "final clash." Underlining mercy as a fundamental attribute of God expresses this radically Christian need.

Francis wants to break the organic link between culture, politics, institution and Church. Spirituality cannot tie itself to governments or military pacts for it is at the service of all men and women. Religions cannot consider some people as sworn enemies nor others as eternal friends. Religion should not become the guarantor of the dominant classes. Yet it is this very dynamic with a spurious theological flavor that tries to impose its own law and logic in the political sphere.[45]

If Spadaro and Figueroa's observations are correct, then *Francis's pontificate stands against the theological-political model that has been shaping ecclesial consciousness for thirty years.* This explains the opposition and misunderstandings. In 2013, the same year Bergoglio became pope, I published a volume entitled *Critica della teologia politica: Da Agostino a Peterson: la fine dell'era costantiniana*[46] [Critique of political theology: From Augustine to Peterson: the end of the Constantinian era]. In it I turned to Ratzinger's teachers, Augustine and Erik Peterson (the latter a great critic of Carl Schmitt), to demonstrate a thesis formulated by Ratzinger himself: "In contrast to its deformations, Christianity has not established Messianism in the political sphere. Quite the contrary; from the start it insisted on leaving the political world in the sphere of rationality and ethical principles. It taught and made possible the acceptance of what is imperfect. To put it another way, the New Testament is aware of political ethics but not of political theology."[47]

---

45. Spadaro and Figueroa, "Evangelical Fundamentalism and Catholic Integralism."

46. Massimo Borghesi, *Critica della teologia politica: Da Agostino a Peterson: la fine dell'era costantiniana* (Genoa-Milan: Marietti, 2013).

47. Joseph Ratzinger, *Church, Ecumenism, and Politics*, trans. Robert Nowell (New York: Crossroad, 1988), 216.

This is an important statement that contrasts not only with left-wing messianism but also with Catholic neoconservative ideology and the "Christianism" described by Brague. In my book, I argued that Ratzinger's distinction was more relevant than ever:

> In its conception of itself, the Christian faith is *essentially* metapolitical; it is political in its consequences. It is political in that the *civitas Dei*, according to the image suggested by the *Letter to Diognetus*, is the soul of the *polis*, lives in it even without identifying with it, seeks its good. But it is not realized *through* politics. It is a theology *of* politics, not a political theology. This means that it does not reach the political *directly* but through ethical-juridical mediation. It does not seek or accept *identity* with the political. This is prevented by its eschatological reserve, the gap between grace and nature. Political theology, on the contrary, is "dialectical." For it, the theological moment is realized *through* the political and the political *through* the theological. In passing "through," in being realized through other-than-self, the two moments undergo a *metamorphosis*. It is in this sense that *political theology represents a formula of secularization*: of the theological, which identifies the *civitas Dei* with the *civitas mundi*; and of the political, when, in the sense of Löwith or Voegelin, it becomes a political religion.[48]

The Catholic neoconservative movement, which since the 1980s has taken the place of the Catho-Marxist messianism of the 1970s, is a conservative political theology, a right-wing variant of left-wing political theology. Like the latter, the former also conceives faith as an entirely earthly message in its means and its end. It uses faith as a driving force for secularization. For this reason, its development is closely connected to American politics and particularly to the presidencies of Ronald Reagan and George W. Bush. This movement reached its peak at the time of the American war against Saddam Hussein, in 2003–2004, and then declined as the devastating consequences of that conflict—including many thousands of deaths and the massive exodus of the Christian community from the lands of Nineveh and Babylon—became clear. Its golden age was the first decade of the new millennium, following the global shock provoked by the Islamist demolition of the World Trade Center towers in New York.

---

48. Borghesi, *Critica della teologia politica*, 12–13.

That event inaugurated what the historian Emilio Gentile has called "the *era of theopolitics*."[49] Gentile writes,

> The Bush era also coincided, after September 11, with the awakening of the American civil religion, which had seemed to be dormant for some time. The American civil religion, or more simply the American religion, is a special religion, because it arose out of the political sacralization of the United States as a nation blessed by God. The cornerstone of this civil religion is the belief that the Creator gave the American people the values of democracy as a gift, so that the American people might make them a gift to all peoples of the world. The United States has considered itself, since its birth, the only genuine "democracy of God."[50]

The messianic investiture that marked the Bush era represented a metamorphosis of the political, which becomes religious, and of the religious, which becomes political. "In this change, one clearly sees the tendency of the Republican Party to transform *civil religion*, understood as a form of sacralization of politics unconnected to the ideology of a single party or movement, into a *political religion*, understood as the sacralization of the politics of a single party or movement, which arrogates to itself the monopoly of defining good and evil according to its own ideology."[51] It is a process that, after Bush, also characterized the Democratic messianism promoted by Barack Obama.

What is clear is that every time a theological movement follows a political one, it shares its successes and defeats; it gives up its own autonomy. This is the fate of political theologies. The Catholic neoconservative movement dissipated with Bush's declining second term. It did not disappear, however. It simply transformed. The accents remained, the basic motivations that the neoconservatives had implanted in the Catholic conscience: the moral agenda in the foreground, focusing on a small set of select values; the relativist opponent; the emphasis on Christian-Western identity in an anti-Islamic key; a Manichean dualism about the forces of good and evil. In a criticism of leading Catholic neocon intellectuals (Richard

---

49. Emilio Gentile, *La democrazia di Dio: La religione americana nell'era dell'impero e del terrore* (Bari: Laterza, 2008), xv. On the theological-political turning point provoked by 9/11, see Borghesi, *Critica della teologia politica*, 270–82.

50. Gentile, *La democrazia di Dio*, v.

51. Gentile, *La democrazia di Dio*, 226.

Neuhaus, George Weigel, and Robert George), the American legal scholar and theologian Cathleen Kaveny observes how they have modified traditional Christianity in a dualistic, dichotomous sense:

> [They] urged bishops to present Catholic teaching in a way that distorted key concepts and divided the Body of Christ. The most egregious of their strategies was to present the thought of Pope John Paul II in stark, dualistic terms—which led them to celebrate Republican Catholics as warriors for the culture of life and to castigate Catholics who voted for the Democrats as minions of the culture of death. But a culture isn't reducible to a political party. And building a culture of life required far more than opposition to abortion—it also required care for the vulnerable. No American political party is the party of saints.
>
> Some might say that his functionalist conception of religious community was motivated by a good end: his passionate desire to end abortion and restore traditional sexual morality. But here's the irony of Neuhaus's project: in treating theological belief and commitment as mere instruments of political will, Neuhaus's view of religion resonated more with Feuerbach, Marx, and Leo Strauss than with the church fathers. In separating his own church of the politically pure from the hoi polloi of the body of Christ, his ecclesiology better reflects Protestant sectarianism than Roman Catholicism. And in decrying powerful "elites" even as he went about creating his own elite force for the Republican Party, his political tactics bore more than a passing resemblance to Saul Alinsky's.
>
> Pope Francis isn't trying to drive conservative Catholics out of the church. But he has decisively put a stop to their efforts to eject everyone else.[52]

What the Catholic neoconservative movement bequeathed, then, is the sectarian and Manichean inclination to divide society between the pure and the impure. The great post-2001 crusade against the "axis of evil," the war of the "Christian" West against the Islamist invasion, and the defense of the roots of the West against progressive nihilists are all points of a strongly dichotomous political-religious strategy. It is a Manichaeism that was not avoided by the counterpart Democratic Party, which participated in the radicalization of libertarian individualism. It is this libertarian individualism that, in the second decade of the new millennium, allowed the Catholic neoconservative movement to stay

---

52. Cathleen Kaveny, "First Things First," *Commonweal*, January 27, 2016, https://www.commonwealmagazine.org/first-things-first.

alive even when the evaporation of the Islamic threat and the obviousness of the Iraqi debacle made clear that it was, intellectually, spent.

While the presidency of Barack Obama (2009–2017) contained strong elements of harmony with Catholic social teaching, its policy on abortion and the Obamacare provision that forced Catholic organizations to pay for contraception and abortive medicines in their health care coverage resulted in a complicated relationship with the church. The easily anticipated consequence was that many more Catholics drifted to the right. The administration also exacerbated the Manichean ideology it had committed to overcome.[53]

With a relativist opponent in the Oval Office, the Catholic neocon movement found new momentum and new unity. The American church chose to concentrate on defending a small set of nonnegotiable values in a relentless struggle against the Democratic Party, which they portrayed as a lost world, with the result that "for decades, the scene has been dominated by an undeniable polarization and radicalization of positions between the two sides on moral and ethical issues, which mirrors the polarization and radicalization within the American religious world on issues of sexual, family, and marriage ethics; immigration; and religious freedom."[54]

---

53. On the dialectic between the Obama presidency and the Catholic American world, see Alessandro Gisotti, *Dio e Obama: Fede e politica alla Casa Bianca* (Cantalupa: Effatà Editrice, 2010), 72–125.

54. Faggioli, "Il cattolico Biden non potrà sanare." In a 2010 address, then-Archbishop of Denver Charles Chaput argued that the contrast between the US episcopate and the Democratic Party was due to ideas made popular by President John F. Kennedy. Chaput criticized Kennedy's September 1960 statements to the Greater Ministerial Association, an organization of Protestant pastors in Houston, about the separation of church and state in the United States, words that would initiate the secularization of American politics. See Charles J. Chaput, "The Vocation of Christians in American Public Life," March 1, 2010, https://www.ewtn .com/catholicism/library/vocation-of-christians-in-american-public-life-3681.

A response to Archbishop Chaput came from the Italian Catholic social scientist Luca Diotallevi, who noted "the risk that some of the 'evangelical' or neoconservative positions most widespread in the American Protestant world, but also in some fringes of the Catholic world, might adopt the paradigm of Westphalia, meaning that they might tend to propose again a relationship between politics and religion in which the latter becomes an instrument (albeit valuable and well rewarded) of the former. In some passages of his talk, Archbishop Chaput seems to accept the view according to which if one does not want indifferent political institutions, then the separation between Church and state must be rejected." "Separating Church and State Isn't Just an Option, It's a Must," in Sandro Magister, "Saving the Catholic Kennedy. A Reply to Archbishop Chaput," Settimo Cielo

This dualism took on new and decidedly more radical tones with the shift, in the second decade of the twenty-first century, from a neoconservative to a populist ideology. Catholic neoconservative universalism, which had championed America's mission to spread democracy around the globe, gave way to a preoccupation with walls and borders. Globalization, this populism insisted, had lied. It had not fulfilled its promises, and it enslaved the people. The Catholic neocons gave way to theo-populists who hoisted crosses rather than flags, not to unite but to divide. The heralds of American democracy were replaced by antimodern and anticonciliar traditionalists like Archbishop Viganò. The consequence, writes Jesse Russell, is that "as the Catholic Church appears divided into increasingly polarized camps, consisting of traditionalists, on one hand, and progressives, on the other, the Catholic neoconservatives, who attempted to find a theological *via media* between the two camps, have found themselves increasingly isolated. Furthermore, in the realm of geopolitics, seemingly amorphous forms of populism appear to be gaining support among large swathes of the population from Brazil, to the United States, to Italy, and to even countries like Japan, thus threatening the neoconservative project of global liberal world order under American hegemonic rule."[55]

Such a threat was thwarted with the advent to the presidency of the anomalous Donald Trump, the norm-smashing billionaire not entirely to the liking of the old religious neocons Michael Novak and George Weigel.[56] Trump became an idol of those who opposed the "deep state" and Francis's "deep church." He was the populist president who brought

blog, *L'Espresso*, April 11, 2010, https://chiesa.espresso.repubblica.it/articolo/1342853bdc4 .html?eng=y.

Archbishop Chaput replied to Diotallevi via Magister's blog with "Kennedy Case: The Bishop Flunks the Professor," Settimo Cielo blog, *L'Espresso*, April 21, 2010, https://chiesa .espresso.repubblica.it/articolo/1342971bdc4.html?eng=y.

55. Jesse Russell, "The Winter of (Neo)Conservative Discontent," The Religious Studies Project, November 15, 2019, https://www.religiousstudiesproject.com/response /the-winter-of-neoconservative-discontent/.

56. Prior to the 2016 election, Weigel coauthored, with Robert P. George, an anti-Trump manifesto, "An Appeal to Our Fellow Catholics," *National Review*, March 7, 2016, https:// www.nationalreview.com/2016/03/donald-trump-catholic-opposition-statement/. Regarding Michael Novak on the subject, see the interview "Vi spiego perché Trump ha conquistato gli americani," La Nuova Bussola Quotidiana, June 18, 2016. See also Giuliano Ferrara, "Mi spiace, ma non capisco certo trumpismo," *Il Foglio*, November 12, 2016, the first in a series of articles extremely critical of Trump and his politics, written by a leader of neoconservatism in Italy.

populists back under the American aegis. Thus the sovereignists, from the Hungarian Orbán to the Italian Salvini, were anti-European and, at the same time, decidedly "Americanist." In Trump's hands, populism was a pawn to weaken the German-led European Union, and religion—the harsh, integralist sort, preoccupied with identity—served as the perfect tool for geopolitical conflicts and for doing political damage to the world authority most threatening to polarizations, conflicts, and the status quo in the balance of power: Pope Francis.[57]

This book is the second I have written about Pope Francis. The previous one, *The Mind of Pope Francis: Jorge Mario Bergoglio's Intellectual Journey*,[58] was the first in-depth study on Bergoglio's thought, his teachers, and his philosophical and theological formation. It responded to the objections of those who, starting from the European and North American prejudices, doubted the cultural formation of the "Latin American" pontiff, a rich and complex formation that has, at its core, the model of "polarity" derived from the philosophy of the French Jesuit Gaston Fessard and from the antinomic anthropology of Romano Guardini. It is thanks to this model, which is at the center of "Bergoglian thought," that Francis can oppose the false polarizations of contemporary Manichaeism and the Catholic neoconservative and nationalist political theologies. *This is a point of capital importance that largely eludes commentators.*

In his critique of political theology, Bergoglio follows his teacher Guardini, who wrote in 1967, a year before his death,

> In the *Frankfurter Allgemeine Zeitung*, there was an article by the correspondent from the Vatican on a recently published book by Prof. Guitton. He summarizes the result of various talks with Pope Paul there and shows the spiritual character and intention of the pope: not simply to govern, but to establish a dialogue with those who each time represent the "other." The

57. See Iacopo Scaramuzzi, *Dio? In fondo a destra: Perché i populismi sfruttano il cristianesimo* (Verona: Emi, Verona 2020) and Flavia Perina, "La nuova Lega, ultraconservatrice e dura contro le idee di Papa Bergoglio," *La Stampa*, March 30, 2018. Representative of this thinking was the second National Conservative Conference, held in Rome February 3–4, 2020, on the theme "God, Honor, Nation: President Ronald Reagan, Pope John Paul II, and the Freedom of Nations." Among the featured speakers were Victor Orbán, Giorgia Meloni, Rod Dreher, Roberto de Mattei, Christopher DeMuth (president of the American Enterprise Institute), Antonio Martino, and Anna Maria Anders (Polish ambassador to Italy). See https://nationalconservatism.org/natcon-rome-2020/.

58. Massimo Borghesi, *The Mind of Pope Francis: Jorge Mario Bergoglio's Intellectual Journey*, trans. Barry Hudock (Collegeville, MN: Liturgical Press, 2018).

essence of this approach consists in the fact that the other does not appear as an adversary, but as "opposed," and the two points of view, thesis and antithesis, are brought to unity. Then the author cites the names of personalities who support the same method, and for Germany he cites mine. Considering the importance that the idea of dialogue has today, then he sees that the right time has come for my book on Opposition. We have already said this explicitly as well. The theory of opposites is the theory of confrontation, which does not take place as a fight against an enemy, but as a synthesis of a fruitful tension, that is, as the construction of concrete unity.[59]

This theory of "opposites" is a theory of comparison and synthesis that rejects the friend-enemy dialectic that constitutes the essence of Carl Schmitt's political theology, dominant in the contemporary religious scene.[60] It is the theory that underpins the theoretical framework of *Evangelii Gaudium*, *Laudato Si'*, and *Fratelli Tutti*. In his conversation with Austen Ivereigh, *Let Us Dream: The Path to a Better Future*, Francis makes his debt to Guardini clear. Thanks to this Italian-German thinker, Bergoglio's thought is neither irenic nor Manichaean. It is *catholic*, based on the distinction between "opposition" and "contradiction."

> Guardini gave me a startling insight to deal with conflicts, analyzing their complexity while avoiding any simplifying reductionism: there exist differences in tension, pulling apart, but all coexist within a larger unity.
>
> Understanding how apparent contradictions could be resolved metaphysically, through discernment, was the topic of my thesis on Guardini, which I went to Germany to research. I worked on it for some years, but

---

59. Romano Guardini, Letter to Jacob Laubach of November 21, 1967, cited in Hanna Barbara Gerl-Falkovitz, "Introduzione a R. Guardini," in *Scritti di metodologia filosofica*, Gerl-Falkovitz, ed., *Opera omnia*, vol. 1 (Brescia: Morcelliana, 2007), 22. Emphasis mine. The book by Jean Guitton that Guardini refers to is *Dialogues avec Paul VI* (published in English as *The Pope Speaks: Dialogues of Paul VI with Jean Guitton* [New York: Meredith Press, 1968]).

60. On the opposition between the dialogical-polar model and the political theology of Carl Schmitt, see Rodrigo Guerra López, "Amistad social o conflicto político," *El Eraldo de México*, November 16, 2020. See also the interview with Guerra López, "Existen algunos sectores que han entrado en una deriva ideológica de la fe," Aleteia, December 14, 2020. For a comparison of Romano Guardini and Carl Schmitt, see Massimo Borghesi, *Romano Guardini: Antinomia della vita e conoscenza affettiva* (Milan: Jaca Book, 2018), 45–52. On Guardini's idea of polar opposition, see Borghesi, *Romano Guardini: Dialettica e antropologia*, 2nd ed. (Rome: Studium, 2004).

I never finished writing it up. But the thesis has helped me a lot, especially in managing tensions and conflicts. . . .

One of the effects of conflict is to see as contradictions what are in fact contrapositions, as I like to call them. A contraposition involves two poles in tension, pulling away from each other: horizon/limit, local/global, whole/part, and so on. These are contrapositions because they are opposites that nonetheless interact in a fruitful, creative tension. As Guardini taught me, creation is full of these living polarities, or *Gegensätze*; they are what make us alive and dynamic. Contradictions (*Widersprüche*) on the other hand demand that we choose, between right and wrong. (Good and evil can never be a contraposition, because evil is not the counterpart of good, but its negation.)

To see contrapositions as contradictions is the result of mediocre thinking that takes us away from reality. The bad spirit—the spirit of conflict, which undermines dialogue and fraternity—turns contrapositions into contradictions, demanding we choose, and reducing reality to simple binaries. This is what ideologies and unscrupulous politicians do.[61]

One of these contrapositions that dissolve into contradiction is currently that between fundamentalism and relativism. Contemporary culture, politics, and religion are dominated by the contrast between liberal postmodernism and an ethical reaction to it, between progressivism and traditionalism. It is the dialectic that divides Republicans and Democrats in the United States. Francis's pontificate seeks to reach beyond this dialectic, and this explains the misunderstanding to which it is subject. This "reaching beyond" finds its expression in the idea that "the Jesuit must be a person whose thought is incomplete, in the sense of open-ended thinking."[62] It is an expression that is also subject to misunderstanding or distortion, as if to say the pope doesn't think. In reality, what is in question here is the *form* of thought. Francis made this clear in his conversation with Ivereigh:

I learned this way of thinking from Romano Guardini. It was his style that captivated me, first of all in his book *The Lord*. Guardini showed me the importance of *el pensamiento incompleto*, unfinished thinking. He develops

61. Pope Francis, in conversation with Austen Ivereigh, *Let Us Dream: The Path to a Better Future* (New York: Simon & Schuster, 2020), 78–79.

62. Pope Francis, with Antonio Spadaro, *My Door Is Always Open: A Conversation on Faith, Hope and the Church in a Time of Change*, trans. Shaun Whiteside (London: Bloomsbury, 2013), 24.

a thought but only takes you so far before he invites you to stop to give space to contemplate. He creates room for you to encounter the truth. A fruitful thought should always be unfinished in order to give space to subsequent development. With Guardini I learned not to demand absolute certainties in everything, which is the sign of an anxious spirit. His wisdom has allowed me to confront complex problems that cannot be resolved simply with norms, using instead a kind of thinking that allows you to navigate conflicts without being trapped in them.

The way of thinking that he proposes opens us to the Spirit and to the discernment of spirits. If you don't open up, you can't discern. Hence my allergy to moralisms and other -isms that try to resolve all problems with prescriptions, equations, and rules. Like Guardini, I believe in objective truths and solid principles. I am grateful for the solidity of the Church's tradition, the fruit of centuries of shepherding humanity and of *fides quaerens intellectum*, faith seeking reasoning and understanding.[63]

Truth is objective and firm in its essence. It opens up, however, in discernment. Bergoglio brings together Guardini and St. Ignatius in a fruitful and original way. Discernment always takes place in a tension through which truth is made manifest. "Discernment," Francis says, "allows us to navigate changing contexts and specific situations as we seek the truth. Truth reveals itself to the one who opens herself to it. That is what the ancient Greek word for truth, *aletheia*, means: what reveals itself; what is unveiled. The Hebrew vowel *emet*, on the other hand, connects truth to fidelity, to what is certain, what is firm, what does not deceive or disappoint. So truth has these two elements."[64]

Truth is objective and, at the same time, requires the moment of persuasion, of certainty. A Christianity accepted only as a dogmatic system, as an ideology that offers security in an uncertain world, does not change one's life and does not bring joy. This is the problem with "Christianism." Hard as a stone, muscular, it flaunts faith as a possession and not as an undeserved grace. *Truth-in-itself* must, on the contrary, become *truth-for-me*. It must move toward gratitude. Otherwise, even if formally true, it remains "abstract"; it does not touch the heart, the self, in its deepest reality. This is the lesson of John Henry Newman, which Bergoglio joins with Guardini's.

---

63. Pope Francis, *Let Us Dream*, 55–56.
64. Pope Francis, *Let Us Dream*, 55.

Like John Henry Newman, whom I declared a saint in October 2019, I see the truth lying outside us, always beyond us, but beckoning to us through our consciences. It is like a "kindly light" we reach not normally through reason but "through the imagination, by means of direct impressions, by the testimony of facts and events, by history, by description," as he wrote in *Grammar of Assent*. Newman was convinced, as I am, that in embracing what often appear at first sight to be contradictory truths and trusting in the kindly light to lead us, we will eventually come to see the greater truth that lies beyond us. I like to think that we do not possess the truth so much as the truth possesses us, constantly attracting us by means of beauty and goodness.

This is an approach to truth quite distinct from the epistemology of post-truth, which demands that we choose sides rather than hear evidence. Yet it doesn't mean thinking in set ways that are closed to new possibilities; it contains both an element of assent and an element of continuous searching. That has been the tradition of the Church: her understanding and beliefs have expanded and consolidated over time in openness to the Spirit, according to the principle enunciated in the fifth century by Saint Vincent of Lérins: "They strengthen with the years, develop with time and become deeper with age."[65]

* * *

This book analyzes the Catholic neoconservative movement, beginning with a consideration of its early leaders, Michael Novak first, and then George Weigel and Richard John Neuhaus. Their attempt to "hijack" the pontificate of John Paul II first, and that of Benedict XVI later, brought them to the height of American and, at times, global Catholic intelligentsia. Their influence, even in the Italian ecclesial context, has been conspicuous and little investigated. But understanding it goes a long way

---

65. Pope Francis, *Let Us Dream*, 56–57. "This mention of Newman brings to mind his well-known words in his *Essay on the Development of Christian Doctrine*, a book that coincided chronologically and spiritually with his entry into the Catholic Church: 'Here below to live is to change, and to be perfect is to have changed often.' Naturally, he is not speaking about changing for change's sake, or following every new fashion, but rather about the conviction that development and growth are a normal part of human life, even as believers we know that God remains the unchanging center of all things." Pope Francis, "Christmas Greetings to the Roman Curia," December 21, 2019, http://www.vatican.va/content/francesco/en/speeches/2019/december/documents/papa-francesco_20191221_curia-romana.html.

toward explaining the resistance that has been met by Pope Francis in some segments of the church, especially in the United States. Opposition to Francis, to his fundamental documents *Evangelii Gaudium*, *Laudato Si'*, and *Fratelli Tutti*, is based on a vision of the world devised by these Catholic neoconservatives.[66]

On the other hand, we also cannot understand Bergoglio's pontificate without a conscious questioning of the ideological frame that movement has built around the church. A rethinking of the narrow moral agenda, the primacy of the missionary dimension and of dialogue over the dialectical dimension, and the fresh consideration of Catholic social teaching in all its breadth rather than the partial and distorted Catho-capitalist version—these are all points that mark the distance between the "field hospital" and the culture wars. The call for a church that goes forth, the primacy of grace and evangelical freedom, the preferential option for the poor that has been obscured in the conscience of Catholics in the rich regions of the planet are all elements of the "reform" of the church in progress.

＊   ＊   ＊

I would like to thank the apostolic nuncio to the United States, Archbishop Christophe Pierre, who has worked so hard to open the church in the United States to an accurate understanding of Pope Francis. Archbishop Pierre helped to promote, with Fr. Thomas L. Knoebel of Sacred Heart Seminary, the international symposium held in Milwaukee (October 8–11, 2018) on "Discovering Pope Francis: Theological, Philosophical, Cultural and Spiritual Perspectives," the first conference in the United States dedicated to the pope's thought. From that conference, which included the participation of some of the most qualified specialists

---

66. Notable here is the publication of George Weigel, *The Next Pope: The Office of Peter and a Church in Mission* (San Francisco: Ignatius Press, 2020). The book was sent as a gift by Cardinal Timothy Dolan, the Archbishop of New York, to other cardinals of the church. See Salvatore Cernuzio, "I conservatori Usa pensano già al Conclave: esce libro sul 'nuovo Papa': E l'arcivescovo di New York lo regala ad altri cardinali," Vatican Insider, *La Stampa*, July 17, 2020. Regarding the case of Archbishop Viganò, Weigel has offered public support for the former Vatican nuncio in "Why We Stay, and the Viganò Testimony," *First Things*, August 28, 2018.

in Bergoglio's thought, a volume of proceedings with a preface by the pope, was published.[67]

A special thanks to Cardinal Gualtiero Bassetti, president of the Italian Episcopal Conference, with whom I have had the opportunity to share an esteem and affection for the person and magisterium of Francis. Thanks to all the friends I mentioned in the dedication, involved in different ways in promoting Francis's thought. I have benefited greatly from their insights, observations, and writings. Among the latter, I recall the important contribution of Austen Ivereigh, *Wounded Shepherd: Pope Francis and His Struggle to Convert the Catholic Church.*[68] Thanks also to Vincenzo Di Alessandro for the helpful guidance on the work of David Schindler, the American disciple of Henri de Lubac and Hans Urs von Balthasar, opponent of the Catholic neoconservative theology. Finally, as always, I thank my family—my wife Carmen and my children Daniela, Luisa, Alessandro—for sharing and enduring the "monastic conditions" that the writing of each book requires.

67. Brian Y. Lee and Thomas L. Knoebel, eds., *Discovering Pope Francis: The Roots of Jorge Mario Bergoglio's Thinking*, foreword by Pope Francis (Collegeville, MN: Liturgical Press, 2019).

68. Austen Ivereigh, *Wounded Shepherd: Pope Francis and His Struggle to Convert the Catholic Church* (New York: Henry Holt, 2019).

The Fall of Communism and the Hegemony of Catholic Americanism

The Church after the Fall of Communism

When Jorge Mario Bergoglio became pope, taking the name Francis, on March 13, 2013, he took the helm of a church devastated by clergy sex abuse crimes and cover-ups and further roiled by the lesser scandal that had become known as Vati-leaks. But that same church was marked by another legacy that shaped Catholic consciousness, one that had been taking shape since the 1980s, with the advent of the era of globalization.

After the years immediately following the Second Vatican Council—which were marked by intense theological disputes and, in some segments, an attempt to understand Christianity through a Marxist lens—the church seemed to establish, with the pontificate of John Paul II, a renewed sense of identity and balance. In his first documents, the encyclicals *Redemptor Hominis* and *Laborem Exercens*, John Paul brought a renewed awareness of the church's foundation—"Christ the center of the universe and of history"—and of its social commitment, specifically in defense of the dignity of work. Inspired by the popular struggles of the *Solidarność* trade union movement in Communist Poland, *Laborem Exercens* became the pope's social manifesto. It took up the Polish model and proposed it to Christians and all people as an authentic liberation movement, based on the radical rejection of violence.

The pope's approach found an echo in Latin American Catholicism. Upon the publication of *Laborem Exercens* in 1981, a group of South

American Catholic intellectuals that included Alberto Methol Ferré, Hernán Alessandri, and Joaquín Allende immediately began to discuss—primarily in the journal *Incontri*[1]—implications for the Latin American context. Their perspective was notably different from the pro-Marxist and pro-revolutionary ideas the theologian Gustavo Gutiérrez had recently proposed in his well-known 1971 book, *A Theology of Liberation*.[2] But it was not reactionary. Rather, their reflection upon the Polish experience presupposed the profound turning point for the Latin American church represented by the important gathering of the continent's bishops in Puebla, Mexico, in 1979, which combined an appreciation of popular religiosity with a preferential option for the poor and the struggle for justice. It is a model that was articulated in the "theology of the people" developed by the Argentine school of Rio de La Plata, in the work of Lucio Gera, Rafael Tello, Justino O'Farrel, Gerardo Farrell, and Juan Carlos Scannone.[3] Gutiérrez would himself come to embrace it as an authentic form of liberation theology, in his self-criticism that he included in the 1988 edition of his book, in which he questions the Marxist primacy of praxis that he had previously advocated: "What we see here is an authentic spirituality—that is, a way to be Christian. It is from this rich experience of the following of Jesus that liberation theology emerges; the following constitutes the practice—at once commitment and prayer—on which liberation theology reflects."[4] Another who shared this approach was Jorge Mario Bergoglio.

John Paul II's social-political vision, shaped by opposition to Communist totalitarianism in Poland, was not conservative. In *Laborem Exercens* he wrote:

1. See Alver Metalli, ed., "Dottrina sociale, Polonia, 'Laborem exercens,'" *Incontri: Testimonianze dall'America Latina*, November-December 1981, 8–20. See also the editorial "Nel destino della Polonia il Risorgimento dell'America Latina," *Incontri: Testimonianze dall'America Latina*, January-February 1982, 3–6.

2. Gustavo Gutiérrez, *A Theology of Liberation: History, Politics, and Salvation*, trans. Candida Inda and John Eagleson (Maryknoll, NY: Orbis, 1973, rev. ed. 1988).

3. On the Argentine "theology of the people," see Juan Carlos Scannone, *La teología del pueblo: Raíces teológicas del papa Francisco* (Maliaño: Sal Terrae, 2017). On the use of the category of people in the perspective of Pope Francis and of Juan Carlos Scannone, see Emilce Cuda, *Para leer a Francisco: Teologia, etica e politica* (Turin: Bollati Boringhieri, 2018).

4. Gutiérrez, *A Theology of Liberation*, 19.

In order to achieve social justice in the various parts of the world, in the various countries, and in the relationships between them, there is a need for ever *new movements of solidarity of* the workers and *with* the workers. This solidarity must be present whenever it is called for by the social degrading of the subject of work, by exploitation of the workers, and by the growing areas of poverty and even hunger. The Church is firmly committed to this cause, for she considers it her mission, her service, a proof of her fidelity to Christ, so that she can truly be the "Church of the poor."[5]

As cardinal in Buenos Aires and later as pope, Bergoglio embraced this. John Paul II marked out a path by which the church could avoid the two siren calls of reactionism and revolution.

Throughout the 1980s, John Paul was an undisputed protagonist upon the international stage. The fall of Soviet Communism that followed a series of events set in motion by the labor movement in Poland can in large part be attributed to him. However, the outcome of the Soviet collapse was not all that he had hoped for. While the gains for religious and civil liberty were clear, hopes for the rebirth of faith from the East—*ex Oriente lux*—were illusory. Neither the East nor the West became more receptive to the church after the fall of Communism. Having lost its historical adversary and therefore able to abandon the principled moral-religious stance that allowed it to claim a moral superiority over Soviet atheism and materialism, the West largely became more materialistic. With the fall of Carthage, Rome could abandon the ethical idealism of wartime.

This explains why the era of globalization coincides with a much more radical secularization of Western life than occurred during the 1960s and 1970s. The primacy of the economy, with a new type of financial capitalism, coincides with the decline of politics, ethics, and religion. The *ideal* that stood in contradistinction with Marxist *ideology* disappeared, and a cynical and soulless pragmatism based on an individualistic, Hobbesian-Darwinist anthropology triumphed. Faced with this "anthropological mutation," which had been clearly foreseen in the 1970s by Pier Paolo Pasolini, the church stood bewildered and unprepared. Conditioned by more than seventy years of an adversarial stance against totalitarianism

---

5. Pope John Paul II, *Laborem Exercens*, September 14, 1981, http://www.vatican.va /content/john-paul-ii/en/encyclicals/documents/hf_jp-ii_enc_14091981_laborem -exercens.html, 8.

and persecution, it bore a *forma mentis* that could not decipher the vacuum it faced.

Furthermore, while the West had won its victory over Communism, the new Christian-social conscience that might have replaced the Marxist conscience in the struggle for justice and rights was weak or absent. In Latin America, the development of the theology of the people by the Argentine school was a singular positive exception. But after the criticism of liberation theology by the Congregation for the Doctrine of the Faith, the theoretical and practical support for a *new* theology of liberation that Rome had promised never materialized.[6] A preoccupation with ecclesial order and an orthodoxy that failed to include social doctrine prevailed over missionary dynamism and attentiveness to social realities. *Redemptor Hominis, Laborem Exercens,* and *Redemptoris Missio* were each splendid documents, manifestos that articulated the bold program of John Paul II's pontificate, and yet beginning in the late 1980s, the church withdrew into itself, disinterested in both mission and the social-political common good.

This tendency became stronger when, with the fall of Communism, even liberation theology lost its charm and appeal. In Latin America, the vacuum it left was filled by a theology of order, an ecclesial conformism that abandoned the poor to their fate. It was clear that the church had no idea how to take advantage of the situation, and so it abandoned its appointment with history. As Alberto Methol Ferré—one of the protagonists of the Latin American Catholic *Risorgimento* and Bergoglio's friend and "philosopher"—declared in 2006, "In a certain way, the 'evaporation' of liberation theology has diminished the drive of the Latin American church as a whole to assume the condition of the poor with courage. I believe the church is paying the price for getting rid of liberation theology too easily. Liberation theology should have offered its full contribution

---

6. The Congregation for the Doctrine of the Faith published two documents on liberation theology. The first, *Instruction on Certain Aspects of the "Theology of Liberation"* (*Libertatis Nuntius*), was published in 1984. The second, *Instruction of Christian Freedom and Liberation,* came in 1986. While the first text offered a systematic critique of the theological and philosophical deviations of liberation theology in its Marxist elements, the second expressed a more positive appreciation of the same theology by correctly focusing on the theme of liberation. But even the second document appears more concerned with addressing the possible problems than with offering a positive reflection on the topic.

after the fall of Communism, not withered away with Marxism. Today it is urgent to make up for its absence."[7]

This opinion was shared by Cardinal Bergoglio. On April 16, 2007, less than a month before he would lead the fifth great gathering of the Latin American church, at Aparecida in Brazil, Bergoglio wrote to the Italian journalist and Vatican expert Lucio Brunelli: "We will see you in Aparecida. As an interpretive key, I believe, like you, that we need to get out of the dialectic with the theology of liberation. For me the key must be evangelization, the kerygma in the identity of Latin America today. For the fifth conference, the end will not be a document but the 'continental mission,' the proclamation of Jesus Christ."[8]

Like Methol Ferré, Bergoglio saw the fall of Soviet Communism as an opportunity for the church to finally take seriously the link—emphasized by Pope Paul VI in *Evangelii Nuntiandi* in 1975—between evangelization and human development without the fear of being accused of Communist sympathies. To do this, it was necessary to start afresh from evangelization, because from there the categories of justice, the common good, and the option for the poor received their vigor and meaning. This would make it possible to "get out of the dialectic with liberation theology." It would provide a critical opportunity to move beyond the stark good-bad dialectic with which liberation theology had been approached.

Marxism was mistaken, and its consequences were both violent and destructive of authentic human freedom. But Marxism's denunciation of the violence of unbridled capitalism and the unjust structures that produced social inequalities was accurate. Overcoming the problematic version of liberation theology would allow the church to address its just demands. Such a transition ought not mean, as it in fact did within conservative fringes of Latin American Catholicism, an uncritical transition to a *liberal* neocapitalism with no concern for the oppressed. This was not any kind of triumph, but simple, adialectic opposition, in which the figure of the opponent remained. It was a conservative position rather than a progressive one. It put the church in the role of a simple pawn in

---

7. Alberto Methol Ferré and Alver Metalli, *Il papa e il filosofo* (Siena: Cantagalli, 2014), 114.

8. Cited in Lucio Brunelli, *Papa Francesco: Come l'ho conosciuto io* (Cinisello Balsamo: Edizioni San Paolo, 2020), 32.

a game of interests, one player on the field, one party in the struggle. On the contrary, as Methol Ferré clearly wrote:

> Engaging in and orienting a real historical process obviously requires the *conditio sine qua non* of knowing the other, of deeply penetrating the logic of current models, of delving into them in order to be able truly to move beyond them, in order to respond to reality in a true way. If I am nothing more than resistant, if I say, "Hegel and Marx are atheists, and that's all I need to know," and I close myself off from any further consideration, this is not a way forward. The theologians of the last century clearly recognized the atheism of Hegel and Marx and denounced it. But that wasn't enough. What was necessary was to penetrate deeply into their motivations, to discover the new problems that they revealed. But that was never done. And so today a couple of generations of Catholics try in vain to assimilate and understand Hegel and Marx. And many will die of "indigestion," because it is not possible to "consume" Hegel and Marx with impunity and the task of moving beyond them is not easy.[9]

This theoretical and practical moving beyond Marxism did not happen. The social teaching of the church, expressed frequently by John Paul II, nevertheless fell into oblivion, and the church withdrew into a closed, clerical, autonomous space. The more the church abstracted itself from history, the more *clericalized* it became. In this transformation, from the socially engaged Catholicism of the 1970s to the disengaged Catholicism of the 1990s, the result was a new expression of American Catholicism.

As the United States transitioned from the Carter to the Reagan presidency, a significant metamorphosis took place in the church there. The secularization of the North American landscape and in particular of the Democratic Party pushed Catholics into the Republican sphere, with its typically Protestant combination of defense of the family and the free market. As Massimo Faggioli has written:

> The theological-political victory of doctrinal politics in the Vatican over liberation theology had brought with it the elimination of one of the themes of the Second Vatican Council: the poor. In this cultural and ecclesial climate, what emerged particularly strongly was the American Catholic

---

9. Alberto Methol Ferré, "La Chiesa latinoamericana nella dinamica mondiale," in Methol Ferré, *Il Risorgimento Cattolico Latinoamericano* (Bologna: CSEO, 1983), 133.

Church's conservative school of the Reagan era, or the U.S. Catholicism that between 1973 (the Supreme Court decision to legalize abortion) and 1980 (the election of Ronald Reagan to the presidency) had moved to a large extent from the Democratic Party (which had been the natural political home of recent Catholic immigrants for almost a century) to the Republican Party. From the late eighties onward, "Catholic Reaganism" also affected the American hierarchy, and gave a decisive boost to the theological formulation of the "culture wars" between the different key elements of American culture, even within Catholicism.

The winning side of political Catholicism in the United States, represented by the conservative and neoconservative strains, chose two pillars for its identity: a pro-life anti-abortion stance that was isolated from the "social question"; and an economic culture oriented towards free market that was against the public sector and the regulation of the market by politics. In the American "culture wars," two extremes tend to meet: the radical progressive and the conservative, both substantially (but to different extents) oblivious to the great tradition of social Catholicism.[10]

With the disappearance of Communism, Catholicism lost its "social" soul, as if it had only been an expedient tool to be used for beating an adversary on its own ground. The individualism that has marked the era of globalization also infected the Christian conscience. Everything expressive of community, solidarity, or equality was dismissed as part of the "bad" legacy of the radical left. This was the case not only in the eyes of Christians but also in those of the new left, which, in order to legitimize itself and erase its past, forged a new progressivism that was uninterested in people as a category.

Being on the left, after 1989, meant cultivating an individualistic, radical liberalism that elevated physical and individual desires as a model of human progress in general. Poverty, social inequalities, workers' rights, economic justice, and collaboration between the state and civil society in management of the economy disappeared from the view of the new left. It became libertarian and pleasure-seeking, measuring quality of life solely by one's personal sense of psychosocial well-being. Thus the left, the liberal right, and the church each abandoned social concerns as a locus of politics and change. The church's embrace of conservative

10. Massimo Faggioli, *Pope Francis: Tradition in Transition*, trans. Sean O'Neill (New York: Paulist, 2015), 80–81.

positions, in reaction to a relativistic and optimistic postmodernism, coincided with an ecclesial "retreat," a closure from and distrust of a world perceived as hostile, alien, enemy. The adversary, once Marxism, was now relativism and then—following the terrorist attacks of September 2001— also Islamism, and sensing its own weakness, the church closed itself within a besieged fortress.

Christian commitment in the world meant culture wars, defending a set of specific values—unborn life, heterosexual marriage, rejection of euthanasia, and so on—that were rejected by the dominant culture. The dialectical model was imposed, with dialogue and mission dismissed; it was also a militant model, understood only in relation to the enemy of the moment. But it was dialectic only when it came to life issues, not economic ones; in the latter case, a decisive conformism reigned. The rejection of the spirit of secularization was accompanied by an unconditional embrace of a capitalist model, which, ironically, was the real engine of the very secularization that was supposed to be the enemy. Hence the impotence of a struggle that bears within itself a contradiction: opposition to the relativism and individualism created by economic processes that are accepted enthusiastically. The religious conscience had nothing to say about the logic of "waste" that allowed the rejection of the handicapped, the unproductive elderly, the terminally ill, and the poor. It opposed such a logic when it came to abortion or euthanasia, and yet it avoided critical engagement with the structural processes that nourished the "purge" dynamics. And so the struggle against secularization presupposed its acceptance as a "destiny" that left Christians with two options from which to choose: either existence as tiny communities outside of history (Rod Dreher's "Benedict Option"[11]) or an organic alliance with political conservatives in the hope that power, a new *kathèkon*, would be able to stop the advance of the enemy. In either case, the new evangelization—encouraged by John Paul II especially with his splendid encyclical *Redemptoris Missio*—was abandoned, left, at best, to individual initiative.

The Catholic culture that resulted, and that Pope Francis inherited, was one that had left behind both social doctrine *and* new evangelization. It was an essentially "ethical" Catholicism, polarized on a few foundational values, the model of which was expressed in the great alliance between

11. See Rod Dreher, *The Benedict Option: A Strategy for Christians in a Post-Christian Nation* (New York: Penguin, 2017).

John Paul II and Ronald Reagan during the 1980s. It was a "tactical" alliance, determined by a common adversary, that became *ideological*, adopting an *ontological* guise. Catholicism of the last thirty years is *essentially* conservative. It seeks order, moral certainties, clear opponents, bright boundaries. It does not like to be "without a country," *in partibus infidelium*, on the "threshold," to use Péguy's term. It wants to be among "the faithful," among its own, and relentlessly fight the eternal battle, devoid of sentimentality, against the infidels.

This *forma mentis* is the result not only of a historical process but also of an intellectual one, given life by a small group of thinkers who, in the United States, played a fundamental role in the intellectual formation of American Catholicism, which became a pilot for the entire Western world after the fall of the Berlin Wall. Among them, the most prominent figures were Michael Novak, George Weigel, and Richard John Neuhaus.

From Antimodernism to Liberal-Conservative Modernism: Michael Novak's Catho-capitalism

In 1982 Michael Novak, whose intellectual biography included an appreciation of the ideals of "Christian socialism," published a book called *The Spirit of Democratic Capitalism*. In it Novak, who would within a decade become a leading American Catholic intellectual, asks himself: "The Catholic Church has heretofore learned from the intellect of Greece and Rome, Germany and France. Why not also from America?"[12] Novak

12. Michael Novak, *The Spirit of Democratic Capitalism* (New York: American Enterprise Institute/Simon & Schuster, 1982), 249. On Novak and his thought, see J. David Hoeveler, "Michael Novak: Capitalism and Catholicism," in Hoeveler, *Watch on the Right: Conservative Intellectuals in the Reagan Era* (Madison, WI: The University of Wisconsin Press, 1991), 233–69; Flavio Felice, *Capitalismo e cristianesimo: Il personalismo economico di Michael Novak* (Soveria Mannelli: Rubbettino, 2002). Among Novak's works, see esp. *A New Generation: American and Catholic* (New York: Herder and Herder, 1964); *The Open Church: Vatican II, Act II* (New York: Macmillan, 1964); *Belief and Unbelief: A Philosophy of Self-Knowledge* (New York: Macmillan, 1965); *The Experience of Nothingness* (New York: Harper and Row, 1970); *Ascent of the Mountain, Flight of the Dove: An Invitation to Religious Studies* (New York: Harper and Row, 1971); *The Rise of the Unmeltable Ethnics: Politics and Culture in the Seventies* (New York: Macmillan, 1972); *Freedom with Justice: Catholic Social Thought and Liberal Institutions* (San Francisco: Harper & Row, 1984); *Will it Liberate? Questions about Liberation Theology* (New York: Paulist, 1986); *Free Persons and the*

advocates an *American* Catholicism, a Catholicism modeled on the American lifestyle. In some ways he offers himself as the Catholic Max Weber.[13] In the early twentieth century, Weber had published *Protestant Ethics and the Spirit of Capitalism*, which demonstrated the importance of Calvinist puritanism in the formation of modern capitalist ethics. Novak revises and updates the Weberian perspective by substituting Catholicism for Calvinism. The encounter between Catholicism and modernity, advocated by the Second Vatican Council, becomes an alliance between Catholic ethics, founded on freedom and the rights of the person, with modern political economy. Novak certainly does not seek a clericalization of the economic system nor an integralist version of society. He makes clear that the American political system does not put God at the center:

> In a genuinely pluralistic society, there is no one sacred canopy. *By intention* there is not. At its spiritual core, there is an empty shrine. That shrine is left empty in the knowledge the no one word, image, or symbol is worthy of what all seek there. Its emptiness, therefore, represents the transcendence which is approached by free consciences from a virtually infinite number

---

Common Good (Lanham, MD: Madison Books, 1989); *The Hemisphere of Liberty: A Philosophy of the Americas* (Washington, DC: AIE Press, 1990); *The Catholic Ethic and the Spirit of Capitalism* (New York: Free Press, 1993); *Business as a Calling: Work and the Examined Life* (New York: Free Press, 1996); *The Fire of Invention: Civil Society and the Future or the Corporation* (Lanham, MD: Rowman & Littlefield, 1997); (with Jana Novak) *Tell Me Why: A Father Answers His Daughter's Questions About God* (New York: Pocket Books, 1998); *On Cultivating Freedom: Reflections on Moral Ecology,* ed. Brian C. Anderson (Lanham, MD: Rowman & Littlefield, 1999); *On Two Wings: Humble Faith and Common Sense at the American Founding* (New York: Encounter Books, 2003); *The Universal Hunger for Liberty: Why the Clash of Civilizations Is Not Inevitable* (New York: Basic Books, 2003); (with Jana Novak) *Washington's God: Religion, Liberty, and the Father of Our Country* (New York: Basic Books, 2007); *No One Sees God: The Dark Night of Atheists and Believers* (Cincinnati: St. Anthony Messenger Press, 2009); *All Nature Is a Sacramental Fire: Moments of Beauty, Sorrow, and Joy* (South Bend, IN: St. Augustine Press, 2011); (with William Simon) *Living the Call: An Introduction to the Lay Vocation* (New York: Encounter Books, 2011); (with Elizabeth Shaw) *The Myth of Romantic Love and Other Essays* (London: Routledge, 2013); *Writing from Left to Right: My Journey from Liberal to Conservative* (New York: Image Books, 2013); (with Paul Adams) *Social Justice Isn't What You Think It Is: Rescuing a Forgotten Virtue* (New York: Encounter Books, 2015).

13. "He was the first to assay the questions we take up afresh" (Novak, *The Spirit of Democratic Capitalism,* 36). On Weber, see 36–39.

of directions. (Aquinas once wrote that humans are made in the image of God but that since God is infinite He may be mirrored only through a virtually infinite number of humans. No concept of Him is adequate). Believer and unbeliever, selfless and selfish, frightened and bold, naive and jaded, all participate in an order whose *center* is not socially imposed.[14]

For Novak, this "empty shrine" is not, however, completely empty. He continues,

Human beings, according to the Declaration of Independence, are endowed with inalienable rights by the Creator. Abraham Lincoln and other presidents have freely reverenced the Almighty. On coins and notes of deposit one reads: "In God we trust." Is not God at the center? For those who so experience reality, yes. For atheists, no. Official religious expressions are not intended to embarrass or to compromise those who do not believe in God. They have a pluralistic content. No institution, group, or person in the United States is entitled to define for others the content signified by words like "God," "the Almighty," and "Creator." These words are like pointers, which each person must define for himself. Their function is to protect the liberty of conscience of all, by using a symbol which transcends the power of the state and any other earthly power. Such symbols are not quite blank; one may not fill them in with any content at all. They point beyond worldly power. Doing so, they guard the human openness to transcendence.[15]

Religious freedom thus becomes the legitimizing principle of the American political system. But it is a legitimacy that yields to another principle derived from Christian ethics: solidarity.

A "sacred canopy" of this sort—practical rather than creedal—allows for unity in practice, diversity in belief.

By contrast, traditional and socialist societies offer unitary vision. They suffuse every activity with symbolic solidarity. The human breast hungers for such nourishment. Atavistic memories haunt each free person. The "wasteland" at the heart of democratic capitalism is like a field of battle, on which individuals wander alone, in some confusion, amid many casualties. Nonetheless, like the dark night of the soul in the inner journey of the

14. Novak, *The Spirit of Democratic Capitalism*, 53.
15. Novak, *The Spirit of Democratic Capitalism*, 53–54.

mystics, this desert has an indispensable purpose. It is maintained out of respect for the diversity of human consciences, perceptions, and intentions.[16]

This sphere of individuality, "sacred" to democratic capitalism, is the value around which Novak's entire theoretical construction revolves. Despite the counterweights and retaining walls he invokes to govern the rules of the market, his conception remains deeply *individualistic*. "Solidarity—not only in practical cooperation but in moral values and meaning—is the common aim of all social systems except democratic capitalism."[17] One notes, then, that to Novak, *cooperation between capitalism and modern Christianity excludes the idea of solidarity*. It also excludes any critical appraisal of the liberal model. In a short chapter on "A Theology of Democratic Capitalism" toward the end of his book, Novak offers, with an evident sense of anxiety, a list of the theological points called upon to legitimize the capitalist form of the economy. From broad theological doctrines such as the Trinity and the Incarnation of Christ, Novak boldly offers a hermeneutic that draws very specific conclusions—about, for example, the federal budget. Where this all leads is to a Christianity that is "humble" and "realistic," one that calls us to accept "the world as it is," dismissing any utopianism or desire for change; the invitation is to "modest hopes," "illusionless hopes."[18]

> The single greatest temptation for Christians is to imagine that the salvation won by Jesus has altered the human condition. Many attempt to judge the present world by the standards of the gospels, as though the world were ready to live according to them. Sin is not so easily overcome. A political economy for sinners, even Christian sinners (however well intentioned), is consistent with the story of Jesus. A political economy based on love and justice is to be found beyond, never to be wholly incarnated within, human history. The Incarnation obliges us to reduce our noblest expectations, so to love the world as to fit a political economy suitable to it, nourishing all that is best in it.[19]

From this, says Novak, results the system of classical political economy that starts from the idea of sinful humanity and does not attempt to

16. Novak, *The Spirit of Democratic Capitalism*, 54–55.
17. Novak, *The Spirit of Democratic Capitalism*, 65.
18. Novak, *The Spirit of Democratic Capitalism*, 340–42.
19. Novak, *The Spirit of Democratic Capitalism*, 343–44.

subvert its nature. The correspondence that Novak proposes between capitalism and Catholicism is based not on the assumption that grace can "humanize" nature but on an extrinsic dualism, between natural and supernatural, for which the action of the Christian in the world must remain circumscribed within the ecclesial enclosure. Every attempt to transfer Christian ideals into history results in utopias, intolerance, sectarianism. This transfer is legitimate only where Christian values coincide with liberal-capitalist ones—for example, in the case of "competition." In the latter case, Novak writes, "it does not seem to be inconsistent with the gospels for each human being to struggle, under the spur of competition with his fellows, to become all he can become."[20] Thus, in a striking reversal of terms, in this "bourgeois Christianity" it is the economy that dictates the ethical model rather than vice versa. And this despite Novak's insistence, in *The Spirit of Democratic Capitalism* and in subsequent works, that this "spirit" is the result of a threefold convergence between economics, morality, and politics: "Montesquieu's dictum that the English were known throughout Europe for three distinctive excellences—piety, commerce, and liberty—pleased Weber."[21]

It also pleased Novak, the new "Catholic Weber," who nevertheless was notably uninterested in explaining in any detail how the Catholic *ethos* might temper modern capitalism at all.[22] The problem is complicated by an ambiguity that marks the Novakian legitimation of capitalism: that of the meaning to be accorded to sin.

On one hand, Novak insists that capitalism is, in contrast to socialism, the superior system precisely because it starts from the idea of the imperfection of humanity. Since economics presupposes an anthropology, capitalism, founded on the idea of sinful man, is the system that corresponds best to human nature. Realism excludes any consideration of change: selfishness remains selfishness, generosity remains generosity. The economy is a system based on selfishness, not on generosity, and Christianity must surrender to this reality by keeping generosity in its proper place, which is in spheres of life other than the economic.

On the other hand, though, Novak's description of capitalism goes beyond simple realistic acceptance of the immovable data of human

---

20. Novak, *The Spirit of Democratic Capitalism*, 348.

21. Novak, *The Spirit of Democratic Capitalism*, 40.

22. Novak would attempt to recalibrate the relationship between ethics and the economy in his 1993 book *The Catholic Ethic and the Spirit of Capitalism*.

nature. It includes even an element of apologetics: "The world as Adam faced it after the Garden of Eden left humanity in misery and hunger for millennia. Now that the secrets of sustained material progress have been decoded, the responsibility for reducing misery and hunger is no longer God's but ours."[23] His realism turns from pessimistic to optimistic; instead of the Christian conversion of hearts, which is valid only for individuals, *capitalism is a model capable of turning evil into good*. It offers an economic theodicy, at the heart of the liberal-Enlightenment economy, that Novak fully embraces. Capitalism overcomes the power of sin by turning sin against itself. The power of the system, it turns out, is that it transforms evil into good.

The pages of *The Spirit of Democratic Capitalism* devoted to Adam Smith, the first theorist of modern capitalism, are illuminating of Novak's thinking.[24] The crux is Smith's doctrine of the "invisible hand" with its "doctrine of unintended consequences."[25]

> In political economy, there are two self-frustrating ways to defeat sin. One is to convert individual hearts. The other is to construct a system which imposes virtue by force. Democratic capitalism chose a third way. Through close study, its founders observed that in political economy personal intentions characteristically lead to unintended consequences. There is a gap between "moral man" and "not-so-moral society." Thus, political economists must pay less attention to individual intentions and more attention to systemic even if unintended consequences. . . . This doctrine of unintended consequences is central in the theory of democratic capitalism. It represents the conservative strain within the Enlightenment. It is counter-rationalist.[26]

One might observe that rather than being "counter-rationalist," the model Novak proposes is in fact "hyper-rationalist." He claims the ability of the rational to triumph not *over* the anarchy of appetites and desires but *through* anarchy itself. *Logos* asserts itself through chaos. Selfishness and the power of sin are overcome not through the conversion of hearts or through the socialist dictatorship of virtue, but through the "third way" of democratic capitalism, a way that contains within itself, within its very

23. Novak, *The Spirit of Democratic Capitalism*, 28.
24. On Adam Smith, see esp. pp. 120–24; 145–50.
25. Novak, *The Spirit of Democratic Capitalism*, 89.
26. Novak, *The Spirit of Democratic Capitalism*, 88–89.

structural model, the capacity of self-regulation. It is the typical theodicy of classical economic liberalism that Novak embraces, failing to subject it to even a moment's criticism. The beneficial effects of capitalism are the work of *the system* and not of the more or less generous intentions of individuals or communities. Capitalism is therefore the most "realistic" system not only because it accounts for the sinful nature of humanity and does not pretend to modify it; it is also the system that overcomes sin through a "mechanism of forces" that overturns individual selfishness into the collective good.

> The doctrine of unintended consequences turns the eyes of the political economist away from the moral intentions of individuals and toward the final social consequences of their actions. More than that, it turns his attention to systems *qua* systems. This led to the insight that, among competing alternatives, the hopes for a good, free, and just society are best reposed in a system which gives high status to commerce and industry.[27]

As was the case in the thought of the French structuralists of the 1970s, often influenced by Marxism, for Novak what drives historical change is not the decisions and actions of people but the structure—in this case the capitalist system.

> It is the *structure* of business activities, not the intentions of businessmen, that are favorable to rule by law, to freedom, to habits of regularity and moderation, to a healthy realism, and to demonstrated social progress— demonstrably more favorable than the structures of churchly, aristocratic, or military activities. It is in the interests of businessmen to defend and to enlarge the virtues on which liberty and progress depend.
>
> This view stands on its head the usual accusation against democratic capitalism. Those who prefer ecclesiastical, aristocratic, or martial values commonly deplore the values of a society undergirded by the moral imperatives of business. Yet democratic capitalism looks to the record, rather than to the intentions, of rival elites. *None had produced an equivalent system of liberties. None had so loosed the bonds of station, rank, peonage, and immobility. None had so raised human expectations. None so valued the individual.*[28]

---

27. Novak, *The Spirit of Democratic Capitalism*, 89.
28. Novak, *The Spirit of Democratic Capitalism*, 91. Emphasis mine.

One striking thing about Novak's uninhibited praise of capitalism is the singular convergence of Marxism and anti-Marxism. It is Marxist in that the economic structure is capable of generating the ethical super-structure and anti-Marxist in the moral elevation of capitalism imagined as the best of all possible worlds. "None so valued the individual"—not even, we may conclude, the Christian religion. Christian faith and ethics have no role in shaping the economy, in disciplining our worst instincts, or in promoting forms of solidarity and equity. On the contrary, Christianity, after having generated the ideal conditions for a market society, is called to model itself on capitalism, abandoning any critical ambitions that would reflect an antimodern spirit. Given a choice between Christian and secular Providence, Novak opts, following the Enlightenment model, for the latter.

At one point, he writes of the concept of "invisible hand" in Adam Smith's *An Inquiry into the Nature and the Causes of the Wealth of Nations*:

> The metaphor, simply put, draws attention to unintended consequences. The *motives* of individuals, it suggests, are not the same as the *social consequences* of their actions. The logic of economic behavior lies on a plane different from that of the logic of motives. Actually, the socialist conception of "structural sin" makes a similar point. Regardless of the moral rectitude of individual agents, socialists say, *the system* of which they are a part leads to injustice. One must inspect the "invisible hand" of the system, not simply the visibly expressed motives of its participants. Whether one regards it as sinful or as beneficial, there is, in any case, a system, a logic, an order, beneath the seeming individuality of individual choices. This is Smith's central point.
>
> Market systems are not, then, as anarchic as intuition may lead one to suppose.[29]

Here Novak acknowledges, surprisingly, the similarity between his structuralist conception of the system, which produces an ethical order

29. Novak, *The Spirit of Democratic Capitalism*, 114. Novak goes on: "Interestingly enough, then, a system which on the face of it leaves historically unprecedented liberty to economic agents—both in supply and in demand—and which involves an array of motives as complex as the mixed motives of millions of individuals, remains orderly. The order is far from perfect. Yet, compared to other systems, an amazing array of complex functions seems to work. A market system embodies order, on a level different from the level of the motives and intentions of those who make it happen. This is one meaning of the metaphor 'led by an invisible hand'" (115).

regardless of the intentions of individuals, with the Marxist model. Novak's democratic capitalism is based on the same theoretical model as its Communist opponent: it is a structure without a "subject." Both depend, consciously or not, on the Hegelian philosophical paradigm of history dominated by the inexorable process of Reason that "uses" the passions of individuals to realize its Order. Both Novak and historical-dialectical materialism posit an immanent Providence that produces, through (respectively) the interaction of egoisms or the contradictions of capital, a harmonious world.

> Adam Smith's hope was that the self-love of human beings might be transformed into a social system which benefited all as no other system had ever done. Thus his purpose in granting human self-interest its due was to transform it into a system of order, imagination, initiative, and progress for all. Such a system would, he thought, evolve interests larger than those of self-love, sentiments of love and gratitude for the system itself as a good of order. Each individual would then participate in a good society, in such a way that his self-love would come to include the whole. And the work of democratic capitalism will not be done until a sound material base has been laid beneath every human life on this planet. The bourgeois ideal, though measured, is spacious. It is not utopian, but it rewards big dreams.[30]

In his book, Novak pulls off, probably unintentionally, a metamorphosis of Catholicism. The result of his legitimation of "democratic" capitalism is *Catho-capitalism*, Christianity's embrace of the "bourgeois" spirit. Thus did Novak provide *the formula for the secularization of American Christianity in the 1990s.*

Contrary to his "liberal" premises, according to which no political-economic system can bring about the kingdom of God on earth, Novak idealized, in the kingdom of the imperfect, the capitalist model as the best of all possible worlds. It is the only real kingdom, since the heavenly one concerns only the *eschaton* and the end of history. The justification of American liberalism based upon the neoscholastic dualism between grace and nature means elevating the plan of nature to the effective goal of a preliminary salvation. Capitalism is not heaven, but it is heaven on earth. Expanding its influence around the world is a task that American Catholics cannot neglect. Its presence guarantees well-being and overcomes the

---

30. Novak, *The Spirit of Democratic Capitalism*, 149–50.

utopian dreams that are the true scourge of peoples. And thus neo-Pelagianism, secularization, and bourgeois ideology converge in a single process, the result of which is a new form of Catholic Americanism. Novak's faith is typical of the Scottish neo-Enlightenment of the late 1700s: a secular theology of well-being accompanied by virtuous outcomes typical of gentlemen.

This being the case, the great success of *The Spirit of Democratic Capitalism* within the North American Catholic world is striking. *A text philosophically dominated by the Hegelian model of history prompted a decisive abandonment of the Catholic social teaching.* It is not charity that modulates an idea of solidarity capable of functioning as the regulating concept of a historical process; on the contrary, it is the "mechanism" of the system and the technical progress produced by capitalist logic that ensure general well-being. Novak notes, approvingly, "John Locke once wrote that the inventors of new economic processes and new products—quinine, for example—were greater benefactors of humankind than earlier givers of charity."[31] He goes on, "Even the mine owners who played such an unsavory role at Lattimer Mines must, in all justice, be given credit for the inventive genius which opened new worlds to those they 'exploited.' No elite on earth has been without its victims, but not all have equally liberated and enriched the many."[32]

As for Hegel, for Novak too the successes and progress of history—in this case, of the capitalist system—justify the victims. Ideological progress represents true theodicy, the rational justification of evil as a function of good. Nonetheless, to the reader who is not watching carefully, he appears on the public scene not as a Hegelian in disguise but as the one who offers Catholic legitimacy to neocapitalism, allowing Catholics to finally feel "modern."

In the Reagan era, Novak became *the author who reconciled—with no critical distance whatsoever—Catholicism, capitalism, and modernity.* His work represents *the Catholic manifesto for the era of globalization*, the manifesto of *Catholic Americanism.* A profound dualism comes to light in Novak's work between the defense of the values of life, with the fight against abortion and euthanasia, and the total acceptance of the liberal-capitalist model celebrated as a direct expression of personal freedom introduced

---

31. Novak, *The Spirit of Democratic Capitalism*, 27.
32. Novak, *The Spirit of Democratic Capitalism*, 27.

into the world by Christianity.[33] Thanks to Novak, and to the intellectuals who subsequently embraced his perspective, Catholic Americanism became the *forma mentis* of the hegemonic Catholic conservatism throughout the final twenty years of the twentieth century.[34] He expressed the reaction and disillusionment with respect to the period of protest of the 1970s, the result of which was an ethical and ideological progressivism that pushed Catholics into the ranks of the Republican Party. The long season of Democratic dominance among American Christians, which marked the 1960s, was interrupted by three assassinations: of John Kennedy in 1963, Robert Kennedy in 1968, and Martin Luther King also in 1968. Following these, racial conflict, radical feminism, and the question of gay rights blocked the reform positions and pushed Catholics to the right.[35]

This was the arc followed by Michael Novak himself who, in the opening pages of his volume, offers some brief biographical notes. Here he confesses his youthful enthusiasm for "Christian socialism"[36] and his

---

33. The defense of Christian values in public is also very nuanced in Novak. He writes in *The Spirit of Democratic Capitalism* that "the political system of democratic capitalism cannot, in principle, be a Christian system. Clearly, it cannot be a confessional system. But it cannot even be presumed to be, in an *obligatory* way, suffused with Christian values and purposes. Individual Christians and their organized bodies may legitimately work through democratic means to shape the will of the majority; but they must also observe the rights of others and, more than that, heed practical wisdom by respecting the conscience of others even more than the law alone might demand. On the question of abortion, for example, no one is likely ever to be satisfied with the law, but all might be well advised not to demand in law all that their own conscience commands" (351).

34. See Patrick Allitt, *Catholic Intellectuals and Conservative Politics in America, 1950–1985* (Ithaca, NY: Cornell University Press, 1993); Gary Dorrien, *The Neoconservative Mind: Politics, Culture, and the War of Ideology* (Philadelphia: Temple University Press, 1993).

35. On the movement of Christians in the United States toward conservative positions, see Patrick Hynes, *In Defense of the Religious Right: Why Conservative Christians Are the Lifeblood of the Republican Party and Why That Terrifies the Democrats* (Nashville: Thomas Nelson, 2006); Blandine Chelini-Pont, "Catholic Colonization of the American Right: Historical Overview," in Marie Gayte, Blandine Chelini-Pont, and Mark Rozell, eds., *Catholics and US Politics after the 2016 Elections: Understanding the "Swing Vote"* (London: Palgrave Macmillan, 2018), 43–61; Jesse Russell, "The Contradictions of Catholic Neoconservatism," in Paul Gottfried, ed., *The Vanishing Tradition: Perspectives on American Conservatism* (Ithaca, NY: Cornell University Press, 2020), 85–98.

36. Novak, *The Spirit of Democratic Capitalism*, 22. On Novak's shift from left to right, see his autobiography, *Writing from Left to Right*. A summary of this change is also offered in the chapter "Errand into the Wilderness" in his *On Cultivating Freedom: Reflections on Moral Ecology.*

aversion to modern Protestantism, liberalism, and capitalism. "As I read the European Catholic intellectuals of the past two centuries—Lamennais, de Maistre, Chesterton, Belloc, Scheler, Maritain, and many others—I was won over by the contrast they drew between British (Protestant) philosophy and Catholic philosophy. On the one side, they and I lined up individualism, utilitarianism, pragmatism; on the other side, personalism, community, 'solidarism.' "[37] This was the classic position of Catholic antimodernism, largely supported by the scholastic philosophy that reigned until the Second Vatican Council, a position that he reversed when Novak perceived that he felt trapped within categories that forced him into a parallel world, alien to the real one. The result, as we have seen, was an embrace of the modern economic and political system as unsurpassable goals.

In Novak, then, we witness a process that was typical of preconciliar Catholicism, which shifted suddenly from a reactionary stance to a progressive one, from antimodernism to modernism. It was, however, a "conservative" modernism, very different from the postmodern progressivism of the new left with its ethical relativism. Conservative modernism was liberal on the economic ground and traditional with regard to the political values of Old America. The identification between religion and nation is understood only in the context, typically American, of their distinction. Christianity supports the secular nature of the public square and guarantees its autonomy. A similar process takes place with regard to the economy. This appeal to religious values as the foundation of public ethics, albeit a secular ethics, is opposed to those who demand a totally secularized version of democracy. Conservatives claim their modernity in the face of those Catholics who, faithful to the social doctrine of the church, continue to criticize the faults of a "pure" and unreformed capitalist system. Conservative modernism is thus a singular mixture of nationalism and capitalism. From this double adhesion, celebrated as a *full reconciliation with the modern spirit*, Catholic Americanism was born, and it is the ideology that has permeated the ecclesial world in the era of globalization.

Of this ideology Novak is the true *maître à penser*, its foundational theorist and its commentator. His limitations were well understood by the Italian scholar Agostino Giovagnoli, who observed in 1987:

---

37. Novak, *The Spirit of Democratic Capitalism*, 23.

Starting from a Catholic *Weltanschauung* that was decidedly inadequate for understanding the reality of the modern world, he suddenly found himself immersed in a new and unexpected situation. In this way, his initial rejection of capitalism turned into an embrace that equaled the strength of his previous opposition. This is expressed in a book [*The Spirit of Democratic Capitalism*] that is in many ways deliberately provocative in its shining partisanship, which makes it so easy to read, while dealing with arguments that are certainly not light. It is precisely the mirror-like reversal from a complete rejection to an enthusiastic embrace that makes this volume such a singularly clear illustration of the difficult journey of American Catholics in their encounter with the modern world. What makes this text captivating is, among other things, the broad criticism reserved for the socialist shift made by so many of Novak's Catholic friends and fellow travelers. Novak effectively demonstrates many unconvincing and culturally inadequate elements of this socialist shift. But one wonders if he is not a participant, albeit on different positions, at least in part, in the same cultural landscape. Rather than a complete change of perspective, what he experienced is a reversal of point of view. While his initial judgment was rooted in the magisterium of the church vis-à-vis the modern world, in his later thinking the modern world became the point of reference for judging the church.[38]

It is this "reversal" that explains Novak's open criticism of the church's social teaching. He writes, "Pope Pius XI said that the tragedy of the nineteenth century was the loss of the working classes to the church. An even deeper tragedy lay in the failure of the church to understand the moral-cultural roots of the new economics."[39] For Novak, "[Catholic thought] has tended, particularly because of the Vatican's location within Italy, and also because of the great strength of still largely feudal societies of the Latin world, the Austro-Hungarian Empire, and Ireland, to rest uncomfortably in the past with only a tenuous connection to liberal societies. In a word, it has stood outside of and has, I think, misread the liberal democratic capitalist revolution."[40]

---

38. Agostino Giovagnoli, "Cattolicesimo e capitalism: A proposito del libro di M. Novak," *Appunti di cultura e di politica*, November-December 1987, 18.

39. Novak, *The Spirit of Democratic Capitalism*, 17–18.

40. Novak, *The Spirit of Democratic Capitalism*, 25.

A truly surprising judgment, reminiscent of the Protestant Hegel's assessment of Catholic countries. Offered in the context of the second half of the twentieth century, in light of the industrialized countries of the new Europe of 1982, Novak's reference to "still largely feudal societies of the Latin world" is anachronistic and beyond any logic. He is measuring the social doctrine of the church against some nonexistent Arcadia rather than the advanced industrial world. The anti-Roman and anti-Latin prejudice of the Anglo-Saxon world is clear.

Giovagnoli wrote,

> These "anti-Roman" expressions reveal Novak's thought to be, more than anything else, very "American." It is reminiscent of the proud "Americanism" of the beginning of the century, widespread then among American Catholics, and even more of the powerful American Catholicism of the age of Pius XII, of which the most famous exponents, such as Spellman and Cushing, brought their demands even to Vatican II. Like those bishops, Novak too represents a typical form of adherence, above all empirical, to the American model of life. It is what could be defined as a "reconciliation" with Protestantism on an economic-political level, very different from an ecumenism of a religious nature, and one that does not imply an abandonment of rather conservative positions on the theological level. In the controversy against the Latin American episcopates for their critical positions toward the United States, Novak is clearly targeting a Latin-type Catholicism, more precisely Spanish and Portuguese.[41]

The Catholic Neoconservative Movement and *Centesimus Annus* as "Decisive Break"

Giovagnoli's framing of the question—North American Catholicism versus "Latin" Catholicism—helps us grasp the nature of the ecclesial "heritage" that Francis, the South American pope, would face at the moment of his election: the American (United States) model that was imposed on Western Catholicism during the 1980s and 1990s. Thanks to its dominance, a theology of capitalism stood in distinction from and opposition to what remained of the theology of liberation; the church of the opulent world was profoundly detached from the church immersed in the reality of the poor. The Hegelian dialectic between lordship and

---

41. Giovagnoli, "Cattolicesimo e capitalism," 18.

bondage existed *within* the church, giving rise to an intellectual contradiction between two incompatible points of view.

In this process, Novak was certainly not the only one to give shape to the Catholic Americanism whose strength lay in supporting the ascendant momentum of the Reagan moral-economic-political model. In addition to Novak, the Catholic neoconservative movement included Richard John Neuhaus, George Weigel, and Robert Sirico.[42] It was a very active group of intellectuals who, in the span of a few years, managed to establish

42. Richard John Neuhaus (1936–2009), a Lutheran pastor who became Catholic in 1991, was the founder of the Institute for Religion and Public Life, the Free Society Seminar based in Krakow, and the monthly journal *First Things*, a key publication of the Catholic conservative movement. His books include *The Naked Public Square: Religion and Democracy in America* (Grand Rapids, MI: Eerdmans, 1984); *The Catholic Moment: The Paradox of the Church in the Postmodern World* (New York: Harper Collins, 1987); and *Catholic Matters: Confusion, Controversy, and the Splendor of Truth* (New York: Basic Books, 2006).

George Weigel, a senior fellow of the Ethics and Public Policy Center, was president and founder of the James Madison Foundation. He gained notoriety through his monumental biography, *Witness to Hope: The Biography of Pope John Paul II* (New York: Harper Collins, 1999). Among his books are *The Final Revolution: The Resistance Church and the Collapse of Communism* (New York: Oxford University Press, 1992); *The Truth of Catholicism: Ten Controversies Explored* (New York: Harper Collins, 2001); *The Cube and the Cathedral: Europe, America, and Politics Without God* (New York: Basic Books, 2005); *God's Choice: Pope Benedict XVI and the Future of the Catholic Church* (New York: Harper Collins, 2005); *The End and the Beginning: Pope John Paul II—The Victory of Freedom, the Last Years, the Legacy* (New York: Doubleday, 2010); and *The Irony of Modern Catholic History: How the Church Rediscovered Itself and Challenged the Modern World to Reform* (New York: Basic Books, 2019).

Robert A. Sirico is a priest and founder, in 1990, of the Acton Institute, a think tank based in Grand Rapids, Michigan, that has as its purpose the promotion of the encounter between Catholicism and capitalism. His books include *Catholicism's Developing Social Teaching* (Grand Rapids, MI: The Acton Institute, 1992); *Defending the Free Market: The Moral Case for a Free Economy* (Washington, DC: Regnery Publishing, 2012); and *A Moral Basis for Liberty* (Grand Rapids, MI: The Acton Institute).

On neoconservative Catholicism, see Weigel, "The Neoconservative Difference: A Proposal for the Renewal of Church and Society," in *Being Right: Conservative Catholics in America*, ed. Mary Jo Weaver and R. Scott Appleby (Bloomington, IN: Indiana University Press, 1995); Flavio Felice, *Prospettiva "Neocon": Capitalismo, democrazia, valori nel mondo unipolare* (Soveria Mannelli: Rubbettino 2005); Felice, *Neocon e teocon: Il ruolo della religione nella vita pubblica statunitense* (Soveria Mannelli: Rubbettino, 2006); Francesco Martini, "Ritorno al Vangelo: la sfida dei Catholic neocons," *Limes*, April 12, 2013, https:// www.limesonline.com/i-neocons-vogliono-una-chiesa-samaritana/44918.

themselves as the shapers of the American Catholic conscience. The group was part of a neoconservative galaxy dotted with intellectuals, disappointed by the left and by the politics of the Democratic Party, whose historical leader was the American Jewish journalist Irving Kristol.[43]

A school of thought slowly began to take shape and became the most incisive right-wing think tank starting in 1981, when Ronald Wilson Reagan's presidency began. Taking into account their backgrounds, the socialist Michael Harrington (1928–1989) ironically baptized these intellectuals as "neocons," to distinguish them from the traditional conservatives led by Russell Kirk. In Italy, however, Kristol and his disciples were inadequately defined "theocon," overlooking the fact that, as Novak attests, "Neocons were not in the beginning, nor are they now, distinguished primarily by religion or morals. The cutting issue was political economy and, in particular, dissatisfaction with the growing list of failures of the left-wing imagination."[44]

Novak's observation about the genesis and ideology of the conservative movement in general is correct, though the movement's strong Jewish component calls for more nuanced consideration of the theological-political motivations involved.[45] It is also correct with regard to the genesis of his 1982 work on democratic capitalism, the motivations for which were dictated by a "secular" desire to break away from the traditional Catholic vision of the market and to reconcile with the modern

43. See Irving Kristol, *Neo-Conservatism: The Autobiography of an Idea* (New York: The Free Press, 1995). See also Novak, "Twice Chosen: Irving Kristol as American," in *The Neoconservative Imagination: Essays in Honor of Irving Kristol*, ed. Christopher DeMuth and William Kristol (Washington, DC: AEI Press, 1995), 73–82.

44. Lorenzo Montanari and Luca Sandonà, "Nove domande a Michael Novak," *Cultura & Identità* 4, March-April 2010, 24–25. Novak's observation is offered in "Neocons: Some Memories," *National Review Online*, May 20, 2003, https://www.nationalreview.com /2003/05/neocons-michael-novak/.

45. See Jim Lobe and Adele Oliveri, eds., *I nuovi rivoluzionari: Il pensiero dei neoconservatori americani* (Milan: Feltrinelli, 2003). On neoconservatism, see Dorrien, *The Neoconservative Mind*; Michael Gerson, ed., *The Essential Neoconservative Reader* (New York: Perseus, 1997); Gerson, *The Neoconservative Vision: From the Cold War to the Culture Wars* (Seattle: Madison, 1997); Christian Rocca, *Esportare l'America: La rivoluzione democratica dei neoconservatori* (Milan: I libri del Foglio, 2003); Alain Frachon and Daniel Vernet, *L'Amérique des néo-conservateurs: L'illusion messianique* (Paris: Éditions Perrin, 2010); Gottfried, *The Vanishing Tradition*.

political economy. *Support for the capitalist system is at the origin of the conservative movement*, a meeting point between Jewish and Catholic authors, each having moved away from initially left-leaning stances. The religious elements of their thinking came later. These were not, in the beginning, decisive. In fact, Novak's prominence grew in relation to his identity as a "Catholic" philosopher. *He became a key figure because he defended, for the first time, the theoretical agreement between Catholicism and capitalism*, a stance that has, in a nation like the United States, inhabited by millions of Catholics, substantial political value.

His academic and political experience supported his mission. Since 1978, he had held the George Frederick Jewett Chair in Religion, Philosophy, and Public Policy at the American Enterprise Institute in Washington, DC. He also taught at Harvard, Stanford, SUNY Old Westbury, Syracuse, and Notre Dame. He had headed the United Nations Commission on Human Rights since 1981 and served in 1986 as the head of the American delegation to the Conference on Security and Cooperation in Europe. But it was in the 1990s that Novak became a public figure. He received twenty-seven honorary degrees (including four in Latin America and three in Europe) and a bevy of prestigious awards and prizes, including the Anthony Fischer Prize (1992) from Margaret Thatcher, the Templeton Prize for Progress in Religion (1994) in a ceremony at Buckingham Palace, and the Catholic Culture Medal from the School of Catholic Culture in Bassano del Grappa, Italy (1999). Like a kind of dual-faced Janus, Novak brought together in his thought two very distant subjects: the Austrian school of the liberal economists Ludwig von Mises and Friedrich von Hayek and the social tradition of the Catholic Church. He wrote a book on von Hayek on the occasion of the centenary of his birth,[46] while his interest in von Mises, who emigrated to the United States in 1940, was rooted in his shared interest in the alliance between the church and capitalism that the Austrian economist set out in the final pages of his 1922 book, *Socialism*.[47] Novak credited von Mises's book *Anti-Capitalistic*

46. Novak, *The Legacy of Friedrich von Hayek* (Chicago: Liberty Fund and the Committee on Social Thought at the University of Chicago, 2005).

47. Ludwig von Mises, *Socialism: An Economic and Sociological Analysis*, trans. J. Kahane (Indianapolis: Liberty Fund Indianapolis, 1981). In chapter 29 of the book, von Mises criticized both socialism and Christianity for their critique of capitalism, arguing that it was rooted, as for Nietzsche, in the *resentment* of the weak against the strong. "Jesus'

Mentality as being especially important in his intellectual formation.[48] It confirmed for Novak the magic formula of classical capitalism: "action in the interests of myself and action in the interest of others do not conflict, since the interests of individuals come together in the end."[49]

Through Novak, the ethical-economic model of the Austrian school, adverse to welfare and solidarity in economic matters and colored by Nietzschean thought, came to be understood as normative for the Catholic vision of society. It is a mix of perspectives, highly casual from the intellectual point of view, that was accepted by the American Catholic establishment when Novak, supported by Weigel, Neuhaus, and Sirico, became the most authoritative interpreter, in the United States, of John Paul II's 1991 encyclical *Centesimus Annus*.

Published just after the definitive collapse of Soviet Communism, the document was critical of capitalism. Celebrating the centenary of Leo XIII's landmark encyclical *Rerum Novarum*, John Paul insisted upon the earlier document's continued relevance.

> The content of the text [*Rerum Novarum*] is an excellent testimony to the continuity within the Church of the so-called "preferential option for the poor," an option which I defined as a "special form of primacy in the exercise of Christian charity" [*Sollicitudo Rei Socialis*, 42]. Pope Leo's Encyc-

---

words are full of resentment against the rich, and the Apostles are no meeker in this respect. The Rich Man is condemned because he is rich, the Beggar praised because he is poor. . . . Up to the time of modern socialism no movement against private property which has arisen in the Christian world has failed to seek authority in Jesus, the Apostles, and the Christian Fathers, not to mention those who, like Tolstoy, made the Gospel resentment against the rich the very heart and soul of their teaching. This is a case in which the Redeemer's word bore evil seed" (379). In its opposition to wealth, economic freedom, and modern liberalism, von Mises said, Christianity, which is the true root of socialism, would have a destructive effect: "Liberalism . . . transformed the world more than Christianity had ever done. It restored humanity to the world and to life" (382). To avoid the crisis of the system, there is only one solution, and it is the same one proposed by the positivist Auguste Comte: an alliance between the church and capitalism, such as to modify the "dissolving" effects of Christian ethics. "Might not the Church reconcile itself with the social principle of free cooperation by the division of labor? Might not the very principle of Christian love be interpreted to this end?" (381).

48. Novak, *The Spirit of Democratic Capitalism*, 27n24. See von Mises, *The Anti-Capitalistic Mentality* (South Holland, IL: Libertarian Press, 1972).

49. von Mises, *Socialism*, 357.

lical on the "condition of the workers" is thus an Encyclical on the poor and on the terrible conditions to which the new and often violent process of industrialization had reduced great multitudes of people. Today, in many parts of the world, similar processes of economic, social and political transformation are creating the same evils.

If Pope Leo XIII calls upon the State to remedy the condition of the poor in accordance with justice, he does so because of his timely awareness that the State has the duty of watching over the common good and of ensuring that every sector of social life, not excluding the economic one, contributes to achieving that good, while respecting the rightful autonomy of each sector.[50]

Already from these lines, the distance that separated Novak's Catho-capitalism from John Paul II was obvious. In contravention of liberal dogma, the pope recognized the state's "duty of watching over the common good" in the face of "the new and often violent process of industrialization." This obviously did not mean a nationalization of the economy and society. Between statism and liberalism there is, however, a third way that the social doctrine of the Church has always proposed.

In this regard, *Rerum Novarum* points the way to just reforms which can restore dignity to work as the free activity of man. These reforms imply that society and the State will both assume responsibility, especially for protecting the worker from the nightmare of unemployment. Historically, this has happened in two converging ways: either through economic policies aimed at ensuring balanced growth and full employment, or through unemployment insurance and retraining programs capable of ensuring a smooth transfer of workers from crisis sectors to those in expansion.

Furthermore, society and the State must ensure wage levels adequate for the maintenance of the worker and his family, including a certain amount for savings. This requires a continuous effort to improve workers' training and capability so that their work will be more skilled and productive, as well as careful controls and adequate legislative measures to block shameful forms of exploitation, especially to the disadvantage of the most vulnerable workers, of immigrants and of those on the margins of society. The role of trade unions in negotiating minimum salaries and working conditions is decisive in this area.

50. John Paul II, encyclical letter *Centesimus Annus* (May 1, 1991), 11.

Finally, "humane" working hours and adequate free time need to be guaranteed, as well as the right to express one's own personality at the workplace without suffering any affront to one's conscience or personal dignity. This is the place to mention once more the role of trade unions, not only in negotiating contracts, but also as "places" where workers can express themselves. They serve the development of an authentic culture of work and help workers to share in a fully human way in the life of their place of employment.

The State must contribute to the achievement of these goals both directly and indirectly. Indirectly and according to the *principle of subsidiarity*, by creating favorable conditions for the free exercise of economic activity, which will lead to abundant opportunities for employment and sources of wealth. Directly and according to the *principle of solidarity*, by defending the weakest, by placing certain limits on the autonomy of the parties who determine working conditions, and by ensuring in every case the necessary minimum support for the unemployed worker.[51]

The vision of the state and society proposed by the encyclical referred clearly to the welfare state, the model that Novak and the neoconservatives rejected. Equally opposed to their thinking was what John Paul II affirmed in the third chapter, titled "The Year 1989": "The crisis of Marxism does not rid the world of the situations of injustice and oppression which Marxism itself exploited and on which it fed. To those who are searching today for a new and authentic theory and praxis of liberation, the Church offers not only her social doctrine and, in general, her teaching about the human person redeemed in Christ, but also her concrete commitment and material assistance in the struggle against marginalization and suffering."[52] John Paul II, in other words, was hoping, after the fall of Communism, for the affirmation of an authentic theology of liberation, free from Marxism but no less committed to the struggle for justice. It was the same dream expressed by Methol Ferré and Jorge Mario Bergoglio.

In the fourth chapter of the document, on "Private Property and the Universal Destination of Material Goods," the pope affirmed that "the Church teaches that the possession of material goods is not an absolute right,"[53] and here he referred to his encyclicals *Laborem Exercens* and *Sol-*

---

51. Pope John Paul II, *Centesimus Annus*, 15.
52. Pope John Paul II, *Centesimus Annus*, 26.
53. Pope John Paul II, *Centesimus Annus*, 30.

licitudo Rei Socialis and to the historic conference of the Latin American church in Puebla in 1979. This was, to the Catholic neoconservatives, an utter heresy. It did not, of course, mean a blanket condemnation of the Western economic system. The pope recognized that "the modern *business economy* has positive aspects. Its basis is human freedom."[54] This was the central truth proclaimed by the neoconservatives, but for John Paul this recognition was delimited by the role of the state, in the economy of the common good, in regulating the selfish instincts that dominate the logic of the market. The pope taught:

> It is the task of the State to provide for the defense and preservation of common goods such as the natural and human environments, which cannot be safeguarded simply by market forces. Just as in the time of primitive capitalism the State had the duty of defending the basic rights of workers, so now, with the new capitalism, the State and all of society have the duty of *defending those collective goods* which, among others, constitute the essential framework for the legitimate pursuit of personal goals on the part of each individual.
>
> Here we find a new limit on the market: there are collective and qualitative needs which cannot be satisfied by market mechanisms. There are important human needs which escape its logic. There are goods which by their very nature cannot and must not be bought or sold. Certainly the mechanisms of the market offer secure advantages: they help to utilize resources better; they promote the exchange of products; above all they give central place to the person's desires and preferences, which, in a contract, meet the desires and preferences of another person. Nevertheless, these mechanisms carry the risk of an "idolatry" of the market, an idolatry which ignores the existence of goods which by their nature are not and cannot be mere commodities.[55]

The "idolatry of the market" was an expression that, from the point of view of the Catholic neoconservatives, could not be uttered. Here John Paul II was violating the dogma behind Novak's "doctrine of involuntary consequences," whereby the market, by itself, by its own internal logic independent of the intentions of individuals, is able to reach, as Leibniz put it, a preestablished harmony. Economic theodicy has no foundation.

---

54. Pope John Paul II, *Centesimus Annus*, 32.
55. Pope John Paul II, *Centesimus Annus*, 40.

For this reason, John Paul said, *"it is unacceptable to say that the defeat of so-called 'Real Socialism' leaves capitalism as the only model of economic organization"*[56]—a statement directly contradicting the neoconservative gospel.

For the pope, overcoming Marxism required understanding its point of truth:

> Marxism criticized capitalist bourgeois societies, blaming them for the commercialization and alienation of human existence. This rebuke is of course based on a mistaken and inadequate idea of alienation, derived solely from the sphere of relationships of production and ownership, that is, giving them a materialistic foundation and moreover denying the legitimacy and positive value of market relationships even in their own sphere. Marxism thus ends up by affirming that only in a collective society can alienation be eliminated. However, the historical experience of socialist countries has sadly demonstrated that collectivism does not do away with alienation but rather increases it, adding to it a lack of basic necessities and economic inefficiency.
>
> The historical experience of the West, for its part, shows that even if the Marxist analysis and its foundation of alienation are false, nevertheless alienation—and the loss of the authentic meaning of life—is a reality in Western societies too. This happens in consumerism, when people are ensnared in a web of false and superficial gratifications rather than being helped to experience their personhood in an authentic and concrete way. Alienation is found also in work, when it is organized so as to ensure maximum returns and profits with no concern whether the worker, through his own labor, grows or diminishes as a person, either through increased sharing in a genuinely supportive community or through increased isolation in a maze of relationships marked by destructive competitiveness and estrangement, in which he is considered only a means and not an end.
>
> The concept of alienation needs to be led back to the Christian vision of reality, by recognizing in alienation a reversal of means and ends.[57]

Communism's foundation in "alienation" was, John Paul knew, reductive and mistaken. But its critique of the alienation that marked the capitalist world deserved attention. In contrast to Novak's position, according

---

56. Pope John Paul II, *Centesimus Annus*, 35 (emphasis mine).
57. Pope John Paul II, *Centesimus Annus*, 41.

to which capitalism is the simple negation of Communism, John Paul II sought a way of moving forward that included critical consideration of this alienation in the post-Communist world. The pope reiterated this point two years later, in an interview with Jas Gawronski published in November of 1993. He said:

> Communism has been successful in this century as a reaction to a certain kind of excessive, savage capitalism that we are all familiar with. We can refer here to the social encyclicals and above all to the first one, *Rerum Novarum*, in which Leo XIII describes the situation of the workers at that time. Even Marx described it in his own way. That was the social reality, there was no doubt, and it derived from the system, from the principles of ultraliberal capitalism. . . .
>
> Of course, it was legitimate to fight the unjust totalitarian system, which called itself socialist or communist. But what Leo XIII says is also true—there are "seeds of truth" even in the socialist program. It is obvious that these seeds must not be destroyed, they must not be lost. Today we need a precise and objective confrontation, accompanied by a keen sense of discernment. Those who advocate capitalism to the bitter end and in any form tend to disregard even the good things achieved by Communism: the fight against unemployment, concern for the poor. In the system of real socialism, excessive protectionism of the State has also brought about negative fruits. Private initiative has disappeared, inertia and passivity have spread.[58]

The pope's position, then, was clear: "*Those who advocate capitalism to the bitter end and in any form tend to disregard even the good things achieved by Communism: the fight against unemployment, concern for the poor.*" And *Centesimus Annus*, the encyclical that reflected on the world after the fall of the Berlin wall, did not indulge in any legitimation of victorious capitalism.

The pope would reiterate this in his 1999 apostolic exhortation, *Ecclesia in America*. There he wrote:

> More and more, in many countries of America, a system known as "neoliberalism" prevails; based on a purely economic conception of man, this

---

58. Jas Gawronski, Interview with Pope John Paul II, *La Stampa*, November 2, 1993, http://www.vatican.va/content/john-paul-ii/it/speeches/1993/november/documents/hf _jp-ii_spe_19931102_intervista.html.

system considers profit and the law of the market as its only parameters, to the detriment of the dignity of and the respect due to individuals and peoples. At times this system has become the ideological justification for certain attitudes and behavior in the social and political spheres leading to the neglect of the weaker members of society. Indeed, the poor are becoming ever more numerous, victims of specific policies and structures which are often unjust.[59]

The judgment was clear and could not be misunderstood. That is what is so surprising about the ease with which the Catholic neoconservatives took possession of *Centesimus Annus*, presenting it as the manifesto of American Catho-capitalism in the nineties. The result was that a text that strongly critical of neocapitalism came to be understood as an apologetics manual of the same. This hermeneutic violence had at its heart a single point, made in the document's paragraph 42, where the pope posed a question:

Returning now to the initial question: can it perhaps be said that, after the failure of Communism, capitalism is the victorious social system, and that capitalism should be the goal of the countries now making efforts to rebuild their economy and society? Is this the model which ought to be proposed to the countries of the Third World which are searching for the path to true economic and civil progress?

The answer is obviously complex. If by "capitalism" is meant an economic system which recognizes the fundamental and positive role of business, the market, private property, and the resulting responsibility for the means of production, as well as free human creativity in the economic sector, then the answer is certainly in the affirmative, even though it would perhaps be more appropriate to speak of a "business economy," "market economy," or simply "free economy." But if by "capitalism" is meant a system in which freedom in the economic sector is not circumscribed within a strong juridical framework which places it at the service of human freedom in its totality, and which sees it as a particular aspect of that freedom, the core of which is ethical and religious, then the reply is certainly negative.[60]

---

59. Pope John Paul II, *Ecclesia in America* (January 22, 1999), 56, https://www.vatican
.va/content/john-paul-ii/en/apost_exhortations/documents/hf_jp-ii_exh_22011999
_ecclesia-in-america.html.

60. Pope John Paul II, *Centesimus Annus*, 42.

It was John Paul's subtle distinction between the two forms of capitalism—in which the acceptable one, according to the pope's own words, barely merits being called capitalism—that allowed the taking of the winter palace. With a clever coup, Novak and his fellow neoconservatives presented themselves as the proponents of a good, "ethical" capitalism as opposed to the bad. All the criticisms that the encyclical addressed to post-Marxist capitalism fell into oblivion, and only paragraph 42 remained. That was the opening they took to suggest the existence of a "break" by John Paul II with the entire tradition of Catholic social teaching, which had been marked from the start by a distrust of capitalism. *Centesimus Annus* had finally brought legitimacy to *The Spirit of Democratic Capitalism*. Novak's work had anticipated and paved the way for the Polish pope's "turning point." This is the interpretation that was repeated countless times in the media and in all the necessary settings, the interpretation that became commonplace in Catholic publications of all kinds, first in the United States and then in Europe: *Centesimus Annus* has opened the doors to ethical Catho-capitalism.

Richard John Neuhaus wrote immediately following the release of the text:

> *Centesimus Annus* is a ringing endorsement of the market economy. The endorsement is, however, joined to powerful challenges . . .
>
> John Paul affirms a "new capitalism." But the term he prefers is simply "free economy." Of course socialism is economically disastrous, but what he calls the "evil" of the system imposed by the communist "empire" is the denial of freedom. Readers will miss the gravamen of this encyclical if they do not recognize that it is, first and most importantly, an argument about human nature. Capitalism is the economic corollary of the Christian understanding of man's nature and destiny . . .
>
> The pope says that we can now see how prescient Leo XIII was in his scathing critique of the socialist idea 100 years ago. . . . According to the pope's argument, interpretations of Catholic social teaching along socialist or semi-socialist lines, together with the idea that the Church proposes a "third way" between capitalism and socialism, are in serious error . . .
>
> The present encyclical must surely prompt a careful, and perhaps painful, re-thinking of conventional wisdoms about Catholic social teaching. It may be, for instance, that the controlling assumptions of the American Bishops' 1986 pastoral letter, *Economic Justice for All*, must now be recognized as unrepresentative of the Church's authoritative teaching . . .

While the bulk of the 114 pages of the encyclical is devoted to economics, its import is to deflate the importance of the economic. Economics, politics, culture—these three define the social order, and the greatest of these is culture. And at the heart of culture is the spiritual and moral.[61]

Here Neuhaus fixed the canonical points of the neoconservative reading of *Centesimus Annus*: the pope affirms a new capitalism governed by a triple order—economic, political, and cultural. There is no "third way" between capitalism and socialism and, for this reason, the criticisms of the capitalist system offered by the United States bishops' 1986 pastoral letter, *Economic Justice for All*, do not represent the teaching of the magisterium in social matters.

In a 1993 interview, Neuhaus returned to the point. The "new capitalism" of *Centesimus Annus* "is in many ways what writers such as Michael Novak describe as democratic capitalism. It is an idea that is historically embodied in a number of advanced societies, not least of all the United States. This is a very significant development in Catholic social teaching that will, in my judgment, nurture a new phase of Catholic social thought with respect to the relationship between a Christian anthropology and a Christian understanding of history as it relates to economics and political justice."[62]

And thus, the circle was closed. The content of *Centesimus Annus* was identical to that expressed by Novak in *The Spirit of Democratic Capitalism*. Novak was not only a good interpreter of the pope; he was also his precursor. Pope John Paul II was a "Novakian" without being aware of it. And Neuhaus's statement was by no means isolated. Even Weigel, in a 2014 article, claimed:

> From its inception with Pope Leo XIII in the late nineteenth century through the mid-twentieth century, modern Catholic social doctrine, for all its insights, had a somewhat abstract, top-down quality. Thus, the strikingly empirical character of *Centesimus Annus*, Pope John Paul II's seminal 1991 encyclical on the free and virtuous society in its political, economic, and cultural dimensions, marked a significant development in the Church's evolving social thought. The basic principles of that tradition remained in

61. Richard John Neuhaus, "The Pope Affirms the New Capitalism," *Wall Street Journal*, May 1, 1991, https://www.acton.org/pub/religion-liberty/volume-1-number-3/initial-reactions-centesimus-annus.

62. Richard John Neuhaus, *Religion and Liberty*, September/October 1993, https://www.acton.org/pub/religion-liberty/volume-11-number-3/centesimus-annus-retrospective.

place, but they now found themselves filled out by a far more attentive reading of the realities of late-modern political and economic life—including the one that Novak powerfully described at the outset of his groundbreaking 1982 book *The Spirit of Democratic Capitalism*: "Of all the systems of political economy which have shaped our history, none has so revolutionized ordinary expectations of human life—lengthened the life span, made the elimination of poverty and famine imaginable, enlarged the range of human choice—as democratic capitalism." Recognizing the truth (and limits) of that insight, *Centesimus Annus* developed Catholic social doctrine's "standpoint" to include the possibilities of empowerment latent in free economies, clearly reflecting Novak's influence. If Catholic social doctrine continues to unfold along the trajectory of *Centesimus Annus*, it will continue to bear the imprint of Novak's thought.[63]

The neoconservatives literally appropriated the pope. They made him the messenger of the gospel of Michael Novak. Like Novak, John Paul was an "innovator," the pope who established the "break" with the whole social tradition of the church from Leo XIII onward.

This was Weigel's blunt assertion in his preface to the 1992 anthology *A New Worldly Order: John Paul II and Human Freedom*, a text whose purpose was to establish John Paul's "liberal" vision in the United States: "*Centesimus Annus* thus marks a decisive break with the curious materialism that has characterized aspects of modern Catholic social teaching since Leo XIII."[64]

The encyclical, we are to understand, establishes a break in Catholic social teaching's inclination to see only the materialistic aspects of the liberal economy. By combining politics, culture, and economics in the same trinomial, *Centesimus Annus* is able to recognize the market economy's "spiritual" nature.[65] This theologically established idealization of

---

63. George Weigel, "American and Catholic: Michael Novak's Achievement," *City Journal*, Winter 2014, https://www.city-journal.org/html/american-and-catholic-13632.html.

64. George Weigel, ed., *A New Worldly Order: John Paul II and Human Freedom: A 'Centesimus Annus' Reader* (Lanham, MD: University Press of America, 1992), 14. Weigel repeated the assertion in his *The Soul of the World: Notes on the Future of Public Catholicism* (Grand Rapids, MI: Eerdmans, 1996), 139.

65. Novak offered the same claims, writing that "in the apostolic exhortation *Ecclesia in America* (1999), John Paul II described the 'neoliberals' as materialists concerned only with market processes, profits, and efficiency, to the detriment of the spirit, values, and human rights"—a vision that Novak disputed because today "even economics would seem, therefore, like physics and other sciences, to stand against materialism" ("Modernità della Dottrina sociale della Chiesa," *Atlantide*, April 2006, 52, 53).

capitalism is at the heart of *A New Worldly Order*; its articles marshal all the evidence that the Catholic neoconservatives can offer. Among the book's contributors are Peter L. Berger, Milton Friedman, Richard John Neuhaus, Michael Novak, and Max L. Stackhouse, illustrious authors who shaped the Catholic conscience in America and beyond more effectively than the bishops, shaping a Catholic world increasingly right-leaning, in part in response to the ethical and relativist progressivism embraced by the Democratic Party.

The ideological manipulation of *Centesimus Annus* was accepted almost without question in the church, and 1991 marked a turning point in the process. Vatican journalist Sandro Magister described the situation in 1997:

> For Neuhaus, Michael Novak, and George Weigel, the troika of American Catholic liberalism, it has been a crescendo of successes. In France, Jacques Garello and Jean Yves Naudet, from the University of Aix-Marseille, back them up. In Great Britain, Kenneth Minogue. In Italy, the theorists of Catholic liberalism—Dario Antiseri, Lorenzo Infantino, plus the minister Antonio Martino who studied with the Jesuits—are welcomed at Rome's Free International University of Social Studies, which is supported by Confindustria [the Italian confederation of industries]. Then there is Giovanni Palladino, president of the Don Luigi Sturzo International Center. And Don Angelo Tosato, professor of biblical sciences at the Gregorian, who was the first to introduce Novak's writings to Italy.
>
> It is in the United States that the new current of Catholic liberalists was born and runs strongest. A fierce platoon came to the symposium held in Rome by the Legionaries of Christ. In addition to Novak, there were Reverend Robert Sirico, Gregory Gronbacher, Jennifer Roback Morse, George Gilder, each with prestigious awards.
>
> Sirico, the son of Neapolitans who emigrated to Michigan, founded the Lord Acton Institute in 1990 and is part of the very exclusive Mont Pélerin Society, which is the global Gotha of pure liberalists. Gronbacher directs the Center of Economic Personalism in Grand Rapids. Roback teaches at George Mason University, Virginia, a stronghold of Public Choice theorists led by the Nobel Prize-winning economist James M. Buchanan. Gilder is a disciple of Henry Kissinger and a great futurologist of politics, as well as a devotee of Opus Dei. All are students of Milton Friedman and Gary Becker, the super-liberalists of the famous Chicago school, but even more of Ludwig von Mises and Friedrich von Hayek, founders of that Austrian school of thought that now serves as the most natural link between Catholic doctrine and the modern free market.

The Catholic liberalists are so convinced of this conjunction that they make themselves apostles of it within the church. The Lord Acton Institute, founded by Father Sirico, even established in its statutes that its "primary purpose is to familiarize the religious community, especially students and seminarians, with the moral dimensions of the free market."[66]

Magister's article clearly captures the influence that these American neo-conservatives wielded in the 1990s within the Catholic world.[67] It was not just a vision of the economy but a true *Weltanschauung*, a vision of the world that corresponds to what we have called here "Catholic Americanism"—a vision that curiously follows that of the capitalistic Calvinism described by Max Weber.

The Catholicization of capitalism represents, we can say, the formula for the Protestantization of Catholicism. Faith is no longer expected to act as the leaven of the dough, a transformative force. More prosaically, it becomes the theological confirmation of a process that moves on its own feet. Novak's economic theology leads, in its adialectical reaction to the theology of revolution, to the complete acceptance of the status quo. The logic of capitalism, its immanent theodicy, whereby, through a sort of miracle, the sum of all selfishness produces harmony and well-being, is lauded and magnified as the heart of the system. For this reason, any ethical-political surplus, celebrated "religiously," always comes too late.

---

66. Sandro Magister, "I cattolici liberisti: Benedetta sia l'impresa," *L'Espresso*, May 15, 1997.

67. In 1991 and 1992, Novak, Weigel, Neuhaus, together with the Polish Dominican Maciej Zieba, offered the first seminar in Liechtenstein for forty graduate students from Europe and North America. In 1994 the seminar moved to Krakow, Poland, and took as its point of reference the study of John Paul II's *Centesimus Annus*. The move east, to a former Soviet-dominated country, had a strategic value. Weigel recalled in 2018, "the 'Centesimus Annus Seminar on the Free Society' began meeting in Poland's cultural and spiritual capital in July 1994—and has met there every summer since. Renamed the 'Tertio Millennio Seminar on the Free Society' in 2000, the seminar has graduated some 900 students; its 27th annual assembly this past July included young adults from the United States, Canada, Poland, Slovakia, Lithuania, Ukraine, Slovenia, and Russia. . . . Now, my faculty colleagues and I can look back on more than a quarter-century of work that has helped form great priests and religious; parliamentarians and civil servants; journalists and academics; doctors and lawyers; successful businessmen and philanthropists; impressive marriages and families; and, most importantly, Catholics who live the joy of the Gospel as missionary disciples in many walks of life" (Weigel, "Full-Immersion Catholicism," *First Things*, May 9, 2018).

The Catho-capitalist model is not opposed to secularization; on the contrary, like the theology of revolution, it is a clear expression of it.

David Schindler's Theological Critique
of the Neoconservative Movement

It was precisely a critique of the secularization of American society in the 1980s that served as a springboard for a strong challenge of neoconservative thought, offered on a rigorously theological level, by a highly regarded American Catholic theologian. In 1986, David L. Schindler was professor of fundamental theology at the John Paul II Institute for Studies on Marriage and the Family in Washington, coeditor of the journal *Communio*, and author of numerous books and essays. He was a leading exponent of the Communio school of theology, inspired by the work of Hans Urs von Balthasar, Henri de Lubac, and Joseph Ratzinger.

Schindler's challenge to the neoconservative movement was prompted by a response by George Weigel to an interview with Ratzinger in which the then-cardinal discussed the "bourgeois" character of America at the time.[68] In a *Crisis* magazine article, Weigel responded to Ratzinger's comments, objecting to the characterization and insisting upon the profoundly Christian soul of America.[69] He wrote:

> In an interview this past April with Lucio Brunelli of the Italian Catholic magazine *30 Giorni*, Cardinal Joseph Ratzinger described dissent among

---

68. Cardinal Joseph Ratzinger, "Interview with Lucio Brunelli," *30 Days* (April 1986). Weigel's response is "Is America Bourgeois?," *Crisis*, October 1986, 5–10, https://www .crisismagazine.com/1986/is-america-bourgeois.

69. Reading Ratzinger's interview, one has, in fact, the impression that Weigel's reaction is not so much motivated by Ratzinger's judgment on "bourgeois Christianity," which only superficially affected America, as by the conclusion of the interview where he targets the opposing fundamentalisms, the Islamic and the North American. Ratzinger explained the Islamist position as a reaction to the Westernist one, typical of the technical-liberal civilization. Ratzinger said, "A hasty and overconfident industrialization had superimposed the models of liberal Western civilization on top of the profound religious values of the Islamic world. But when this process had produced a certain economic power of its own and new intellectual elites, the reaction had to arrive: the awareness of one's own history and culture turned against the claim of exclusivity of the technical and liberal civilization, whose cynicism about the dignity of God and of man arouses anger and aversion." This narrative surely displeased Weigel.

American Catholic moral theologians as the expression of a more perni-
cious disorder: a "bourgeois Christianity in which Christianity is no longer a spur toward new responses and new hope in the face of a decayed
civilization." In "bourgeois Christianity," the Cardinal charged, "Christianity becomes a burden that must be lightened to the greatest possible
extent. . . . This type of Christianity certainly has a strong presence in a
certain social class and also enjoys considerable influence at the level of
the mass media. But there is nothing in it which suggests it has a future.
One can't feel attracted to a Christianity which has no respect for itself."

It would seem that Cardinal Ratzinger was analyzing more here than
the methodological assumptions of this or that American Catholic moral
theologian. He was, in fact, making a summary judgment about the state
of American Catholicism as a whole. That judgment, in turn, rests on
certain perceptions about American society and culture: American Catholicism has become a "bourgeois Church" because it has caved in to the
temptations of a bourgeois culture that is incompatible with Christian
truth claims and the Christian moral life.[70]

Weigel could not allow such an assessment by Cardinal Ratzinger to
stand unchallenged. It depended on a theory of secularization developed
in an Enlightenment-progressive context.

The concept of a decadent, "bourgeois" America fits comfortably with what
was once the dominant historiography of the American Founding. Pro-
gressivist historians like Vernon Louis Parrington and Charles Beard
taught that the intellectual progenitor of the American experiment was
John Locke — the Locke of the Enlightenment, not the Locke who had
been influenced by Thomas Hooker and the Puritan Covenanters. Locke
meant radical individualism. Lockean individualism has bent and shaped
the Founders' and Framers' political understandings such that America
was a republic, not in the classic sense of a community of virtue, but in
the distinctively modern sense of a non-tradition-bound, accidental col-
lectivity in which, so as to pursue their own private interests, men agreed
to basically leave each other alone. The "common good," in such a "bourgeois" republic, would not reflect universal moral norms; it would not be
pursued through what the Greeks and Romans understood by "civic virtue." Rather, the common good in a Lockean republic of radical individualism would be a practical, least-common-denominator arrangement in

70. Weigel, "Is America Bourgeois?"

which the pursuit of various private (usually commercial) interests became a centripetal, rather than centrifugal, force.[71]

It is a vision, Weigel said, that is related to a certain ideological vision: "Given the ideological predispositions of their historiography, it is not surprising that Parrington and Beard advanced this analysis; a secular-positivist worldview and an anti-capitalist animus dramatically colored their view of the Founding and its intellectual origins."[72] To overcome this perspective, a historiographical review of the "roots" of America was necessary. It was a question of bringing to light the religious and communitarian foundations, the "ethics," at the origins of the United States.

The Parrington/Beard hypothesis is, happily, on the wane in contemporary American historiography. It simply ill fits the evidence. No serious student of American political thought denies the profound influence of Enlightenment themes on the thinking of Jefferson, Madison, and the rest. John Locke was indeed an important herald of the American Founding. But no one who has examined modern scholarship on the Scottish, as distinguished from English, Enlightenment, and traced the intellectual long-lines between Edinburgh and Williamsburg; no one who has considered the impact of the Puritan revolution and its "covenanting" impulse on Locke's political thought; no one who has thought about the role played by John Winthrop's sermon on the *Arbella* (". . . Wee shall be as a Citty upon a Hill. . . ."), and Roger Williams's concept of religious toleration as God's will, in fertilizing the cultural subsoil of the American experiment; no one who has reflected on what it meant that the two most Deistic Founders, Jefferson and Franklin, proposed Biblical images for the Great Seal of the United States (themes from the Exodus in both instances)—no one who has thought seriously about any or all of these phenomena can maintain, with a straight face and a clear intellectual conscience, that the American Founding was devoid of a sense of the common good, or that it did not comprehend the linkage between liberty and civic virtue, or that it was essentially "bourgeois" in its reduction of politics to an expression of private property interests. It just wasn't so.[73]

Weigel's revisionism here is clear: he is minimizing the influence of Locke's individualism upon the American spirit and exaggerating that of

71. Weigel, "Is America Bourgeois?"
72. Weigel, "Is America Bourgeois?"
73. Weigel, "Is America Bourgeois?"

the Scottish Enlightenment (as opposed to the English one). The republican idea of Madison and Jefferson finds its nourishment in the ethos of civic virtues. "The assumptions, then, that the deficiencies of modern American moral culture can be traced to the ill-founding of the American experiment, and that the experiment was ill-founded because it was built on the shifting sands of a radical, Lockean individualism, do not meet the test of the present historical scholarship. Whatever their other errors of political theory and practice, the American Founders and Framers were not 'bourgeois,' in the deprecatory senses of the term."[74]

In support of his thesis, Weigel points to two illustrious Catholic thinkers, Jacques Maritain and John Courtney Murray, who believed that "the real herald of the American experiment was St. Thomas, 'the first Whig.'"[75] In short, Ratzinger's secularization hypothesis is not only inaccurate but also obsolete, since the contemporary American spirit was extremely attentive to Catholic values.

> Catholic natural law understandings are essential in a pluralistic democracy trying to determine the right role of religiously-based values in public policy discourse. The ideal of the "communitarian individual" in American democratic capitalism coheres nicely with Catholicism's central social-ethical principles of personalism and the common good. The Church is led by a pope who seems widely respected across the country (discounting such secularist redoubts as the New York Times editorial board and the Ed Asner wing of Hollywood).
>
> If there ever was a "Catholic moment" in America, it would seem to be now. Seizing that moment requires, as Cardinal Ratzinger rightly suggests, regaining our theological nerve. But I would also suggest, with all respect, that it means understanding our historical-philosophical roots, and our present cultural circumstances, in a manner rather different from that conveyed by the image of a "bourgeois Christianity" that has surrendered to a "decayed civilization."[76]

Weigel's opinion, in clear opposition to Ratzinger's, was not shared by David Schindler, whose response ignited a debate that would become one of the most interesting intellectual discussions in the American

74. Weigel, "Is America Bourgeois?"
75. Weigel, "Is America Bourgeois?"
76. Weigel, "Is America Bourgeois?"

Catholic world of the late1980s and the 1990s.[77] In a long essay titled "Is America Bourgeois?" published in *Communio*, Schindler criticized Weigel's optimism about the Christian soul of American society. Weigel, he said, lacked a dualistic vision between faith and history and had failed to look for the interpenetration of the Christian and the human that alone can denote the face of a Christian society. The Balthasarian-Lubacian vision of grace permeating human life from within is different from the scholastic dualism of natural and supernatural. To Schindler, Weigel's vision represented a bourgeois, dualistic, "Cartesian" Christianity.

> There are two very different ways of understanding "soul," and these correspond to what I have suggested is the extroversion of bourgeois Christianity on the one hand and the interiority of Catholic Christianity on the other. These two ways of understanding the soul can be labeled, respectively, Cartesian and Thomistic. The essential difference between them can be seen in the fact that the latter, in contrast to the former, *truly penetrates and orders from within* that of which it is the soul. A Cartesian soul, that is, remains outside and thus orders only in an external manner (in so far as it can be said to order at all) that of which it is the soul. A Thomistic soul in contrast precisely enters into—i.e., is genuinely interior to and thus truly transforms and integrates—that of which it is the soul. The difference I am getting at here, then, can be appropriately described as the difference between extroversion on the one hand and incarnation on the other; and the pertinence of such a difference when we recall the context of religion or religiosity seems to me evident.[78]

The "Cartesian" Thomist Weigel, unlike the "Augustinian" Thomist Schindler, had stopped at the surface-level, sociological image, at the apparent philanthropic altruism. He did not penetrate the profound ontology of the question and failed to fully grasp the point Ratzinger was making in his interview.

Weigel replied to Schindler's objections in another article, "Is America Bourgeois? A Response to David Schindler,"[79] now in *Communio*, in the

---

77. David L. Schindler, "Is America Bourgeois?," *Communio*, Fall 1987, 262–90. For a summary of this debate between Schindler and the neoconservatives, see Mark Lowery, "The Dialogue Between Catholic 'Neoconservatives' and Catholic 'Cultural Radicals': Toward a New Horizon," *Catholic Social Science Review* 3 (1998), 41–61.

78. Schindler, "Is America Bourgeois?," 275.

79. George Weigel, "Is America Bourgeois? A Response to David Schindler," *Communio*, Spring 1988, 77–91.

spring of 1988. Theologian Mark Lowery later summarized Weigel's response by noting that he "emphasizes that the American foundation has roots quite different from those that germinated in the ideology of the Jacobin wing of the French Revolution. As John Courtney Murray noted, medieval Christian political theory provides the deepest roots of the American experiment. Hence, there is not a pure atomism at work in America that would inevitably yield a contemporary bourgeois culture. The empirical evidence shows America to be deeply religious, despite the secular leanings of the 'new knowledge class.' America's religiosity is not pure, but it is genuine and capable of maturing, able to bear a 'Catholic Moment.'"[80]

Weigel shifted the question to the terrain of religious freedom, and he insinuated that Schindler's approach, with its insistent unity of natural and supernatural, risked a return to the theological-political monism that prevailed prior to the conciliar declaration *Dignitatis Humanae* on religious freedom. Schindler's response clearly excluded the integralist alternative to secularization.[81]

One year later, in 1989, the discussion moved to the pages of *30 Days* (the English edition of the Rome-based *30 Giorni*). In addition to Weigel and Schindler, now Richard Neuhaus and Michael Novak joined the fray.[82] The differences among the positions were by now clear, and the debate, which carried on in *Communio* and other publications, did not seem to lead to any common ground.[83] While Schindler persisted in pointing to the profound dualism between grace and nature that marks the Protestant spirit as the true cause of American secularization, the

---

80. Lowery, "The Dialogue," 41–42.

81. David L. Schindler, "Once Again: George Weigel, Catholicism and American Culture," *Communio*, Spring 1988, 92–120.

82. David L. Schindler, "U.S. Catholicism: A 'Moment of Opportunity'?," *30 Days*, May 1989, 57–60; Richard Neuhaus, George Weigel, and Michael Novak, "America Is Not a Secular Society," *30 Days*, June 1989, 52–55; David L. Schindler, "The One True American Religion," *30 Days*, June 1989, 55–59.

83. See Mark Lowery, "The Schindler/Weigel Debate: An Appraisal," *Communio*, Fall 1991, 425– 28 (response by Weigel: 439–49; response by Schindler: 450–72); David L. Schindler, "The Church's 'Worldly' Mission: Neoconservativism and American Culture," *Communio*, Fall 1991, 365–97. See also Michael Novak, "Schindler's Conversion: The Catholic Right Accepts Pluralism," *Communio*, Spring 1992, 145–63; David Schindler, "Christology and the Church's 'Worldly' Mission: Response to Michael Novak," *Communio*, Spring 1992, 164–78.

other participants in the debate argued that the Catholic tradition of natural law (apart from grace and revelation) was capable of transforming American society. For Schindler, grace was a source of transformation of nature; for the neoconservatives, law and natural law guaranteed, correctly understood, the Christian face of society.

With his polemical verve and intellectual agility, Schindler had brought to light the theological presuppositions of Novak and his neoconservative allies. It was a position marked by a profound dualism between the supernatural and the natural order, scholastic in its *forma mentis*, such as to lead to an uncritical and total acceptance of the American political and economic system. Christianity became the legitimation of the existing order. It became Catholic Americanism. This model implied, on the part of Catholics, the uncritical acceptance of both political and economic liberalism. It was an acceptance that, from Schindler's point of view, seemed more like a sort of subordination: "Where do we find in neoconservative thought a serious criticism of Western consumerism and materialism?"[84]

In a 2000 interview with the Italian journalist Paolo Mastrolilli, Schindler commented:

> In the United States there has been a certain exaltation of capitalism by some theologians who have interpreted encyclicals such as *Centesimus Annus* in only one direction. Yet John Paul II himself, in paragraph 26 of that document, warned us about the need to keep in mind some positive aspects of the theology of human liberation. Cardinal Ratzinger criticizes this theology's contacts with Marxism, but he recognizes that, if understood in the right way, it can flow from the Gospel, which invites liberation from sin not only in its private dimension but also in the social dimension, which is the "structural sin" of which the pope spoke. The error, in general, was to read *Centesimus Annus* in isolation from *Sollicitudo Rei Socialis*, from *Evangelium Vitae*, and from the whole body of the teachings of John Paul II. Thus many theologians were surprised when they found, in the recent document *Ecclesia in America*, some criticisms of capitalism, or of neoliberalism, which caught them off guard.[85]

---

84. David L. Schindler, "The Culture of Love" (interview), *Catholic World Report*, October 1994, 49.

85. The interview with Schindler is published in Paolo Mastrolilli, "Ma il Papa non si Usa," *Limes* 1, 2000, 40–41. According to Schindler, this does not mean rejecting the

Acceptance of the spirit of capitalism was the common conviction among the neoconservatives. Neuhaus, for his part, remarked ironically on the criticism of consumerism in *Centesimus Annus*: "It has, in short, all the appearances of being a throwaway line. Should we all consume less and, if so, consume less of what? And how will that help to include the poor within the circle of production and exchange?"[86] Neither Neuhaus nor Novak acknowledged any need for a reform of a "bourgeois" mentality, or even its existence. Christianity, in short, always comes too late, to the point of appearing as an uncomfortable, uninvited guest.

For Schindler, their view of a market that is self-regulated by its own internal logic, to which merely a dash of ethics is added, is unsustainable. As Michael Sean Winters writes:

> Schindler attacks capitalism on similar philosophical grounds: "Novak's position rigs the game: all the while it claims to be creating space or a market for competing moral visions, it is in fact, simultaneously, pouring the Scottish Enlightenment in this putatively 'empty' space or 'free' market." It is refreshing to read someone, anyone, for whom the triumph of market capitalism is not an eschaton, a climax of history, a salvific event.
>
> For Schindler, the relationship between capitalism and Christianity is not at all ambiguous. They are, quite simply, incompatible. The neo-conservatives acknowledge that self-interest is the engine of capitalism, and that self-interest is rooted in sinfulness, but they argue that it can be wiggled into a virtue out of necessity: self-interest can be socially creative, and thus promote the common good. Schindler attacks such consequentialism at its root: "The question rather is twofold: a) whether we recognize that a selfishness become mutual is not yet mutual generosity; and b) whether

---

market economy: "Christianity requires freedom in this area, too, because liberty is part of the truth. Capitalism, however, is only one way of interpreting the free market, and the neoliberal system has a unilaterally economic conception of man, which gives profit the primacy over being. So some market freedom is important, but the Western economic system is not neutral towards it. Liberalism is very insidious, because it hides its own oppressive face. Precisely for this reason, the consumerism of the Western system ends up becoming a subtle deprivation of man's freedom" (41). On Schindler's economic thought, see his *Ordering Love: Liberal Societies and the Memory of God* (Grand Rapids, MI: Eerdmans, 2011). See also Doug Bandow and David L. Schindler, eds., *Wealth, Poverty, and Human Destiny* (Wilmington, DE: ISI Books, 2003).

86. Richard John Neuhaus, *Doing Well and Doing Good: The Challenge of the Christian Capitalist* (New York: Doubleday, 1992), 218.

we recognize that our primary 'exigence' or dynamic remains for the latter, however much we fail to realize it. . . . A mutual selfishness which produces material wealth will, by virtue of its intrinsic dynamic, create a spiritual poverty which is exactly coincident with the production of material wealth."[87]

Schindler's critique strikes at the liberal theodicy at the heart of the neoconservative position. The theological dualism between natural and supernatural led Novak, Weigel, and Neuhaus to an autonomous conception of the world, such as to recognize an (almost) perfect order in its sphere. The kingdom of sin is transformed, by a kind of magic, into one of order and the harmony of passions and interests. This was why their vision can be characterized by saying that grace arrives when the banquet is already over and the guests fully satisfied by the society of well-being. The observation was on target and undermined the theology underlying Novak's social philosophy.

In 1996, Schindler published a book that was hailed as "the most important Catholic text to be published in the United States for some time, because he attempts to apply the idea of Balthasar to the social and political situation in America."[88] In *Heart of the World, Center of the Church: Communio Ecclesiology, Liberalism, and Liberation,*[89] Schindler attempted to mark out, beyond the liberals and conservatives, a Balthasarian "third way," a way that combined freedom and truth beyond the usual perspective of American liberalism. It was an effort that led him to critically engage John Courtney Murray, the main theorist of the reconciliation between Catholicism and modern freedom in the United States, whose theological work paved the way for *Dignitatis Humanae*, the great conciliar document on religious freedom.[90]

---

87. Michael Sean Winters, "David Schindler: Hero," *National Catholic Reporter*, June 28, 2013 (https://www.ncronline.org/blogs/distinctly-catholic/david-schindler-hero).

88. Winters, "David Schindler: Hero."

89. David L. Schindler, *Heart of the World, Center of the Church:* Communio *Ecclesiology, Liberalism, and Liberation* (Grand Rapids, MI: Eerdmans, 1996).

90. On John Courtney Murray, SJ (1904–1967), see Donald E. Pelotte, *John Courtney Murray: Theologian in Conflict* (New York: Paulist Press, 1975); Leon J. Hooper, *The Ethics of Discourse: The Social Philosophy of John Courtney Murray* (Washington, DC: Georgetown University Press, 1986); Walter J. Burghardt, "Tribute to John Courtney Murray, S.J.," *Woodstock Report*, December 1992; Leon J. Hooper, Os Guinness, and Michael J. Perry,

Reacting to the neoconservatives' identification of liberalism, capitalism, and Christianity, Schindler questioned their assumption that Murray's thought lent support to the liberal model. Since the neoconservatives referred often to Murray, it was easy to think he was a key source and support of their dualism. Now Novak certainly referred to Murray in the first pages of *The Spirit of Democratic Capitalism*, but he did so in a way that implied that he, Novak, was bringing to completion an effort that Murray had begun only *in potentia*. "Through the lonely pioneering work of John Courtney Murray, S.J.," Novak wrote, "the experience of religious liberty under democratic capitalism finally, after so much resistance, enriched the patrimony of the Catholic church. *So also, I hope, arguments in favor of 'the natural system of liberty' will one day enrich the church's conception of political economy.*"[91] Murray is cast here as the forerunner of a project that he never, in fact, undertook, like others whom Novak offers as points of reference. "Maritain saw the need for a new theory about the American system, but never gave sustained reflection to it himself. Neither has any other philosopher or theologian. John Courtney Murray, S.J., assayed the political system in *We Hold These Truths* (1960). Walter Lippmann tried to fill the gap with *The Public Philosophy* (1955).

"John Courtney Murray, S.J., and Religious Pluralism," *Woodstock Report* 33, March 1993; Hooper, "Citizen Murray," *Boston College Magazine*, Winter 1995; Hooper, *John Courtney Murray and the Growth of Tradition* (London: Sheed & Ward, 1996); Joseph A. Komonchak, "The Silencing of John Courtney Murray," in Alberto Melloni et al., eds., *Cristianesimo nella storia: Saggi in onore di Giuseppe Alberigo* (Bologna: il Mulino, 1996), 657–703; Komonchak, "John Courtney Murray," in S. Scatena and M. Ronconi, eds., *Libertà religiosa e diritti dell'uomo: Introduzione a* Dignitatis humanae (Milan: Periodici San Paolo, 2010), 109–121; Dominique Gonnet, *La liberté religieuse à Vatican ii: La contribution de John Courtney Murray* (Paris: Éditions du Cerf, 2004); Luca Diotallevi, "La convergenza Montini-Murray," *Nomos* 3 (2015); P. B. Harris, "John Courtney Murray and the Americanization of Religious Liberty at the Second Vatican Council," Nomos 3 (2015); Piergiorgio Grassi, "John Courtney Murray: Un gesuita americano al Concilio Vaticano ii," *Dialoghi* 2 (2015); Barry Hudock, *Struggle, Condemnation, Vindication: John Courtney Murray's Journey Toward Vatican II* (Collegeville, MN: Liturgical Press, 2015); Steven K. Green, "The Path Not Taken: Reinhold Niebuhr, John Courtney Murray, and the American Proposition of Church-State Separation," *Oxford Journal of Law and Religion* 8, no. 1 (2019), 51–70; Stefano Ceccanti, "L'irruzione del diritto costituzionale americano nella Chiesa cattolica," preface to a new edition of John Courtney Murray, *Noi crediamo in queste verità: Riflessioni cattoliche sul "principio americano"* (Brescia: Morcelliana, 2021), i–xiii.

91. Novak, *The Spirit of Democratic Capitalism*, 28. Emphasis mine.

Reinhold Niebuhr in *The Irony of American History* (1952) and in other books also blazed a trail across deserts and mountains, but stopped short of the vision."[92] It is, then, not Murray who espouses the cause of reconciling capitalism and Catholicism. On the contrary, Novak was keen to emphasize that this was his own achievement. By calling into doubt Murray as Novak's source, then, Schindler was only agreeing with Novak on the point.

Schindler's most careful and demanding challenge came in a long 1994 article entitled "Religious Freedom, Truth, and American Liberalism: Another Look at John Courtney Murray."[93] Here he proposed to show "how Murray's dualism is not neutral, even when intended only as a juridical matter; how it leads (logically) to a liberal privatization of religion and hence to secularism; and how, finally, it differs from the theology of de Lubac and John Paul II, in the latter's reading of Vatican Council II."[94] In his criticism, Schindler immediately makes it clear that he is not at all on the side of the conservatives. Revising the notion of religious freedom, as theorized by Murray, does not mean returning to the preconciliar position. "In particular, apropos of the theme of religious freedom, we need to see that the criticism of a certain prevalent notion of religious freedom does not, *a priori*, indicate a ('conservative') retreat from *Dignitatis humanae*; on the contrary, it indicates merely that one's understanding of this notion might differ depending on which theology within the 'progressive' majority at the Council one takes as primary. My intention in this paper is to illustrate this difference, in terms of the theologies of Murray on the one hand, and de Lubac (and Pope John Paul II) on the other."[95]

Schindler's criticism of Murray does not concern the notion of religious freedom that developed consequent to the surrender to liberalism, as the reactionaries lament. For Murray, acceptance of the liberal legal order does not at all imply acceptance of the philosophy and worldview of classical liberalism. The articles of the First Amendment are, for Murray, "articles of peace"; they avoid conflicts, protecting the unity of a nation

92. Novak, *The Spirit of Democratic Capitalism*, 21.

93. David L. Schindler, "Religious Freedom, Truth, and American Liberalism: Another Look at John Courtney Murray," *Communio*, Winter 1994, 696–741.

94. Schindler, "Religious Freedom, Truth, and American Liberalism," 718.

95. Schindler, "Religious Freedom, Truth, and American Liberalism," 700n5.

founded on religious pluralism. But this distinction between legislation and liberal philosophy does not convince Schindler.

> It nonetheless seems to me that this distinction itself requires more dif-ferentiation than Murray gives it. The claim of constitutional indifference (that is, neutrality) is tied, in the case of Murray, to his interpretation of the religion clauses of the First Amendment as "articles of peace." And this interpretation is reinforced by his definition of religious freedom first in negative terms, as an immunity (from coercion). But what happens if it can be shown that the religion clauses, whenever they *actually* mean any-thing, always imply someone's "articles of faith"; and if it can be shown, further, that a religious freedom defined first in negative terms already presupposes *a theory of religion different* from one which would define religious freedom in positive terms, in terms of the person's positive rela-tionship toward God?[96]

This latter perspective involves the relationship between freedom and truth, a relationship suspended and placed in brackets in the liberal ap-proach. In its dualism, liberalism separates the person from God, freedom from truth, the person from other persons, the natural from the super-natural. Hence the criticism of Murray starting from de Lubac's theology: "My point is that Murray did not integrate fully enough into his own work de Lubac's theology of nature and grace: Murray did not see in a sufficiently radical way the cultural implications of de Lubac's nature-grace theology for the 'conservative liberalism' which Murray was at pains to defend as distinctive of (Anglo-) America."[97] Murray's weakness, then, lies in his negative conception of freedom, devoid of a positive valence.

Schindler wrote, "But note the crucial ambiguity: the purely formal definition that Murray defends as primary in American liberalism in fact leaves unmentioned any (positive) sense of openness to God. What it men-tions explicitly is rather the negative relation of 'immunity (from coercion).' Now this may very well *imply*, and for Murray it certainly does imply, a *positive* sense of openness to the transcendent. *But in point of fact this defi-nition of freedom is silent about God and the transcendent order. And silence about God is not yet, in and of itself, an indication of positive openness to*

---

96. Schindler, "Religious Freedom, Truth, and American Liberalism," 702–3.
97. Schindler, "Religious Freedom, Truth, and American Liberalism," 705n11.

God."[98] From this point of view—and this is Schindler's thesis—Murray's dualistic liberalism would not be neutral at all but would constitute the premise and the ratification of the secular face of America. "Murray's dualistic worldview is neither so unequivocally favorable to Christianity nor so unequivocally unfavorable to atheism-secularism as this suggestion assumes. Murray's argument, contrary to its intention, carries a(n) (onto-) logic of liberalism which weights society either toward a certain kind of secularized ir-religion or toward a certain kind of Christianity, neither of which is consistent with an authentic conciliar (Lubacian) Catholicism."[99]

Schindler concludes, "Murray's project thus seems to lead to a privatization of religion. By this, I do not mean that Murray himself endorses privatization: clearly he does not. I mean . . . only that Murray's position contains an equivocation: affirming premises ('articles of peace') that entail privatization while otherwise defending the contrary."[100]

The privatization of religion and secularization of the world—these, Schindler says, are the (unintended) consequences of Murray's liberalism, while Murray, to the contrary, seeks to legitimize the encounter between freedom and American religiosity—the same encounter celebrated by the "thinkers [who] follow Murray in making a simple contrast between European secularism and American religiosity, without differentiating further . . . how American religiosity itself tends of its nature toward inversion into secularism."[101] Who are these "thinkers" who follow Murray? One name springs to mind: Michael Novak.[102]

Novak, Murray's intellectual disciple, represents the secularization of American Catholicism. In contradistinction is the thought of Henri de Lubac. Schindler wrote:

> For Murray, grace's influence on nature takes the form of assisting nature
> to realize its own finality; the ends proper to grace and nature otherwise

98. Schindler, "Religious Freedom, Truth, and American Liberalism," 716–17 (emphasis in the original).

99. Schindler, "Religious Freedom, Truth, and American Liberalism," 720–21.

100. Schindler, "Religious Freedom, Truth, and American Liberalism," 722.

101. Schindler, "Religious Freedom, Truth, and American Liberalism," 725. "My argument, in contrast, influenced by Herberg, is that secularism in America is logically linked to the founding principles of America" (725). The work of Will Herberg, to whom Schindler refers here, is *Protestant Catholic Jew* (Chicago: University of Chicago Press, 1983). For Herberg, the "American Way of Life" is the result of a "secularized Puritanism" (81).

102. See Schindler, "Religious Freedom, Truth, and American Liberalism," 727n23.

remain each in its own sphere. For de Lubac, on the contrary, grace's influence takes the form of directing nature from within to serve the end given in grace; the ends proper to grace and nature remain distinct, even as the natural end is placed *within*, internally subordinated to, the supernatural end. For Murray, then, the result is an insistence on a dualism between citizen and believer, and on the sharpness of the distinction between eternal (ultimate) end and temporal (penultimate) ends. For de Lubac, on the contrary, the call to sanctity "comprehends" the call to citizenship and all the worldly tasks implied by citizenship. The eternal end "comprehends" the temporal ends.[103]

The question that arises is whether Schindler's approach, insisting upon the close connection between grace and nature, leads to a form of confessional state.[104] Is his model workable in the context of the liberal-democratic state? Put another way, is an alternative to Murray that preserves the principle of religious freedom even possible *in practice*? This is the question that Schindler poses. He writes,

> But we now appear to have been backed into a dilemma. On the one hand, Vatican II surely affirmed religious freedom; religious freedom seems to require something like Murray's distinction between state and society; the distinction between state and society seems tied to an understanding of the state as neutral toward anyone's religious theory, hence as non-confessional; and, finally, Murray's dualistic distinction between nature and grace seems essential in securing the non-confessional state.
>
> On the other hand, our suggestion is that Vatican II (in the light of the theology of de Lubac and Pope John Paul II) has embraced an organic-paradoxical understanding of the nature-grace relation. But this would thus seem to call into question the non-confessional state and in turn the

103. Schindler, "Religious Freedom, Truth, and American Liberalism," 732.

104. As Michael Sean Winters observes: "One wonders what a Schindler-inspired polity would look like. No one wants a return to the confessional state, but that would seem to be the natural outcome of Schindler's proposals. He fails to appreciate the varieties of liberalism: he may object to the priority of negative freedom in liberal thought, but he takes no note of the precious complicating fact that liberal thinkers such as Kant favored a positive conception of freedom. What is most troubling, though, is Schindler's inalertness to history: to recognize that regimes built upon negative freedom have entailed less tyranny than any other regimes is a powerful argument in their favor, and one which Schindler does not engage. The absence of ontology has sometimes been a moral and political blessing" (Winters, "David Schindler: Hero").

distinction between state and society, leading finally to a withdrawal of religious freedom.[105]

With his solution, Schindler would like to move beyond the dialectic between liberals and conservatives. He continues,

> It seems to me that we need not accept this dilemma. Indeed, it is the common acceptance of such a dilemma by both "liberals" (e.g., "Murrayites") and "conservatives" (e.g., Lefebvrites) that seems to me to lie at the heart of the impasse following Vatican II. Murrayites and Lefebvrites, however much they do so for opposite reasons, nonetheless converge in their apparent conviction that clear priority of religious truth is incompatible, or at least strongly in tension, with a principled commitment to religious liberty. In what sense is this the case? And what do we propose alternatively, as a way out of the dilemma?
>
> Let me first of all repeat what was stated earlier: Vatican Council II unequivocally affirmed religious freedom and thereby unequivocally rejected "integralism"; and the importance of Murray in these conciliar achievements is indisputable.[106]

Where then, it must be asked, is the real point of contrast between Schindler and Murray if it does not concern the acceptance or rejection of the principle of religious freedom? The crux of the answer is found in the "juridical" conception of the church that guided Murray's reflection in a unilateral way and that led him to neglect the theme of the evangelization of the world. "The problem with Murray in this connection is that he tends to conflate the secular-sacred distinction into a Church-state distinction, that is, even as, in so doing, he understands the Church primarily as a juridical entity. The inevitable consequence is that he hesitates to affirm the need for Christianizing 'the terrestrial and temporal order in its structures and processes,' because to Christianize entails juridicalizing entails a renewed integralism."[107]

On the contrary, according to Schindler, an authentic "*communio* ecclesiology"—theology rooted in the thought of de Lubac and the Second Vatican Council read in the spirit of John Paul II—leads to overcom-

---

105. Schindler, "Religious Freedom, Truth, and American Liberalism," 735.

106. Schindler, "Religious Freedom, Truth, and American Liberalism," 735–36.

107. Schindler, "Religious Freedom, Truth, and American Liberalism," 738n40.

ing the dilemma between integralism and liberalism: "What they both intend is simply that the whole world be inserted within the mission of Jesus Christ: that the whole world thus become a 'civilization of love.' This intrinsic subordination of the world to the finality given in grace must always be maintained simultaneous with the juridical distinctness of state and Church. The former subordination without the latter distinctness entails 'integralism'; the latter distinctness without the former subordination entails secularism. An ecclesiology of *communio* allows us to break through this dilemma."[108]

Communio ecclesiology corrects the lacuna in Murray's juridical ecclesiology and prevents his religious liberalism from becoming a secularizing dualism between private faith and neutralizing public sphere—a secularizing dualism that to Schindler appears to be intimately linked to the "American spirit" dependent on the puritanism of the nation's founders. The critical picture is therefore clear even if, in Schindler's objections to Murray, some gray areas remain. One has the impression, in fact, that Schindler does not adequately value, in practical terms, the distinction made by Fr. Murray between legal liberalism and the philosophical Enlightenment-type *Weltanschauung* that accompanies it in Locke's school. That is, it escapes Schindler that the emphasis on the negative concept of freedom (as noncoercion) is the result of the wars of religion that bloodied Europe during the sixteenth and seventeenth centuries; it is a reaction to ecclesiastical and state absolutism.

This "negative" freedom is, for Murray, a prerequisite to "freely" access the truth, to practice religious, philosophical, and political beliefs without impediment. It is not just a "modern" conception, as progressives and reactionaries seem to think, as does Schindler, for whom the reference to an authentic conception of freedom implies a return to a classical anthropology.[109] It is, rather, an exquisitely Christian conception, derived

---

108. Schindler, "Religious Freedom, Truth, and American Liberalism," 738.

109. See David L. Schindler, *Freedom from Reality: The Diabolical Character of Modern Liberty* (Notre Dame, IN: University of Notre Dame Press, 2017). Here Schindler, in a journey similar to Alasdair MacIntyre's, describes a return to the classic ethical model of politics to fill the "relational" deficit of modern liberalism devoid of a true notion of "common good." It is a precious reflection full of implications. However, there remains the problem of affirming, in a practical-juridical context, the value of the modern notion of freedom, the meaning of which cannot be understood or exhausted starting from the dialectic between "dia-bolic" and "symbolic."

from the evangelical distinction between God and Caesar, spread and defended by the fathers of the church and then placed in the background starting from the Edict of Thessalonica of AD 380, which legitimized the Catholic religion as the only religion of the Roman Empire. It is a conception that the Second Vatican Council reaffirms, in antithesis to totalitarianism, thanks to the rediscovery of its most ancient and original tradition.[110]

Modern liberalism is not simply individualism and the privatization of the faith. It is also heir to the Christian liberalism of the first four centuries and to the revolutionary distinction between church and state made by Christ. For this reason, Schindler's critique, which links Novak to Murray in a single secularizing current, risks complicating the picture. Nonetheless, it remains, in context of this debate of the nineties, one of the most interesting attempts to denounce the ideology of the Catho-capitalism professed by the neoconservatives. The Balthasar-de Lubac-Ratzinger-related journal *Communio* distanced itself from this ideology, considering it to have a hand in the secularization of American Catholicism. The Catholic spirit of democratic capitalism was, in fact, the spirit of bourgeois Catholicism.

America First: The Neoconservatives versus John Paul II and Benedict XVI

David Schindler's criticism of the neoconservatives was certainly important, but it did not do much to slow the spread of their ideas and their influence within a large segment of American and European Catholicism. In the era of post-Communist globalization, these ideas became a cultural hegemony, and this only intensified after the destruction of the Twin Towers in New York on September 11, 2001, as the idea of a battle of the West against an "axis of evil" took root.

The first signs of a weakening of this hegemony came only as the disaster caused by the war in Iraq, which was so strongly supported by the neoconservatives, became clear and with the advent of the Obama presidency in 2008. Criticism of the ideological manipulation of John Paul II's pontificate focused especially on the instrumental and distorted use

---

110. See Borghesi, *Critica della teologia politica*, 25–64.

of *Centesimus Annus* in support of a neoconservative Catho-capitalism. More recently, the scholar Jesse Russell has summarized the critics' point of view by targeting, first, George Weigel's papal biography, *Witness to Hope*. Russell writes, "In his biographies, George Weigel crafts an often misleading portrait of Pope John Paul II as the pope of American liberalism and neoconservativism. Ironically, at the same time, the story of Weigel's biographies contains the story of the rise and fall of the Catholic neoconservative movement in America."[111]

Russell has also criticized the neoconservatives' hijacking of *Centesimus Annus*, writing,

> In the twilight of the twentieth and beginning of the twenty-first century, Catholic theologians and journalists who identified as members of the neoconservative political movement crafted a narrative of John Paul II's encyclical *Centesimus Annus* as representing a sea-change in Catholic social teaching. In this neoconservative reading, the Catholic Church embraced a specifically American style of late twentieth century laissez-faire capitalism. However, an examination of *Centesimus Annus* reveals that the text is consonant with the teaching of twentieth century popes. What is more, recent publications enable us to get a clearer view of how neoconservatives were able to craft their narrative of the encyclical.[112]

Two salient points have been critically noted by recent publications: the neoconservatives' understanding of the economy and the common good and their support for the Bush administration's war against Iraq in 2003.

The ideological use of *Centesimus Annus* had certainly not gone unnoticed. In Italy, the respected philosopher Antonio Maria Baggio critically analyzed Novak's and Neuhaus's work as early as 1995. He wrote,

> Neuhaus is aware of the trend of an increase in the number of the very rich and also of the very poor, but he does not question the system that

---

111. Jesse Russell, "The Neoconservatives and the Pope: Misreading John Paul II in George Weigel's Biographies," *Political Theology* 20 (2019), 24–47 ("Abstract").

112. Jesse Russell, "The Catholic Neoconservative Misreading of John Paul II's *Centesimus Annus* Revisited," *Political Theology* 21 (2020), 172–191 ("Abstract"). By the same author, see "The Contradictions of Catholic Neoconservatism," in Gottfried, *The Vanishing Tradition*, 85–98.

produces it. Indeed, he believes that poverty is essentially the result of non-participation in the economic dynamism of that system; that therefore the free expansion of the activities of production, inserting the poor into work, is sufficient to absorb poverty. But the problem, again, is that the system itself, in its way of functioning, produces areas of marginalization, for example, by eliminating many professional positions and creating new ones, to which the unemployed do not have access. Not only that: precisely in the United States we see a constant growth of an underclass made up of individuals whose brutalization is such as to make them impermeable to any attempt, conducted with traditional methods, to emancipate them.

All this raises the problem of intervention in the system by the state, which Neuhaus and Novak never mention. According to the pope, one can escape poverty by gaining access to property; it is a traditional position of Christian social doctrine. But the system itself in many respects prevents individuals from doing so, just as it prevents many countries from entering the world economic community in a position that is not subordinate to the interests of the stronger countries. In short, there is need for structural reforms, or at least for regulation of both internal and international capitalist dynamics. But Neuhaus and Novak, who theoretically admit, on the basis of the principle of subsidiarity, the intervention of the state, are silent when a specific problem would require it—the situation of poverty in the United States being just such a case.[113]

According to Baggio, "These examples, in conclusion, make clear that the stance of Christian social doctrine toward poverty is, in many of its aspects, rejected by Neuhaus and Novak."[114]

Another scholar who has criticized the neoconservative interpretation of John Paul II's teaching is American theologian John Sniegocki. In a 2006 article, Sniegocki notes that "neoconservative interpretations of the social teaching of Pope John Paul II have become very influential in recent years. These interpretations, put forth by persons such as Michael Novak, George Weigel, and Richard John Neuhaus, center upon the assertion that John Paul II in his 1991 encyclical *Centesimus annus* broke in important ways with previous Catholic Social Teaching (CST) documents

---

113. Antonio Maria Baggio, "Capitalismo ed 'etica cattolica': Osservazioni sull'interpretazione della dottrina sociale cristiana di Richard Neuhaus e Michael Novak," *Nuova Umanità* 6 (1995), 107.

114. Baggio, "Capitalismo ed 'etica Cattolica,'" 108.

and paved the way for an embrace of 'democratic capitalism.' "[115] Seeking to demonstrate the inaccuracy of this assertion, Sniegocki offers a detailed examination of the points that mark the distance between the neoconservative reading of the pope and the texts of his social teaching—the unfounded assertion that after the fall of Communism, capitalism would be the only fully acceptable model; Novak's blindness to the pope's insistence on economic rights and the presence of workers in the management structure of companies; the disregard for the issue of the redistribution of wealth based on the principle of the universal destination of goods; the importance of lifestyle simplification, so incomprehensible to the neocons; the role of the government in regulating the common good; and the topic of consumerism.

The crux of the contrast between the neocons and John Paul II, Sniegocki writes, lies in two different anthropologies. The neocons understand freedom individualistically and treat solidarity only as its corollary. For the pope, on the other hand, freedom and solidarity are the two poles of an antinomy, neither of which can be absolutized to the detriment of the other.

> It is in the name of liberty that the neoconservatives oppose economic rights, seek to minimize the role of the state in economic life (apart from protecting property, contracts, etc.), and oppose most measures to redistribute wealth. Any strong egalitarian values, they state, are "incompatible with respect for liberty." As numerous commentators have highlighted, the economic theory that the neoconservatives uphold (put forth by economists such as Ludwig von Mises and Friedrich von Hayek) is rooted in a very strong methodological individualism. While Novak and the others would deny that they themselves have individualistic anthropologies, a strong case can be made that this individualism is embedded, whether consciously or not, in the overall economic visions that they put forth. In contrast to the neoconservative emphasis on "liberty," Pope John Paul II emphasizes especially the virtue of "solidarity," which places primacy on meeting the basic needs of all. Solidarity, John Paul says, involves "a firm and persevering determination to commit oneself to the common good; that is to say to the good of all and of each individual, because we are all really responsible for all." Pope John Paul II clearly values liberty and

115. John Sniegocki, "The Social Ethics of Pope John Paul II: A Critique of Neoconservative Interpretations," *Horizons* 33, no. 1 (2006), 7.

freedom, as the neoconservatives do, but he grounds his understanding of freedom in a highly communitarian understanding of the human person that sees freedom as being most fully exercised in active concern for the marginalized.[116]

No one who is attentive to John Paul II's teaching will be inclined to crown him as the standard-bearer of capitalism. As Stephen Krason observes, "One should not be so ready to conclude that *Centesimus Annus* abandons the quest for a 'third way.' Clearly, as Professor Novak himself acknowledges, John Paul outrightly rejects a certain notion of capitalism—which essentially means what popes since Leo XIII have called 'liberalism'—along with his rejection of the various varieties of socialism. The above indicates that he makes very clear in *Sollicitudo Rei Socialis* that he believes that liberal capitalism, as practiced, remains flawed, and the fact that *Centesimus Annus* speaks about 'alienation' and 'consumerism' in the West shows that he hasn't changed his mind about that."[117]

The problem with the use that the neocons made of *Centesimus Annus* is therefore clear: the pope did not change his mind in the slightest after 1989, and he did not establish any break in the history of Catholic social teaching.

Novak, Weigel, and Neuhaus's attempts to play fast and loose with the papal magisterium did not stop following the death of John Paul II. Indeed, they became even more overt with the publication of Pope Benedict XVI's social encyclical *Caritas in Veritate* on June 29, 2009.[118] The neoconservative reaction to the document was not at all favorable. Just days after its release, Weigel offered a truly striking assessment. In an article published in the *National Review*, he distinguished its "golden" parts, those he claimed were the work of the pope, from its "red" parts, supposedly the work of the Pontifical Council for Justice and Peace.[119] The pon-

116. Sniegocki, "The Social Ethics of Pope John Paul II," 30.

117. Stephen M. Krason, "Centesimus Annus: Maintaining the Continuity of Catholic Social Teaching: A Response to Professor Michael Novak," *Faith & Reason*, Winter 1991.

118. See Luca Sandonà, "The Reception of *Caritas in Veritate* in the USA: Appreciation and Perplexity," *Oikonomia* 9, no. 2 (June 2010), https://www.oikonomia.it/index.php /en/oikonomia-2010/giugno-2010/704-the-reception-of-caritas-in-veritate-in-the-usa -appreciation-and-perplexity.

119. George Weigel, "*Caritas in Veritate* in Gold and Red," *National Review*, July 7, 2009, https://www.nationalreview.com/2009/07/caritas-veritate-gold-and-red-george-weigel/.

tifical council's approach, Weigel argued, sounded a lot like Paul VI's *Populorum Progressio*, a problematic text from Weigel's point of view:

> In the long line of papal social teaching running from *Rerum Novarum* to *Centesimus Annus*, *Populorum Progressio* is manifestly the odd duck, both in its intellectual structure (which is barely recognizable as in continuity with the framework for Catholic social thought established by Leo XIII and extended by Pius XI in *Quadragesimo Anno*) and in its misreading of the economic and political signs of the times (which was clouded by then-popular leftist and progressive conceptions about the problem of Third World poverty, its causes, and its remedies). *Centesimus Annus* implicitly recognized these defects, not least by arguing that poverty in the Third World and within developed countries today is a matter of exclusion from global networks of exchange in a dynamic economy (which put the moral emphasis on strategies of wealth creation, empowerment of the poor, and inclusion), rather than a matter of First World greed in a static economy (which would put the moral emphasis on redistribution of wealth).[120]

This is a key tenet of the neocons: *Centesimus Annus* corrected Catholic social teaching's anticapitalist stance, which is particularly clear in *Populorum Progressio*. John Paul II versus Paul VI. It was apparently an inadequate "correction," though, since, according to Weigel, *Caritas in Veritate* takes a leap backward, attempting to return to the traditional path of the church's social doctrine. Writes Weigel,

> Now comes *Caritas in Veritate* (Charity in Truth), Benedict XVI's long-awaited and much-delayed social encyclical. It seems to be a hybrid, blending the pope's own insightful thinking on the social order with elements of the Justice and Peace approach to Catholic social doctrine, which imagines that doctrine beginning anew at *Populorum Progressio*. Indeed, those with advanced degrees in Vaticanology could easily go through the text of *Caritas in Veritate*, highlighting those passages that are obviously Benedictine with a gold marker and those that reflect current Justice and Peace default positions with a red marker. The net result is, with respect, an encyclical that resembles a duck-billed platypus.
>
> The clearly Benedictine passages in *Caritas in Veritate* follow and develop the line of John Paul II, particularly in the new encyclical's strong

---

120. Weigel, "*Caritas in Veritate* in Gold and Red."

emphasis on the life issues (abortion, euthanasia, embryo-destructive stem-cell research) as social-justice issues. . . .

But then there are those passages to be marked in red—the passages that reflect Justice and Peace ideas and approaches that Benedict evidently believed he had to try and accommodate. Some of these are simply incomprehensible, as when the encyclical states that defeating Third World poverty and underdevelopment requires a "necessary openness, in a world context, to forms of economic activity marked by quotas of gratuitousness and communion." This may mean something interesting; it may mean something naïve or dumb. But, on its face, it is virtually impossible to know *what* it means.[121]

And the document's reflection on the theme of "gift," Weigel would have us understand, means nothing:

> The language in these sections of *Caritas in Veritate* is so clotted and muddled as to suggest the possibility that what may be intended as a new conceptual starting point for Catholic social doctrine is, in fact, a confused sentimentality of precisely the sort the encyclical deplores among those who detach charity from truth.[122]

Nor is the teaching on redistribution and the creation of wealth— sections introduced, according to Weigel, by the *longa manus* of the justice and peace commission—significant.

> If those burrowed into the intellectual and institutional woodwork at the Pontifical Council for Justice and Peace imagine *Caritas in Veritate* as reversing the rout they believe they suffered with *Centesimus Annus*, and if they further imagine *Caritas in Veritate* setting Catholic social doctrine on a completely new, *Populorum Progressio*–defined course (as one Justice and Peace consultor has already said), they are likely to be disappointed. The incoherence of the Justice and Peace sections of the new encyclical is so deep, and the language in some cases so impenetrable, that what the defenders of *Populorum Progressio* may think to be a new sounding of the trumpet is far more like the warbling of an untuned piccolo.[123]

121. Weigel, "*Caritas in Veritate* in Gold and Red."
122. Weigel, "*Caritas in Veritate* in Gold and Red."
123. Weigel, "*Caritas in Veritate* in Gold and Red."

Weigel's real concern, manifested in his mocking tone, is clear: after all the work the neocons had done to successfully impose their own interpretation of Catholic social teaching, now *Caritas in Veritate* with its anticapitalist slant risked restoring what was clear in *Populorum Progressio.* Despite Novak's reinterpretation of John Paul II, Benedict brings us back to Paul VI. Hence Weigel's political reading of the encyclical, which dissects the document with a scalpel, carefully disentangling Benedict's golden pieces from the justice and peace commission's red ones, the former acceptable, the latter not. It's a truly unique maneuver—and fails to take into account the fact that the encyclical bears the signature with which the pope, in this case Benedict, gives the entire text his authority. But for Weigel, Benedict's signature is merely a benign concession, an act of generosity:

> Benedict XVI, a truly gentle soul, may have thought it necessary to include in his encyclical these multiple off-notes, in order to maintain the peace within his curial household. Those with eyes to see and ears to hear will concentrate their attention, in reading *Caritas in Veritate,* on those parts of the encyclical that are clearly Benedictine, including the Pope's trademark defense of the necessary conjunction of faith and reason and his extension of John Paul II's signature theme—that all social issues, including political and economic questions, are ultimately questions of the nature of the human person.[124]

Weigel's explanation of the 2009 papal encyclical was a clear expression of his distance from papal teaching. *Caritas in Veritate* shattered the illusion that the neocon project was built upon: the identification between Catholicism and capitalism starting from the "turning point" introduced by *Centesimus Annus.* Having presented themselves as apologists for the papacy, the neocons had become, at least in part, its critics. Catholic Americanism had manifested itself for what it was: a form of accommodation and legitimation of the economic and political power that a generation of Catholic intellectuals, veterans of the left, had been granted during the Reagan era.

In a sort of Weigel epitaph, the American scholar Anthony Annett wrote in 2015:

---

124. Weigel, "*Caritas in Veritate* in Gold and Red."

I would contend that few American Catholics in the modern era have surrendered more to the spirit of the age—the age of Reagan and the resurgence of free-market liberalism and aggressive militarism—than George Weigel.

For decades now, Weigel has been a thorn in the side of authentic Catholic social teaching, seeking to baptize economic liberalism and American exceptionalism with the waters of the Catholic faith. Alongside fellow travelers like Richard John Neuhaus and Michael Novak, he has been peddling the idea that *Centesimus Annus*—John Paul II's landmark social encyclical from 1991—represented a decisive break with the past, a significant development of doctrine that saw the Church fully embrace capitalism and free market economics. A simple reading of the encyclical itself exposes the hollowness of such a claim. Yet Weigel et al actually produced an abridged version of the encyclical, which managed to remove the passages that went against their radical reading. Not exactly the height of honesty.

Weigel sprung back into action with the release of Pope Benedict XVI's *Caritas in Veritate* in 2009, which was a profound reflection on the maladies of the modern global economy. This time, Weigel found it too difficult to expunge the offending elements, so he invented his own "encyclical exegesis"—calling on readers to distinguish the authentic "gold pen" of the pope and the false "red pen" of the leftists associated with the Pontifical Council for Justice and Peace.[125]

Compared to Weigel's facile exegetical method, Novak's proved to be a bit shrewder. He did not, however, shy from distinguishing the good parts of *Caritas in Veritate* from the bad, positing, like Weigel, the idea of ambiguity in the text that can be read in different ways.

In his concrete discussions about current affairs, almost every time Benedict seems to give a point to the left, rooted usually in *Populorum Progressio* (1967), he takes it back or qualifies it by drawing on lessons learned in between 1967 and 1991, as recorded in *Centesimus Annus*. His practice follows his intention. He lets both horses run, and does not himself choose to side with either one.

In some ways, this openness seems to be baffling many readers, and making this particular piece of Benedict XVI's writing come across as uncharacteristically waffly and opaque. It often seems to go in two directions at once. Some sentences are almost impossible to parse in practical terms: What on earth does *that* mean in practice?

125. Anthony Annett, "The Enduring George Weigel Problem," *Commonweal*, May 28, 2015, https://www.commonwealmagazine.org/enduring-george-weigel-problem.

This refusal to indulge in ideology has a great strength that compensates for the above-mentioned weakness. Its strength is that it raises the mind to other dimensions of the truth, and avoids squabbles that belong more to the City of Man than to the City of God.[126]

The encyclical, in other words, doesn't allow us to stand on firm ground, and when it does, its solutions, divided between solidarity and subsidiarity, turn out to be ambivalent, usable for the left as well as for the right. In this way, Novak sought to neutralize the pope's teaching. His comments did not actually address any of the key points of *Caritas in Veritate*. Neither he nor Weigel were pleased with it.

Social doctrine was not the only source of friction between the neocons and the popes. A much more concrete issue, since it involved many thousands of human deaths, was that of war.

On March 20, 2003, a coalition led by the United States declared war on Saddam Hussein's regime in Iraq, inaugurating a bloody conflict that was intended to be brief, but that in reality was destined to continue for decades with profoundly negative consequences for the stability of the region: political-religious conflicts, terrorist reactions, the exile of thousands of discriminated and persecuted Christians. The pretext put forward by President George W. Bush and his administration for the declaration of war was that Saddam was a danger to the international community, in possession of chemical weapons of mass destruction, and the source of Islamic terrorism that, since 9/11, had terrorized the world. On February 2, 2003, Secretary of State Colin Powell, speaking to the United Nations Security Council, declared that he was holding the "smoking gun," irrefutable proof that Saddam was in possession of anthrax and deadly biological weapons. No trace of those weapons would ultimately be found, and the famous "smoking gun" turned out to be one of the most sensational lies of the early twenty-first century.

The war in Iraq represented the pinnacle of neoconservative power, their moment of greatest influence in American politics. As Blandine Chelini-Pont writes:

> In the 2000s, under the presidencies of George W. Bush, Catholic thinkers formed an intellectual backbone at the service of the conservative movement,

126. Michael Novak, "Pope Benedict XVI's *Caritas*," *First Things*, August 17, 2009, https://www.firstthings.com/web-exclusives/2009/08/pope-benedict-xvis-caritas.

and their ideas were strongly represented in the entourage of the President. Bush was a parishioner of the Episcopalian Church in Washington and a member of the Methodist Church in Texas, but he was surrounded by intellectuals, counselors, pens, and politicians from the Catholic faith. On the day of his 2001 inauguration, he received the archbishop of Washington to dinner. President Bush Jr. went with his father to the funeral of John Paul II, offering the world the stunning picture of two American Presidents, father and son, gathering at the remains of a Roman pontiff.

Throughout his administration, George W. Bush never ceased to show his reverence for the Catholic religion. His welcoming of Pope Benedict XVI, who visited the United States in April 2008, is also memorable, for the magnificent birthday reception of the pontiff at the White House, with 250 guests, including George Weigel, Michael Novak, and John Richard Neuhaus. According to journalist Daniel Burke, these Catholics had for eight years had a major influence on Bush's speeches, politics, and legacy, "to an unprecedented extent in the history of the United States." . . .

The three "figures" of Catholic conservatism and its neoconservative and intransigent tendencies, Weigel, Novak, and Neuhaus, were very close to this administration and justified in their writings on just war the strong hand of nationalist hawks on defense policy. Acting as the shield or the strong arm of Providence, the salvation of the Christian civilization, the United States was blessed, in their writings and speeches, to start preventive wars, a new concept, in order to preserve itself and the world from the new evil axis of Islam, despite a cautious American episcopate and all attempts of the Holy See to avoid the war in Iraq.[127]

Unlike the neocons, the elderly and sick John Paul II, Reagan's great "ally" in the 1980s, proved to be one of the staunchest opponents of the war. He tried in every way to prevent it, but the American government proved totally deaf to the papal demands. On March 16, 2003, four days before the outbreak of the conflict, John Paul said publicly:

> The next few days will be decisive for the outcome of the Iraqi crisis. Let us pray, then, that the Lord inspire in all sides of the dispute courage and farsightedness.

127. Chelini-Pont, "Catholic Colonization of the American Right," 54–55. On the unreserved support of the neocons for the war against Iraq and on their attempt to influence the stance of the Catholic Church on the matter, see Jesse Russell, "The Catholic Neoconservative at War: The Battle for Control of Catholic Just War Teaching in America," *Politics, Religion & Ideology* 21 (2020), 288–310.

The political leaders of Baghdad certainly have the urgent duty to collaborate fully with the international community to eliminate every reason for armed intervention. To them I direct my urgent appeal: the fate of your fellow-citizens should always have priority.

But I would also like to remind the member countries of the United Nations, and especially those who make up the Security Council, that the use of force represents the last recourse, after having exhausted every other peaceful solution, in keeping with the well-known principles of the UN Charter.

That is why, in the face of the *tremendous consequences* that an international military operation would have for the population of Iraq and for the balance of the Middle East region, already sorely tried, and for the extremisms that could stem from it, I say to all: There is still time to negotiate; there is still room for peace, it is never too late to come to an understanding and to continue discussions.

To reflect on one's duties, to engage in energetic negotiations does not mean to be humiliated, but *to work with responsibility for peace. . . .*

I belong to that generation that lived through World War II and, thanks be to God, survived it. I have the duty to say to all young people, to those who are younger than I, who have not had this experience: "No more war" as Paul VI said during his first visit to the United Nations. We must do everything possible. We know well that peace is not possible at any price. But we all know how great is this responsibility.[128]

The papal warning was clear, and yet, faced with choosing a side, the neocons backed the Bush administration. The intellectual architects of "Catholic Americanism" could only opt for America. So those who had imposed themselves as the American interpreters of the pope's thought, the apologists of John Paul II, did not hesitate to opt for the president over the pope. Weigel and Novak took the field to convince the church and even the Holy See of the war's goodness.[129]

128. Pope John Paul II, "Angelus," March 16, 2003, http://www.vatican.va/content /john-paul-ii/en/angelus/2003/documents/hf_jp-ii_ang_20030316.html.

129. Against the neoconservative position, "the most decisive opposition came from Christian pacifists like Stanley Hauerwas, whom *Time* magazine had named 'theologian of the year' in 2001. Rejecting the position of the journal *First Things*, edited by the Catholic priest and theologian Richard John Neuhaus, in support of the war in Iraq, Hauerwas argued that one could not be Christian without being pacifist" (Gentile, *La democrazia di Dio*, 198–99). See Stanley Hauerwas, *War and the American Difference: Theological Reflections on Violence and National Identity* (Grand Rapids, MI: Baker Academic, 2011); also Borghesi, *Critica della teologia politica*, 267–70.

Weigel, for his part, in a dense series of articles on the just war tradition, forcefully justified the idea of American-led preemptive war to restore "international order."[130] In a 2008 interview, he downplayed the contrast with the pope, as if it were a matter of secondary importance: "Yes, it's true—on Iraq the Pope and the American president arrived at different judgments on how the international community should bend the resistance of the dictatorial and bloodthirsty regime. What I want to remember, however, is that, though there was a different assessment in the case of Saddam Hussein, there have been other situations and other crises that have seen the Holy See and the United States cooperate fully."[131]

Excoriating Weigel's behavior, Anthony Annett has written:

> Nowhere has he been more wrong than with the Iraq war. This marks the true nadir of Weigel's career. Completely ignoring his beloved John Paul II, Weigel engaged in mental gymnastics with the just war teaching, twisting and contorting it to defend the indefensible—the unprovoked "preventive" invasion and occupation of Iraq.
>
> The Vatican foresaw the consequences with great clarity. Cardinal Pio Laghi, Pope John Paul's envoy, implored Bush to come to his senses. He sketched out *three negative consequences*—immense suffering for the Iraqi people, a huge deterioration in Christian-Muslim relations, and greater political instability across an already-unsettled region. Everything the Vatican predicted has come to pass with a vengeance. But the Bush administration didn't listen. No doubt comforted by the alternative magis-

130. George Weigel, "Reality of Terrorism Calls for a Fresh Look at Just War Tradition," *The Catholic Difference*, September 20, 2001; "Just War: An Exchange: Debate with Paul J. Griffiths," *First Things* 122 (April 2002), 31–36; "Just War and Pre-Emption: Three Questions," *The Catholic Difference*, October 2, 2002; "What is the Just War Tradition For?," *The Catholic Difference*, December 4, 2002; "The Peace That Is Possible," *The Catholic Difference*, January 8, 2003; "Moral Clarity in Time of War," *First Things*, December 2002; "The Just War Case for the War," *The Catholic Difference*, March 31, 2003; "No Just War Possible?," *The Catholic Difference*, April 2, 2003; "The Force of Law, the Law of Force," *The Catholic Difference*, April 30, 2003; "Iraq and Just War, Revisited," *The Catholic Difference*, April 21, 2004; "World Order: What Catholics Forgot," *First Things* 143 (May 2004), 31–38; "Iraq and Just War, One More Time," *The Catholic Difference*, June 9, 2004; "Abu Ghraib and Just War in Iraq," *The Catholic Difference*, July 13, 2004; "Who Wants War? Exchange with Paul J. Griffiths," *First Things* 152 (April 2005), 10–12; "Iraq: Then and Now," *First Things* (April 2006); "Just War, Iraq Wars," *First Things* (April 2007).

131. Pino Buongiorno, "Tutti cercano di capirmi dall'esterno: Ma io posso essere solo compreso dall'interno" (interview), Centro Risorse, February 24, 2005, http://www .didaweb.net/risorse/scheda.php?id=6269.

terium of Weigel and allies, they went in with guns blazing. This set in motion a catastrophic train of events, including the utter annihilation of the ancient Christian community in Iraq. Not only did Weigel once again provide cheap intellectual cover for his political overlords, but he has never taken any personal responsibility whatsoever for the evil consequences that flowed from his dreadful advice.[132]

Weigel's judgment was shared fully by Neuhaus and Novak. In a May 2003 article, Neuhaus did not hesitate to attack the pope directly for his opposition to the war.

His most devoted admirers acknowledge that the Pope bears a measure of responsibility for this unhappy circumstance. And it is a mildly amusing nuisance to hear chronic dissenters from firm magisterial teaching on faith and morals proclaim that, on war and peace, they are loyal to the Pope, while the champions of magisterial teaching are, in fact, dissenters. Well, let them have their little fun while they can. With respect to providing moral clarity about war and peace, it must candidly be admitted that this has not been this pontificate's finest hour. But nobody should be shaken too severely. Flannery O'Connor said that we sometimes suffer more from the Church than for the Church. And it is really not suffering so much as it is a matter of disappointment, and more than a little embarrassment.[133]

Novak, for his part, was no less committed to justifying the expediency of the war in Iraq.[134] On February 10, 2003, he was in Rome, at the

---

132. Annett, "The Enduring George Weigel Problem."

133. Richard John Neuhaus, "The Sounds of Religion in a Time of War," *First Things*, May 2003, https://www.firstthings.com/article/2003/05/the-sounds-of-religion-in-a-time-of-war. On Neuhaus's efforts to justify the war theologically, see "A Curious Encounter with a Philosopher from Nowhere," *First Things* 120 (February 2002), 77–96; "Internationalisms," *First Things* 148 (December 2004), 64–68; "Iraq and the Moral Judgement," *First Things* 156 (October 2005).

134. See Michael Novak, "'Asymmetrical Warfare' & Just War: A Moral Obligation," *National Review*, February 10, 2003; Novak, "Civilian Casualties & Turmoil," *National Review*, February 18, 2003; Novak, "War's First Day: Conversations with a European Friend," *National Review*, March 28, 2003; Novak, "Mars & Venus: U.S. vs. Europe on the War," *National Review*, April 2, 2003; Novak, "An Iraqi Democracy?," *National Review*, April 8, 2003; Novak, "The Winning of a Just War," *National Review*, April 9, 2003; Novak, "A Free Iraq," *National Review*, April 28, 2003; Novak, "Errors of Mass Destruction," *National Review*, June 12, 2003; Novak, "Context: The Big Picture on American Deaths in Iraq," *National Review*, August 28, 2003; "Game Plan Iraq," *National Review*, October 20, 2003.

Center for American Studies, to deliver a conference lecture entitled "'Asymmetric Warfare' and Just War," the text of which was published on the same day by the *National Review*. Novak illustrated, in great detail, the danger of Saddam Hussein and criticized the Jesuits of *La Civiltà Cattolica* for their opposition to the war. The real reason for Novak's coming to Rome, however, was not the conference but a direct invitation from the US ambassador to the Holy See, Jim Nicholson, who had commented to *L'Espresso* two weeks prior, "There are many Catholic intellectuals engaged in this discussion. Michael Novak, George Weigel, and others argue that the criteria of analysis must change. I will bring Novak to Rome in early February for a symposium organized by our embassy, specifically dedicated to applying the theory of the just war to the new world situation."[135] The purpose of Novak's Roman visit was thus clear. As Lucio Brunelli wrote,

> The pope preaches against war. And Emperor Bush decided to send his best court theologian to Rome to change his mind. At the initiative of the American ambassador to the Holy See, a symposium will be held in Rome on February 10 to demonstrate the ethical character of the doctrine of preventive war. Leading the work will be Michael Novak, a Catholic intellectual with a progressive past but converted, in Reagan's time, to the word *neoconservative*. His notoriety dates back to the early eighties when *Time* magazine gave space to his lashing criticism of the pastoral letter of the US bishops against the nuclear rearmament policy pursued by the White House.[136]

Novak's Roman mission had no effect at the Vatican, and in particular on Pope John Paul II, who remained adamant that the reasons given by the Bush administration for declaring war were insufficient. The neocons had gone from being paladins of the pope to his adversaries.

---

135. "Saddam è il diavolo, Intervista a Jim Nicholson," *L'Espresso* 5 (January 23–30, 2003). Nicholson recalled Novak's trip to Rome in his book *The United States and the Holy See: The Long Road* (Rome: 30 Days Books, 2004).

136. Lucio Brunelli, "L'assedio di Bush al Papa," *Vita*, January 30, 2003. The U.S. bishops' letter that he refers to is *The Challenge of Peace: God's Promise and Our Response: A Pastoral Letter on War and Peace* (May 3, 1983). Novak's "response" to the letter in fact preceded its publication: "Moral Clarity in the Nuclear Age," *National Review*, April 1, 1983; republished in Michael Novak, *Moral Clarity in the Nuclear Age* (Nashville: Thomas Nelson, 1983), which included a foreword by Billy Graham and an introduction by William F. Buckley, Jr.

Novak's presence in Rome did, however, have one lasting effect: on February 10, the day of the conference at the Center for American Studies, he was received at Palazzo Madama by the president of the Italian Senate, Marcello Pera. The meeting marks the beginning of the Italian branch of the neoconservative movement.

Neoconservatives and the Church in Italy

Pera's meeting with Novak in February 2003 marks the beginning of Pera's rise as a leading figure in the Italian Catholic world. Almost two years later, in November 2004, he coauthored a book with Cardinal Joseph Ratzinger, *Without Roots: The West, Relativism, Christianity, Islam* (which included, in its English edition, an introduction by George Weigel).[137] Shortly thereafter, Ratzinger became Benedict XVI. His election as pope did not interfere with the publication of a new volume by Ratzinger, *Christianity and the Crisis of Cultures*, which featured an introduction by Marcello Pera.[138] Pera, then, a former professor of philosophy formed in the school of Karl Popper, thus became the new pope's intellectual interlocutor. He suddenly held a prominent place in the Catholic world.

The time was right. After the tragedy of September 11, 2001, and the rise of the Islamist threat, large sectors of the secular world gave new consideration to the limits of postmodern culture, the relativism that placed all religions on the same level, and the rejection of the values of the West and modernity. Thus was repeated in Italy the process that, in America in the 1970s, led Novak and Neuhaus from the left to conservative positions. It was the season of the neocons, given strength by the climate of war that was blowing strongly after September 11.

Pera fit comfortably into this current and became one of its central figures. His contribution to *Without Roots*, entitled "Relativism, Christianity, and the West," offered two proposals: first, that Europe build a "civic religion" capable of uniting believers and unbelievers in the face of the moral dissolution caused by relativism, and second, that Europe rediscover the will to fight that was, he said, essential to opposing the

---

137. Joseph Ratzinger and Marcello Pera, *Without Roots: The West, Relativism, Christianity, Islam*, trans. Michael F. Moore (New York: Basic Books, 2006).

138. Joseph Ratzinger, *Christianity and the Crisis of Cultures*, trans. Brian McNeil (San Francisco: Ignatius Press, 2006).

Islamic threat. In a section titled "The New Spirit of Munich," Pera urged Europeans to stand with the United States in its "preventive war" against Saddam Hussein.

> Europe has not accepted this rationale [of preventive war]. It applied its veto in the United Nations Security Council. It has split between those who participate in the Coalition of the Willing and those who do not, between those who send troops for reconstruction and security and those who refuse to do even that much. And it is rotting. It is rotting and crying out, with slogans of uneven persuasion but equal substance: "No war!" "No preventive war!" "No unilateral war!" "No war that has not been legitimated by international organizations!" . . . .
>
> How did this come to pass?
>
> Because Europe does not know where to begin looking for its identity, it cannot speak in a single voice, affirm a single strategy, or assert a single supranational or strategic interest—apart from the occasional pipe dream of local hegemony—on matters pertaining to its own faith and security. . . . Because it believes that the terrorist war is an act of reaction rather than of aggression. Because it has experienced and enjoyed peace for sixty years and is thus inclined to believe that peace is a natural state and a natural right, and that perpetual peace can indeed exist. . . .
>
> So why take the risk of fighting? Is there a war perhaps? I answer yes, there is a war, and I believe that the responsible thing to do is to recognize it and to say so, regardless of whether the politically correct thing to do is to keep our mouths shut. . . .
>
> If there is a war, and it is a just war waged in self-defense, would it not be permitted by Christianity? Has not Christianity waged similar wars in the not-so-distant past?[139]

Pera's call to arms was for a front capable of opposing both postmodern relativism and the Islamic threat. The war was the cement for a possible conservative liberal-Christian bloc, closely linked to the American model, as suggested by the very notion of "civic religion."

But Ratzinger failed to grasp the nuance of Pera's words; he read the criticisms of relativism on a purely moral level and then expressed an unalloyed appreciation for them: "I am most grateful," he wrote, "for all

---

139. Marcello Pera, "Relativism, Christianity, and the West," in Ratzinger and Pera, *Without Roots*, 41–45.

that you explained so carefully in your lecture, and I agree with you completely on everything."[140] Notably, this "on everything" was circumscribed by what Ratzinger had written several pages earlier: "In this context I would like to leave aside the issue of my possible judgment of President Bush's policies and the war in Iraq, which would require a concrete assessment of the facts and therefore go beyond the scope of the problems that I, as a theologian, can and wish to address publicly."[141]

In fact, Cardinal Ratzinger had already offered that judgment very clearly, in an interview with *30 Days* the previous year, in April 2003. His comments there are worth attention.

> *Your Eminence, a question about current events, in some way connected to the Catechism. Does the coalition war on Iraq come within the canons of the "just war"?*
> RATZINGER: The Pope has very clearly expressed his thoughts, not only as the thoughts of an individual, but as the thoughts of a man of conscience occupying the highest functions in the Catholic Church. Of course, he has not imposed this position as a doctrine of the Church, but as the appeal of a conscience enlightened by the faith. This judgment of the Holy Father is convincing from a rational point of view also: reasons sufficient for unleashing a war against Iraq did not exist. First of all it was clear from the very beginning that proportion between the possible positive consequences and the sure negative effect of the conflict was not guaranteed. On the contrary, it seems clear that the negative consequences will be greater than anything positive that might be obtained. Without considering then that we must begin asking ourselves whether as things stand, with new weapons that cause destruction that goes well beyond the groups involved in the fight, it is still licit to allow that a "just war" might exist.
>
> *In an editorial in* La Stampa *Barbara Spinelli praised the stance taken by John Paul II against the war in Iraq, inspired by "Christian realism".* . . .
> RATZINGER: When I said that the Pope's stance is not a question of the doctrine of the faith but is the outcome of a judgment made by an enlightened conscience, and that has its own rational perspicuousness, I meant to say just that. It is a position of Christian realism that, without doctrinal

---

140. Joseph Ratzinger, "Letter to Marcello Pera," in Ratzinger and Pera, *Without Roots*, 127–28.

141. Ratzinger, "Letter to Marcello Pera," 107.

quibbles, assesses the factors in the real situation by keeping in mind the dignity of the human person as the highest value to be respected.

There's been no lack on either side of the conflict of repeated invocations to Allah and to God. . .
RATZINGER: That language seems very sad to me. It's an abuse of the name of God. Neither side can rightly claim to be doing what they're doing in God's name. The Holy Father has many times stressed that violence cannot be employed in the name of God. Seeing that we've been speaking of the Catechism, it's as well to remember what the Second Commandment tells us: "Thou shalt not take the name of the Lord thy God in vain."[142]

The cardinal's opinion was clear and firmly acknowledged the points of disagreement with the Catholic neoconservatives. According to Ratzinger, John Paul II's statement against the war did not represent a mere personal opinion but was "convincing from a rational point of view," particularly from the fact "that proportion between the possible positive consequences and the sure negative effect of the conflict was not guaranteed. On the contrary, it seems clear that the negative consequences will be greater than anything positive that might be obtained." John Paul II, in other words, used the same "just war" doctrine to criticize the war that Novak and Weigel had used to support it. Thirdly, Ratzinger also called into question the theological-political notion of the war, according to which the conflict with Iraq represented a moment in the struggle between the "Christian" West and Islamism—a notion dear to the neocons.

The *30 Days* interview in 2003 made clear the thoughts that Ratzinger chose to obscure in his 2004 dialogue with Pera (published in 2005) in the interest of emphasizing a point of agreement in their mutual critique of moral relativism. Ratzinger's silence, however, seemed to give Pera's

142. Gianni Cardinale, "The Catechism in a Post-Christian World: Interview with Cardinal Joseph Ratzinger," *30 Days*, April 2003, https://www.30giorni.it/articoli_id_775_l3.htm?id=775. In the same issue of the magazine, journalist Marco Politi wrote, "In his recent meeting with the French minister Dominique de Villepin, John Paul II indicated the course that the Holy See means to take: to allow the Iraqis to decide on their own future and on their own resources, to give the United Nations the central role in the transition to peace. We already know that the hawks around Bush are mocking these demands. World public opinion seems, however, to be taking the side of the 'old man of Rome'" (Politi, "The First Stations of the Cross of the 21st Century," *30 Days*, April 2003).

position the indirect endorsement of the theologian who had, in the meantime, become pope.

Benedict's esteem for the president of the Italian Senate cannot, however, be called into question. Proof of this is the letter he sent Pera on September 4, 2008, which Pera published in his book *Why We Should Call Ourselves Christians: The Religious Roots of Free Societies*.[143] In comments he offered at a public presentation of the book, Cardinal Camillo Ruini, then president of the Italian Episcopal Conference, recalled the history of the relationship between Ratzinger and Pera and then noted, "In the letter published in the book that we present this evening, the pope not only expresses great appreciation and consent for the book itself, but in turn takes a stand, with brief but precise and meaningful statements, on the main issues it faces."[144]

Ruini expressed his full agreement with Pera's text. The recovery of the West's Christian soul and the fight against moral relativism was at the heart of the "cultural project" that the Italian bishops under Ruini's lead had been trying to carry out for years.[145] And while Ruini saw in Pera a helpful strategic ally, Pera saw the same in Ruini. The bond with Ratzinger allowed the nascent Italian Catholic neoconservative movement to avoid the conflicts with the Vatican that the American neocons had experienced with John Paul II because of his opposition to the US war. Gaetano Quagliariello, a close collaborator of Pera in the Magna Carta Foundation, of which we will speak, makes this point in his 2006 book, *Cattolici pacifisti teocon*[146] (Catholic pacifist theocon). After describing with disapproval the "prophetic pacifism of Wojtyla," Quagliariello applauded the "closing of the parenthesis" and the new dialogue on the theme of the "roots" shared by unbelievers and Catholics that Ratzinger's election to the papacy had prompted. Pope Benedict, according to Pera and Quagliariello, made it

143. Marcello Pera, *Why We Should Call Ourselves Christians: The Religious Roots of Free Societies*, trans. L. B. Lappin (New York: Encounter, 2008).

144. Cardinal Camillo Ruini, "'Perché dobbiamo dirci cristiani: Il liberalismo, l'Europa, l'etica': La presentazione del card. Ruini del nuovo libro di Marcello Pera," *Europaoggi*, December 4, 2008.

145. On the vision of the church advanced by Cardinal Ruini during his tenure as president of the Italian Episcopal Conference (1991–2007), see Marco Damilano, *Il partito di Dio: La nuova galassia dei cattolici italiani* (Turin: Einaudi, 2006).

146. Gaetano Quagliariello, *Cattolici pacifisti teocon: Chiesa e politica in Italia dopo la caduta del muro* (Milan: Mondadori, 1996).

possible to bridge the distance that had been created with the neocons during the last phase of Wojtyla's pontificate.

It was a distance that had led the Italian historian and politician Ernesto Galli della Loggia, another prominent figure who promoted closer ties between the liberal world and an American-style church, to lament in 2003 the papal pacifism and that of Europe in general. Criticizing the social democratic and Christian cultures that had guided post-war Europe, Galli della Loggia compared them with the bellicosity of American politics and culture: "Motivated by the historical catastrophe of European nationalisms—whose meaning they were ideologically alien to—those [social democratic and Christian] cultures repudiated anything to do with war, and thereby contributed to further entrenching the widespread attitude of the European public spirit, which no longer even wanted to hear about armies and weapons, seeing in them only the symbols of its own ruin."[147] In this way, Galli della Loggia said,

> a difference with the United States has taken shape that could not be clearer. While overseas there remains a strong sense and exercise of state sovereignty—the death penalty is the most paradigmatic manifestation of this— and while war and democracy, far from being considered opposites, are seen there not only as perfectly compatible but even in some sense as complementary, none of this is so with us. We Western Europeans, who have turned in disgust from the ideas of sovereignty and war, are now able to think of the "political" only in a weak sense, where it is substantially reduced on the one hand to procedures and on the other to the sphere of rights ("human," individual, and civil).[148]

What Galli advocated was, on the contrary, a strong political-religious sovereignty for which reference to God is an expression of the power of the social body and of the state.

> And since we've done this, how can we be surprised that in today's Europe of rights and peace, even God and his name have become unspeakable? That both are absent from the draft European constitution, whereas in the United States they dominate public discourse? And yet: there is an ances-

147. Ernesto Galli della Loggia, "Europa e America: Il grande freddo," *Corriere della Sera*, February 23, 2003.

148. Galli della Loggia, "Europa e America: Il grande freddo."

tral link, very deep and psycho-cultural in nature, between the dimension of violence and that of the sacred, between war and God—"the God of hosts" as, not by chance, the most ancient texts of our religious tradition repeatedly describe him.[149]

For Galli della Loggia, religion was essentially political theology, a point of synthesis between violence and the sacred, faith and war. And so the secular face of the Catholic neoconservative soul, in its identification of religion and national spirit, came fully to light. This perspective, after the Wojtyla parenthesis, seemed to enjoy new relevance thanks to a series of historical conjunctures: the terrorist-religious tragedy of September 11, the Western coalition against the "axis of evil," the election of Benedict, and the alliance he sought between unbelievers and Catholics in the fight against relativism. The premises of this alliance, in fact, predated September 11. Already in the 1990s, the new American orientation, after the fall of Communism, made its effects felt not only in Italian politics but also in the Italian church.

In September 1994, "a historic 'marriage' was celebrated within the Vatican walls. Two cultures that have always been antithetical to each other, Catholic doctrine and capitalism, have symbolically united in a great embrace."[150] The secular Italian publishing house Leonardo Mondadori released the Italian editions of Richard John Neuhaus's book *Doing Well and Doing Good: The Challenge to the Christian Capitalist*, Michael Novak's *The Spirit of Democratic Capitalism*, and George Weigel's *The Last Revolution: The Resistance Church and the Collapse of Communism*. The neocons had entered the Italian publishing market in force.

In April 1997, Novak was in Rome, accompanied by Robert Sirico, for an international congress marking the fifth anniversary of the promulgation of *Centesimus Annus*. The event was organized by Sirico's Acton

149. Galli della Loggia, "Europa e America: Il grande freddo." For a critique of Galli della Loggia's position, see Massimo Borghesi, "Il 'Dio degli eserciti' e il 'Papa soldato,'" *30 Giorni* 3 (2003), 36–37; also in Borghesi, *Critica della teologia politica*, 327–30. The links between religion and war is a constant theme in Galli della Loggia's work. See also the dialogue between him and Cardinal Ruini, "L'Occidente e l'anima cristiana alla riscoperta dei valori perduti: La religione e le forze politiche, economiche e militari nella storia," *Corriere della Sera*, May 30, 2009.

150. Orazio la Rocca, "Il catto-capitalismo entra in Vaticano," *La Repubblica*, September 28, 1994.

Institute and the Legionaries of Christ's Pontifical Athenaeum Regina Apostolorum.[151] Sandro Magister wrote of it, "The novelty is absolute. Never in such an august assembly of the church have there been so many praises of the good capitalist, the true and genuine capitalist, not his false double, all greed and theft, that his critics like to call 'savage.' In short, after having left capitalism in the hands of Protestants for centuries, even the Catholic Church today begins to bless it. And the choir of blessing gives itself the pope as its patron and his encyclical *Centesimus Annus* as its magna carta."[152] With the help of the Legionaries of Christ, one of the most right-wing Catholic organizations of that time, Novak and Sirico attempted to repeat in Italy the *Centesimus Annus* operation they'd carried out so successfully in the United States.

The end of the nineties saw a broadening of consensus. In 1998 the Liberal Foundation, founded with the purpose of serving as a bridge between Italy's Democratic Party of the Left (a social-democratic political party) and the Italian People's Party (a Christian-democratic party inspired by Catholic social teaching), moved to the right in the direction of Forza Italia with its president Ferdinando Adornato. It took American Catholic neoconservatism as a model and expressed it in its monthly magazine *Liberal*.[153] On the ecclesial level, the American reading of social doctrine found an echo in the cultural project that the president of the Italian Episcopal Conference, Cardinal Camillo Ruini, was carrying out

151. The proceedings were published the following year: John-Peter Pham, ed., *Centesimus Annus: Assessment and Perspectives for the Future of Catholic Social Doctrine* (Vatican City: Libreria Editrice Vaticana, 1998). Over the next few years, Neuhaus would resolutely defend Fr. Marcial Maciel, the founder of the Legionaries of Christ, from several accusations of sexual abuse of minors (see "Feathers of Scandal," *First Things*, March 2002). Later he would have to retract this position (see Andrew Sullivan, "Neuhaus and Maciel: For the Record," *The Atlantic*, February 15, 2009). On this matter, see J. Paul Lennon, *R. J. Neuhaus Duped by the Legion of Christ: His "Feathers of Scandal" Defense of Legion of Christ Sexually Abusive Founder, Fr. Marcial Maciel* (Scotts Valley, CA: CreateSpace, 2010). George Weigel, too, after having defended Maciel's innocence, had to retract (see "Next Acts in the Legionary Drama," *First Things*, May 5, 2010). Neuhaus and Weigel's vigorous defense of Maciel contributed to the delayed awareness, in the United States, of the priest's grave crimes.

152. Magister, "I cattolici liberisti."

153. See Gianni Baget Bozzo, "Mettiamo insieme S. Tommaso e Adam Smith," *Liberal*, February 1997, 58–59.

at the same time. Prominent among Ruini's lay collaborators were Ernesto Galli della Loggia and the Italian political scientist Angelo Panebianco. Magister, an astute ecclesial observer, explained,

> Angelo Panebianco . . . comes from a secular perspective, but he fully agrees with Ruini and the pope on school equality [that is, equal treatment of private and public schools by the Italian government] and many other topics. Panebianco, who is also a columnist for *Corriere della Sera*, is the cardinal's most esteemed non-Catholic political scientist. Twice in the last year he and [Lorenzo] Ornaghi [vice rector of Università Cattolica del Sacro Cuore in Milan] crossed pens from their respective journalistic positions—last August with two consecutive pairs of alternating editorials. A very friendly exchange, with agreement on the faults of progressive Catholic thought and an exaltation of liberal Catholicism with an Anglo-Saxon flavor, "from Tocqueville to Lord Acton."
>
> Another secular political scientist close to Ruini is Ernesto Galli della Loggia, also a columnist for *Corriere*, as well as the weekly *Liberal*, which is a nice combination. It bears the curious tagline, under the header: "A meeting point between Catholics and the secular world." And it has a trio of cofounders who couldn't be more Ruinian: Galli della Loggia, Ruini himself, and the editor Ferdinando Adornato. *Liberal* has a quasi-monopoly on the cardinal's rare extra-ecclesiastical public appearances. It promotes conferences, publishes political manifestos (the latest, in recent days, on school equality). He establishes relationships with titans of industry and finance. The magazine's owner, Cesare Romiti, a lifelong Catholic with a penchant for grand politics, is also a favorite of Ruini.[154]

During the late nineties, Cardinal Ruini was busy weaving a web of relationships that foreshadowed what would become the Catholic neoconservative movement in Italy during the first decade of the new millennium. The points of agreement: support for a certain set of moral values in politics, a full acceptance of the capitalist system, and embrace of the American model. Magister wrote,

> And on the subject of economics? Here too Ruini is singing a different song than the rest of the chorus. On October 1, in address to the professors of [the Università Cattolica del Sacro Cuore], he told them to remove from

154. Sandro Magister, "Il Vangelo secondo Camillo," Settimo Cielo blog, *L'Espresso*, November 18, 1999.

their minds the idea that the free market necessarily starves "the weakest segments of the population." It was music to the ears of pure liberalists, both secular thinkers like Antonio Martino and Angelo M. Petroni and Catholics like Dario Antiseri and Lorenzo Infantino. In international politics he is a realist, and at *Avvenire* [a Catholic newspaper owned by the Italian Episcopal Conference] he has always given space to the views of those who support the war against Serbia, despite the different Vatican line. The pacifists, the one-sided ones, can't stand them.[155]

On the subject of war, Magister, a "Ruinian," was overstating the reality; it was more his personal opinion than that of the cardinal. This was clear in an impassioned article published after the attack on the Twin Towers in New York.

On September 26, in *Corriere della Sera*, Angelo Panebianco subjected to severe criticism what he considers "the most precious fifth column of Bin Laden and associates in the West: cultural relativism."

Panebianco writes from a secular perspective. But his criticism converges fully with the concern for the "theological relativism" within the church that Cardinal Joseph Ratzinger has been addressing for years. Just as theological relativism places all religions on the same level, so the cultural relativism targeted by Panebianco places all cultures and civilizations on the same level. The danger of it is that "in the eyes of the followers of radical Islam, it represents irrefutable proof that Western civilization is a decadent civilization that can be defeated." Panebianco has also accused sectors of the Catholic Church of taking a prejudicial stance against the West and the United States. A very lively dispute ensued. On September 24, in opening the work of the board of the Italian Episcopal Conference, Cardinal Camillo Ruini largely made this criticism his own. He described Christians who see the United States as "the cause and synthesis of the evils of the world" as "pseudo-moralists." And he urged the church to undertake a "positive" reestablishment of its centuries-old relationship with the West.[156]

In the article Magister was careful not to mention the words of John Paul II on the importance of peace and dialogue in the present moment,

155. Magister, "Il Vangelo secondo Camillo."

156. Sandro Magister, "Pace e guerra: I cattolici divisi," Settimo Cielo blog, *L'Espresso*, October 1, 2001.

referring instead to an editorial in *L'Avvenire*, written by Piero Chinellato, that advocated an American response "that justifies a use proportional to the force," in a way that implied that this was Ruini's position.[157] In

157. Magister's attempt to soften John Paul II's stance against the Iraq war was evident in an article that bore the title, "War in the Gulf: What the Pope Really Said." He wrote,

> There is a war in Iraq. It has been strongly opposed by the Catholic Church—opposed but never condemned, according to the words of its supreme authority, the pope. The media did not make clear their omission of this sentence. They have almost always reported the words of John Paul II as if they were an absolute anathema against this war, if not against all wars. But there is no trace of this condemnation in any of the frequent, pressing speeches in which the pope has called for peace in Iraq. . . . In all of his interventions, the pope preaches peace as an absolute imperative, an inescapable horizon for every decision by governments and individuals. Yet he never goes so far as to define the war in Iraq "a crime against peace," as, for example, two of his collaborators—Archbishops Jean Louis Tauran and Renato Martino—have. The pope's words stand out for their intensely religious character. The passages on how concretely to build peace in the Gulf are rare and extremely measured. And they take the form of a "discourse on the method," not a precept. . . . The pope is uncompromising only on the ultimate goal of peace, not on the ways to get there. And the peace he preaches is essentially that "which comes from God." (Magister, "Guerra nel Golfo: Quell oche il Papa ha detto davvero," Settimo Cielo blog, *L'Espresso*, March 20, 2003).

It is clear that Magister's hermeneutic dissolves John Paul II's clear and firm opposition to the war into a mere "religious," edifying, metahistorical discourse. In May 2003, Magister wrote,

> Along with Italy and Spain, Poland is the third Catholic country in Europe that has sided with the United States in support of the war in Iraq. But with a strong peculiarity, compared to the two other nations. While in Italy and Spain the church and Catholic opinion have opposed the war *en masse*, in Poland the opposite has happened. The church and Catholics have largely supported it, and without feeling themselves to be out of harmony with the pope. There is an important weekly in Poland that fully represents this balance between support for war and obedience to the head of the church. It is *Tygodnik Powszechny*, the voice of a group of Catholic intellectuals of great prestige. It is printed in Krakow and has always had Karol Wojtyla as a supporter and friend and also as a writer before he became pope. . . . Among the signatures there are also those of the Americans George Weigel, Michael Novak, and Edward Luttwak. (Magister, "I cattolici di Polonia partono per l'Iraq: Con l'America e con il Papa," Settimo Cielo blog, *L'Espresso*, May 12, 2003).

Immediately after September 11, 2001, Magister had published an article entitled "US Bishops: This Is Why This Is a Just War" ("Vescovi Usa: Ecco perché questa è una guerra giusta," Settimo Cielo blog, *L'Espresso*, September 21, 2001).

reality, the cardinal's words on September 24, on the occasion of the Italian Episcopal Conference board meeting, sounded different. Magister reported it in an article whose title made clear his agenda: "Ruini: We Are All Americans."[158] He wrote, "There is no doubt, the cardinal said, about the right—indeed, the necessity and the duty—to fight and neutralize, as far as possible, international terrorism and those who, at whatever level, make themselves its promoters or defenders. However, it is equally important and indispensable that this right and duty be exercised not only through the use of force of arms—to always be kept as limited as possible, without indiscriminate reprisals—but also and primarily by working to eliminate the reasons and problems that feed the terrorism or give rise to it."[159]

Ruini's words had a nuance that Magister ignored. In his post–September 11 articles, the journalist undertook an effort similar to that of the American Catholic neocons with respect to *Centesimus Annus*: to Americanize the church and to depict both the pope and the president of the Italian Episcopal Conference as war hawks.

On one point, however, Magister was right: the secular interlocutors in Ruini's cultural project were all close to the neocon world, from Pera to Panebianco, from Galli della Loggia to Giuliano Ferrara, the founding editor of the right-leaning daily newspaper *Il Foglio*. The latter made his newspaper a key instrument for the popularization of Catholic neoconservative ideology in Italy. Ferrara was a full-throated champion of the American war against Iraq and, at the same time, a staunch promoter and participant in the culture wars. Like Pera, Ferrara presented himself as the secular apologist of Benedict's pontificate. The fight against moral relativism and the defense of the Christian and liberal-capitalist West were the cornerstones of a strategy that made his newspaper the reference point for the new pro-American Catholic right, a hegemony that was interrupted with the election of the Latin American Bergoglio in 2013.

158. Sandro Magister, "Ruini: siamo tutti americani," Settimo Cielo blog, *L'Espresso*, September 24, 2001.

159. Magister, "Ruini: siamo tutti americani." On September 16, 2002, Ruini, referring to a possible war against Iraq, reiterated his opposition to "a preemptive war, which would have unacceptable human costs and very serious destabilizing effects on the entire Middle East and probably on all international relations." In Gianni Cardinale, "Niente giustifica una guerra in Iraq," *30 Giorni* 11, no. 12 (2002), 28.

In a September 2013 editorial, Ferrara described, in a way that is enlightening, his admiration for and difference from the pope. His words shed light on the distance that separates the church of Francis and Catholic conservative ideology.

> The Catholic Church is an unfaithful bride. That summarizes, in a single sentence, the new church that is poor and for the poor, the field hospital of mercy, gauzy good feelings rather than Wojtyla's angelic army and Ratzinger's cathedral of reason, two fearful dimensions that made the modern world tremble. The call is great: what is needed is to revive the Christian piety that was weakened through the dominant rationalism according to which the aim has been—unlike the approach of Ignatius's companion Peter Faber—the strengthening of bodies rather than the salvation of souls. Now the Gospel is made to stand against doctrine. That beautiful and wild book, which is also a mysterious and confused memorial, that book that we have been trying to explain for twenty centuries, because simplicity is difficult, becomes the fever of goodness and human understanding against the catechetical cynicism of doctrine, against the little precepts.
>
> The world has put the Catholic Church and Christian thought on trial and condemned them, and the church responds by absolving the world. What a brilliant idea, what a Columbus's egg. Not only does the church absolve the world; it borrows its methods, draws us evangelically toward an old modernist subjectivism, toward its root, toward the morality of intentions. I am not scandalized at all, and I remain a convinced papist, a curious admirer of the relativism of the Jesuits, of their discernment, but my wounds are not curable in that hospital. It is not that I do not believe; it is that believing or not believing has no effect on me. I don't seek forgiveness for my sins, I am not contrite; it will happen, but not now. There is time. My devotion to Christianity and to the church does not arise from private devotion, from faith or from the experience of a benevolent confession and absolution; rather, as I said, it is rooted in the role of Christian ideas and culture in the public sphere and from the theological use that the last two popes before Francis made of human reason, as a fourth virtue after faith, hope and charity. . . .
>
> Francis's hospital is a different kind of thing. It is a living thing, a political response, a laudable, scandalous, but admirable attempt at survival. This is why I like Francis's infidelity, in a certain sense. But I am a secular person, interested in a complete reason for the mystery, not the Gospel as a holy and sublime nursery rhyme; and finally we see true devout atheists at work, those for whom the church is fine if it administers the faith,

mumbles politically correct sentiments, and leaves more or less enlightened reason alone. It is also a great satisfaction. This energetic and shrewd man frees the restless conscience of sinners, because he is as smart as he himself claims, but at the same time keeps reminding his people about the devil, because he does not lack ingenuity. I hope that the Jesuit will know how to behave as the confessors of kings and the casuists and the great missionaries once did: I hope he remembers the fact that the church forgives, the world does not.[160]

In his editorial, Ferrara eloquently notes the points that distance him from the vision of "the Jesuit" who is pope. Moral intransigence, interest in ideas and philosophical reasoning and doctrine—these are the fixed points. Mercy, charity, forgiveness, repentance, grace—all this belongs to the "private" conscience, outside of time and history. Ferrara is interested in reason, not the Gospel. He has no interest, and doesn't try to hide it, in understanding that other dimension that does not belong to him. For Ferrara, who comes from socialist realism, the mercy of which Francis speaks is an expression of weakness or, more subtly, of the Jesuit cunning to enchant the world.[161] In any case, in the years preceding Francis's elec-

160. Giuliano Ferrara, "La sposa infedele," *Il Foglio*, September 21, 2003. [Translator's note: A "Columbus's egg" (*uovo di Colombo*) is an idiomatic expression used to refer (in this case, sarcastically) to an amazing idea or discovery that seems simple or obvious after the fact.]

161. In February 2014, *Il Foglio* published an open letter to Pope Francis ("Lettera a Papa Francesco," February 11, 2014), signed by Ferrara and many prominent figures of the conservative Catholic world, which amounted to a demand that the pope engage more directly in the culture wars to defend the conservative moral positions. Ferrara further clarified the demands in a subsequent article: "Ecco, il modello americano è di minoranza combattiva, una risorsa per Francis," *Il Foglio*, February 23, 2014. The letter to Pope Francis touched off in the Italian media a heated debate that made clear the differences between the papal perspective and the Catholic neoconservative approach. See Vincenzo Tondi della Mura, "Lettera al Foglio: Quei finti 'laici' che chiedono al Papa di fare politica," *Il Sussidiario*, February 19, 2014; Federico Pichetto, "Io non firmo perché sono Cristiano," *Il Foglio*, February 20, 2014, and Ferrara's response, "Non importa la firma, ma l'ignavia," *Il Foglio*, February 20, 2014. See also Maurizio Caverzan, "Reazioni sconcertate nella Chiesa alla richiesta di un gruppo di intellettuali," *Il Giornale*, February 24, 2014. In one of the more notable reactions, the Italian singer-songwriter Giovanni Lindo Ferretti insisted that the pope ought not to be expected to fit our categories: "For days I have been reading and rereading the 'Letter to Pope Francis.' I agree on everything, I could sign it as a commitment, because it makes me extremely nervous. The Holy Father

tion, Ferrara made every effort to support Benedict's pontificate "ideologically." In fact, he is one of the main interlocutors of Cardinal Ruini's ambitious cultural project. This led to *a singular paradox: not one of the intellectuals chosen as central interlocutors of the Italian Episcopal Conference cultural project was Catholic.* They were all "devout atheists." The church had outsourced her point of view on history to authors from the liberal world, recognized its cultural and political hegemony, and, in exchange, received the opportunity to intervene and interact in the public square. After the 1970s, a time characterized by Marxist hegemony over the Christian conscience, the ideological subordination was now to the liberal-capitalist right. In both cases, the absence of authentic Catholic thought capable of keeping a critical distance from the times was clear.

From a tactical point of view, Cardinal Ruini's strategy achieved only one real success: the victory in the referendum of June 12–13, 2005, that would have eliminated bans on egg and sperm donation and freezing embryos. The church convinced Italians to avoid voting, and the result was far smaller voter turnout than was needed for the results to be binding. This was an important victory, the credit of which undoubtedly goes to Ruini. In the face of this success, there remained the price to be paid: the clericalization of the church and the renunciation of the formation of a Catholic laity aware of its own history and responsibility. The Italian church became, through the efforts of Catholic neoconservatives and on the advice of the intellectuals at *Il Foglio*, a militant church, focused on moral battles, concerned with the political framework and absent on social issues, forgetting its own missionary dimension. The Italian church took advantage of

---

cannot make up for our political inconsistency, our incapacities, our cultural inadequacy, nor can he nullify the destructive impulses that a deadly freedom imposes by the breaking of the law with globalist pride and pro-European rancor. The Holy Father does not stretch left and right according to the urgencies of anyone's agenda. The authority of the church, which the pope represents, is in itself, in humility and full conviction of conscience, a counter-offensive of prayer: it is in the everyday life of the centuries, of millennia, whatever happens. He is by grace not because we decide, neither in good nor in bad faith. There are ideas, actions, in the journey of our life, which are our business, of laity: men and women not consecrated to divine service, of Catholic faith, of other faiths, without faith. Free and strong, hopefully. Each one considers his own faults, his own shortcomings and, if he cannot do anything else, at least keep watch. No encouragement is required, much less the Pope's permission" ("La lettera di Giovanni Lindo Ferretti all'Elefantino," *Il Foglio*, February 22, 2014).

the favorable historical situation and fully embraced the winning side. The tragedy of September 11, the struggle against Islam, the defense of the "Christian" identity of the West, the United States as defender of a wounded Christianity, the dual struggle against Islamism and relativism, the alliance with liberalism—these were all elements of the *Weltanschauung* welded together by the Catholic neocons who sat in the rooms of power at the White House.

By the time Novak was received by Pera in 2003, as president of the Senate, the land had largely been cleared. Italy—a US ally, together with Great Britain and Spain, in the war against Iraq, while France and Germany were more reticent—had become a laboratory for the Catholic neoconservative movement. On February 14, 2003, the central committee of the Magna Carta Foundation was established in Rome. Marcello Pera was named president, with Gaetano Quagliariello the spokesperson. The organization's constitution was ratified on January 28, 2004. In terms of guiding principles, its reason for being was clear: "After the attacks of September 11, 2001, an axis has been created with American neoconservative thought. Inspired by this, Magna Carta proposes itself as the think tank of reference on foreign policy issues: the issue of identity, the battle against terrorism, and the new international order are the issues on which its attention is focused."[162]

As president of the new foundation, Pera carried out an intense work of public relations and promotion of events. In May he travelled, in his capacity as president of the Italian Senate, to the United States, receiving a warm welcome from the American neocons at the American Enterprise Institute. At the beginning of June 2005, the Magna Carta Foundation sponsored a two-day event in Lucca on "The New Transatlantic Relations." After the war in Iraq, the key concern of Magna Carta was always relations between Europe and the United States. American ambassador Mel Sembler, Paul Berman, Michael Novak, Giulio Tremonti, and Gianfranco Fini all were present.

On December 10, 2004, in the central Italian town of Norcia, the foundation sponsored a conference on "Liberalism, Christianity, and Secularism," aimed at establishing stronger ties with Catholic ecclesial leadership. A Norcia conference would henceforth become an annual event of the

---

162. Margherita Movarelli, *Think tank all'italiana: Storia della Fondazione Magna Carta: Dieci anni di attività tra ideali e politica* (Soveria Mannelli: Rubbettino, 2013), 38.

organization. Buoyed by his public dialogues with Cardinal Ratzinger, who in the meantime had become pope, Pera understood that an encounter between Catholicism and conservative, American-style liberalism was possible.

On August 21, 2005, Pera addressed the Rimini Meeting, a massive annual Catholic festival (named for the city on the northern Adriatic coast where it was held) organized by the Communion and Liberation movement. Pera's address, entitled "Is Democracy Freedom? In Defense of the West," included by-now-predictable criticisms of multiculturalism and pacifism. Not everyone was enthusiastic about what he said. While the event spokesperson acknowledged that Communion and Liberation leadership did not share "necessarily an identity of views"[163] with Pera, it was the comments of Senator Giulio Andreotti, who was also present, that were especially striking. The magazine *Vita* reported,

> Giulio Andreotti returned to criticizing George W. Bush's decision to attack Iraq and accused the Italian government of hypocrisy. "It is a profoundly unjust war," Andreotti said in a press conference at the Rimini Meeting, "justified by the existence of weapons of mass destruction. This was not true, and the Americans knew it." And Berlusconi knew it, too, Andreotti told the audience, which included many Communion and Liberation members. "Berlusconi even spoke of anthrax in the hands of Saddam." Andreotti said the involvement of the Italian military was justified with the "subtlety" that "we are participating in the post-war period and not in the war." . . .
>
> Reacting to the address offered by the president of the Senate Marcello Pera at the Rimini Meeting, Andreotti said, "No to the equation of terrorism with Islam. There are non-terrorist Muslims and non-Islamic terrorists." Speaking of the dangers associated with religious fundamentalism, Andreotti observed, "Woe to those who do not keep their eyes open, but there is also a lot of hypocrisy." He added, "In Italy there are some areas where demonstrations against immigrants are held in the morning and then in the evening, they recruit them to work in the countryside and in industries."[164]

163. Gian Guido Vecchi, "Pera e l'immigrazione, CL prende le distanze," *Corriere della Sera*, August 23, 2005. See also "Meeting, CL prende le distanze da Pera," *Vita*, August 22, 2005. On the political background to Pera's Rimini address, see Damilano, *Il partito di Dio*, 156–57.

164. Editorial staff, "Meeting: Andreotti contro Pera e guerra in Iraq," *Vita*, August 24, 2005.

In his firm opposition to the American war, Andreotti was in absolute harmony with Pope John Paul II. Addressing the Italian Senate on May 20, 2004, he said,

> Certainly no one has any nostalgia for the Berlin Wall. But a dangerous international imbalance has followed the dissolution of the Soviet empire and the disappearance of the group of non-aligned countries, leaving America with the singular temptation of the ability to grant or revoke certificates of friendship or villainhood. Attention. The authoritative Condoleezza Rice has complained that their decisive contribution in the victory against the European dictatorships has been forgotten. It has not. We have not forgotten their decisive participation in World War I either. But this is not enough to justify the war in Iraq when, at least the state of the evidence, the reasons given, namely the existence of an arsenal of weapons of mass destruction, have proven unfounded.[165]

Fr. Luigi Giussani, the founder of Communion and Liberation, also insisted on the importance of the pope's perspective. In an article published in *Corriere della Sera*, he wrote:

> In these times the pope has adequate reasons to say no to war, even if war is made by people who believe they have reason to wage it. Therefore let us keep in mind what the pope says, because the judgment belongs to people who have been educated to consider what happens from the point

---

165. Giulio Andreotti, "Sulla guerra in Iraq," *30 Giorni* 5 (2004), 22, 24. In a previous speech in the Senate, on February 19, 2003, Andreotti had already harshly criticized Condoleezza Rice: "Nor can anyone who, like the pope, speaks loudly and without compromise for peace, be considered a disturber. There was a bestial statement—permit me to use the term—from the American National Security Advisor, who said that the Vatican is behaving as usual: it does as it did with Hitler. This is really not fair." Giulio Andreotti, "Dopo la 'tempesta' non c'è mai la quiete," *30 Giorni* 3 (2003), 32. The same issue of *30 Giorni* included an essay by Archbishop Jean-Louis Tauran (whom John Paul II would name a cardinal later the same year) titled "Una guerra di aggressione costituirebbe un crimine contro la pace" (A war of aggression would constitute a crime against peace) (pp. 26–29) and an interview with the Jesuit superior general Peter-Hans Kolvenbach headlined, "Noi al tempo di questa guerra assurda" (Us in the time of this absurd war) (pp. 18–25). It is interesting to note that the first Italian periodical to "discover" Cardinal Jorge Bergoglio was the international monthly *30 Giorni*, which was led by Andreotti. Starting in 2002, the magazine regularly included interviews with Bergoglio, articles about him, and contributions from him.

of view of the law of God and the memory of the people. John Paul II, after having said that it is wrong to make war—wrong because there is no adequate reason—added, "God will judge you," which is a way of warning those who have a duty of historical responsibility for the future of the world (this is why we first feel a deep pity for those who have taken on the terrible responsibility of war).[166]

The Rimini address was not, however, entirely fruitless for Pera. Some intellectuals close to Communion and Liberation were included as speakers at the Magna Carta Foundation's Norcia conference the following year, on the theme of "Freedom and Secularity."[167] On that occasion, Pope Benedict XVI sent a greeting to participants.[168] Prior to this, on October 6, Michael Novak and Pera had met together at a conference for Catholic charismatics in Lucca. Pera's dialogue with the Catholic world became so intense that it began to arouse questions and criticism among the Magna Carta Foundation's largely secular, liberal membership. Concerned, Pera sent an open letter on October 30 to Magna Carta membership and supporters, offering assurances that he was not a believer and explaining his strategy of replacing the hegemony that had long been maintained among Catholics by the political left. "Today this hegemony, this block, this boulder, is wavering and is about to crumble. . . . The

166. Luigi Giussani, "Il conflitto in Iraq: Saddam, Bush e il 'No alla guerra' di Giovanni Paolo II," *Corriere della Sera*, April 8, 2003. The Communion and Liberation press office wrote in a statement: "No, just as Bush the father did not convince us, so Bush the son does not convince us. We cannot understand why Saddam is the worst of all, why he is the most dangerous, why killing him is so essential to the fight against terrorism. On the contrary, compared to other regimes, Saddam's tyranny appears more 'moderate.' There is tolerance toward the Christian churches throughout Iraq; in other countries, no. We are against this war; we are with the pope, who sees it as disproportionate as a method and as an aim and is resorting to all legitimate means to avoid it—to avoid that the poor Iraqis, in addition to human and political oppression, must be exposed to the far more deadly aerial bombardments, and all of us to avoid the consequences of a useless conflict." "No alla guerra, Sì all'America," February 13, 2003.

167. See Movarelli, *Think tank all'italiana*, 91n65. The proceedings of the convention were published as Marcello Pera, ed., *Libertà e laicità* (Siena: Cantagalli, 2006).

168. Pope Benedict XVI, "Lettera al Presidente del Senato Marcello Pera in occasione del Convegno di Norcia 'Libertà e laicità,'" October 15, 2005, http://www.vatican.va/content /benedict-xvi/it/letters/2005/documents/hf_ben-xvi_let_20051015_senatore-pera.html.

world changes, dear friends of Magna Carta, *et nos mutamur cum illo* [and we are changing with it]."[169]

The political intention was clear. Pera was proposing himself as the *maître à penser* for post–Christian Democrat Italian Catholicism disappointed by the secularist, relativist, postmodernist left. This was also what Giuliano Ferrara, with *Il Foglio*, and Galli della Loggia sought: to bring together Catholics and liberal-conservatives into a single bloc of "Westernist" ideology whose key points were the alliance with the United States, even in matters of war, and with Israel. To promote this effort, Pera was in New York on February 6, 2006, at the Crossroads New York Cultural Center and Basic Books, to help launch the English edition of *Without Roots*, the book he cowrote with Ratzinger. The title of the event was "Freedom without Roots: The Predicament of Western Liberalism and the Teaching of Pope Benedict XVI." Other presenters included George Weigel and David Schindler.

On February 23, Pera published a manifesto with the title "For the West: The Strength of Civilization."[170] Commenting on it, journalist Mario Sechi wrote, "The manifesto is the culmination of five years of political work, the natural continuation of the results of the Norcia conference (entitled 'To Caesar and to God') and of the collaboration between secular and Catholic institutions."[171] On September 5, 2006, the Magna Carta Foundation promoted the publication of the Italian edition of George Weigel's book, *The Cube and the Cathedral: Europe, America, and Politics Without God*,[172] with a debate held in Frascati, with Weigel present. These turned out to be the final highlights of an intense period in the growth of the neoconservative movement in Italy.

In 2008 Gaetano Quagliariello took over from Pera as president of the Magna Carta Foundation. With the end of Pera's presidency of the Senate,

169. Cited in Movarelli, *Think tank all'italiana*, 92. Pera's text is "Lettera aperta agli amici di Magna Carta," Fondazione Magna Carta, October 2005.

170. Marcello Pera, "Appello 'Per l'Occidente forza di civiltà,'" in Movarelli, *Think tank all'italiana*, Appendix 3, 145–48.

171. Mario Sechi, "Il Manifesto di Pera per il Polo: 'L'Occidente ritrovi l'identità,'" *Il Giornale*, February 22, 2006.

172. George Weigel, *The Cube and the Cathedral: Europe, America, and Politics without God* (New York: Basic Books, 2005). The book was also the subject of a second event, held in Rome, on December 15, which included the participation of Weigel, Magister, the Italian politician Luca Volontè, and historian Flavio Felice.

due to the fall of the center-right government on April 27, 2006, this Popperian philosopher who was a central figure of the neoconservative movement in Italy mostly stepped back from public life.[173] His absence is already noticeable among the responses offered to Pope Benedict XVI's address at the Fourth National Conference of the Italian Church held in Verona in October 2006. There the pope warned that "the grave risk of detaching oneself from the Christian roots of our society is sensed. This sensation, diffused in the Italian People, is expressly and strongly formulated by many important cultural figures, also among those who do not share, or at least who do not practice, our faith. The Church and Catholic Italians are called, therefore, to welcome this great opportunity."[174] Commenting on the papal speech in *Corriere della Sera*, Galli della Loggia's words might just as well have borne the headline of another article that appeared the previous day in the *La Stampa*: "Ratzinger Launches Holy Alliance with Devout Atheists."[175] Between the two approaches of the Italian church, that of Cardinals Carlo Maria Martini and Dionigi Tettamanzi on one hand and that of Cardinal Ruini on the other, it was clear, Galli della Loggia said, that the pope had opted for the second.

> It seems to me that in Verona, as indeed on other occasions, Pope Ratzinger has chosen between these two lines. . . . With the things he said as well as with those he didn't say, he reconfirmed the position that in the past had too casually been attributed to the stubborn will of Cardinal Ruini alone. He could, we know, have insisted on addressing the theme of peace, immigrants, the condition of the elderly, the role of women, or perhaps talked even more on the laity in the church. He didn't. He obviously spoke of the Christian revolution and then of the exclusion of God from the

173. Already the 2005 book, *Liberalismo, cristianesimo e laicità* (Fondazione Magna Carta/Mondadori, 2005), which collects the proceedings of the Magna Carta Foundation convention of December 10, 2004, brings the Introduction by Quagliariello and a final report by Pera dedicated to Liberals and Christians (pp. 72–86). In it Pera referred to Friedrich von Hayek and indicated the three factors of the identity question: the war in Iraq, the European Constitution, bioethics.

174. Pope Benedict XVI, "Address to Participants in the Fourth National Ecclesial Convention," October 19, 2006, http://www.vatican.va/content/benedict-xvi/en/speeches /2006/october/documents/hf_ben-xvi_spe_20061019_convegno-verona.html. Here the Vatican's English translation is slightly corrected for clarity.

175. Luigi la Spina, "Ratzinger lancia la santa alleanza con gli atei devoti," *La Stampa*, October 20, 2006.

public sphere, of relativism and secularism, of the importance of Catholic schools, of "weak and deviant forms of love," of the agreement that the creative *Logos* seems to have established between subjective reason and that objectified in nature and therefore proper to scientific investigation. And finally he invited the Italian church to be "trustingly open to new relationships . . . that can contribute to the cultural and moral growth of Italy," to "welcome this great opportunity" with regard to "many important cultural figures, also among those who do not share, or at least who do not practice, our faith" but by whom, along with many believers, "the grave risk of detaching oneself from the Christian roots of our society is sensed." You may like it or not, but who are these important cultural figures if not the so-called (contemptuously by their opponents) theocons?[176]

Galli della Loggia's comments would certainly not have displeased Pera, who was, however, quiet. The Magna Carta Foundation, which he started, had in any case fulfilled its task: that of lending support to the model of Western Catho-capitalism advocated by Michael Novak. Proof of this is the opinion of the former president of Italy, the Catholic, liberal Francesco Cossiga, who made reference in 2006 to "Pope John Paul II's *Centesimus Annus*, largely influenced by the liberal thought of 'theocon' Catholics like Novak, Weigel, and Neuhaus."[177] The Catholic neoconservative line regarding *Centesimus Annus* had become so well established that even the former Italian president believed it.

But the success of the Italian neocons during the first decade of the new millennium had begun to fade. Like any political theology, Catholic Americanism depended on the fate of the power to which it linked itself. The George W. Bush presidency ended on January 20, 2009, with the inauguration of Barack Obama. Bush's final years were marked by disappointment over the situation in Iraq and Afghanistan. The anticipated utopia of a new world order remained far off. The economic crisis that began with the collapse of Lehman Brothers in September 2008 unveiled the dark face of an unscrupulous neocapitalism where everything is less than "democratic." The dream of the Italian neocons became a sunset.

176. Ernesto Galli della Loggia, "Due linee: il Papa ha scelto," *Corriere della Sera*, October 21, 2006.

177. Francesco Cossiga, "Perché l'Italia assomiglia alle democrazie popolari? Lettera a Sergio Romano," *Corriere della Sera*, October 12, 2006.

Ernesto Galli della Loggia, one of the leading figures of the Ruinian dialogue between Catholics and the liberal right, took note. In a February 2009 editorial in *Corriere*, with the eloquent title "A Season at Its Sunset," Galli wrote,

> Everything seems to indicate that an Italian season—the season that has gone under the name of encounter or dialogue between the secular world and Catholics—is ending. We understand which season, which encounter I am referring to: the one that opened around the beginning of the nineties, at the time of the crisis of the First Republic and with it of the Christian Democrats, of the center-left, but also of the Communist Party that was in mortal peril since the end of the USSR and that received a decisive boost from the 9/11 attack in New York. Those events, as well as the more general feeling that an entire historical epoch was closing, opened or catalyzed a series of questions and problems concerning Italy and the world: imagining a new location and a new political "mission" for both Catholics and the secular forces not at-tracted into the orbit of the old Communist Party; navigating a new cultural climate opened by impressive technological-scientific advances in areas such as genetic engineering; addressing unprecedented geopolitical tensions, in-creasingly dominated by fundamentalist elements, which seemed to demand a rethinking and reestablishment of the category of the West.[178]

This project, according to Galli della Loggia, led to the "birth of news-papers, journals, books, cultural initiatives," but then it failed to materi-alize into something more solid. There were, he said, two reasons for this. The first was that

> this dialogue, which had a substantially cultural nature (albeit with clear political consequences), found itself highly unbalanced due to the very limited presence on the Catholic side of an educated public opinion that was not oriented to the left. The few Catholic participants involved were mostly young intellectuals, almost always grown up in the movements. . . . The result was that the main participants on the Catholic side were leaders in the hierarchy, the church. Many of these prelates saw an opportunity, in the best case, to step outside of their typical, intellectually unsatisfying roles or, worse, to show off, to acquire a more prominent public image.[179]

178. Ernesto Galli della Loggia, "Una stagione al tramonto," *Corriere della Sera*, Febru-ary 15, 2009.
179. Galli della Loggia, "Una stagione al tramonto."

The not-so-veiled accusation here was that Cardinal Ruini's "cultural project" was marked by clericalism.

The second reason for the exhaustion of the dialogue was given by the "self-referentiality" of the church.

> Self-referentiality means having difficulty in establishing truly equal relation-ships with those outside one's own world, difficulty in understanding that for there to be a real dialogue with anyone, it is necessary to give to the same extent that one receives, not skimping on recognition and visibility, under-standing that if you want to achieve important objectives, you must consider factors beyond only yourself, only your immediate advantage. It has happened so many times, for example, that while showing great interest in dialogue with liberal people from the secular world, the church and its representatives were ready, however, with the same interest (indeed very often more), to meet with the harshest opponents of those, with those intransigent secular people who perhaps reviled others precisely because—full of paradoxes—of the dialogue they had with the Catholic world: they were ready to invite them, to write in their newspapers, to ask for their collaboration.[180]

In other words, the church didn't limit its dialogue to the liberal right but also engaged, from time to time, with other interlocutors. It did not choose a side and pretended to keep its hands free. The article expressed Galli della Loggia's disappointment with the Magna Carta Foundation's project, which was coming to a close. Written less than a month after the election of Barack Obama, it marked the end of the season of neocon-servative growth in Italy. In fact, this end had already been noted by journalist Paolo Bracalini in August 2008, in an article aptly entitled "But What Happened to the Neocons in Italy?"[181] Bracalini wrote,

> At one point it really seemed that the only possible culture for the Italian right was that of the neocons and their theocon cousins. The Kagan, Kristol, Perle doctrines and the establishment of the Republican think tanks (a word unknown until then, but now abused) came to us through *Il Foglio* from Giuliano Ferrara, that tireless Italian apostle of neo-theo-conservatism. The question of Islam, the crisis of the West, pride in Judeo-

---

180. Galli della Loggia, "Una stagione al tramonto."
181. Paolo Bracalini, "Ma in Italia che fine hanno fatto i neo-con?," *Il Giornale*, August 1, 2008.

Christian civilization, the Machiavellian justification (great neocon myth) of the use of force, the weakness of Europe (continent of old people) compared to the strength of the United States (young nation). A foundation for the endless geopolitical discussions after September 11, which in our country had already found a voice in Oriana Fallaci, and which seemed to promise the Italian center-right the solution to the eternal worry: to have its own "culture" of reference and also some aspects of an ideology (with the risks that brought, but also the same persuasive capacity as the opponent). The possibility, in short, of appealing to more than people's concerns for their wallets but also to provide a general political vision on the major issues, to give a conceptual framework for center-right ideas.

Now, if there is speculation in the United States about the extinction of the neocons, what about our neocons (Marcello Pera, Gaetano Quagliariello, and the other intellectuals gathered around the Magna Carta Foundation)? Their weakness was in being followers. A movement born essentially to justify US foreign policy in Asia and to respond to the Americans' obsession with security was not easily transplanted into Italy, and interest in the neocon doctrine was destined to wane once the Iraq problem took a back seat to other concerns, for example, the financial crisis or new forms of poverty.[182]

And so the Catholic neoconservative ideology had reached its sunset. But not entirely. Bracalini concluded,

But it would be a mistake to say that the Italian expression of neoconservatism has left no traces, however weak in itself it now is. The slogans of neo-theoconservatism have been absorbed into aspects of the Italian sensibility, disconnected from their original context, to be used in a less imperative framework. But they are there. How else to explain the prominence of moral questions in politics, with issues such as abortion, contraceptive pills, euthanasia, if not as a derivative of the ephemeral neocon doctrine? Even on the question of Islam, on the Christian identity of Europe, on the dangers of secularism, the neo-theocons have paved the way, without however having the strength to see it all through. And so it is that the interlocutor of our neocons (or what remains of them) is, in the end, no longer the America of George W. Bush, but Pope Benedict XVI. In this

182. Bracalini, "Ma in Italia che fine hanno fatto i neo-con?"

too, the path of Italian-style neoconservatism followed in step with that of its first interpreter, Giuliano Ferrara.[183]

183. Bracalini, "Ma in Italia che fine hanno fatto i neo-con?" A neocon response to Bracalini's *Il Giornale* article was published in *L'Occidentale* on the very same day:

In reality, the answer to the newspaper's question lies in the facts (even if these are not what interests us). The ideas of Marcello Pera, Gaetano Quagliariello, and Magna Carta have largely become common sense at least for the Italian center-right, and this leaps all the more to the eye when one looks at the action and culture of [Italian] government.

The positions on Europe that have prevailed in Parliament are exactly what the so-called Italian neocons called for: pragmatism, de-ideologization, a strong connection with the American ally, a military commitment to defend and affirm democracy in the world as a primary defense against terrorism. These are the bases on which Italy has resumed speaking and believing in a possible future for Europe.

On the Middle East, it is precisely the American and European neocon ideas that are now active: very strong cooperation with Israel, rigid limitation of dialogue with terrorists and their supporters, harshness in relations with Iran and its atomic aspirations, reduction of UN rhetoric, etc. *Il Giornale* talks about the public's flagging interest in the Iraq problem as one of the reasons why the neocons would no longer have a hold in the Middle East, but that flagging interest is due to the simple fact that the war was won in Iraq and then also peace, thanks to the success of the original neocon ideas on that front. The Petraeus surge arose from there. It is incredible that *Il Giornale* does not understand this.

And again, the salient feature of neocon reflection has always been directed towards the search for a space and a public role for religion understood both as a personal experience of faith and as a heritage of tradition and identity. How can we not see that, apart from the clamor of Italian secularism, these ideas have widely established themselves in politics and in the Italian public debate? Ethical and biopolitical issues now have full citizenship in the public arena and those who blame the church for meddling on these fronts are increasingly on the sidelines.

Finally, two words about our home: the Magna Carta Foundation and *L'Occidentale*: We are here, having over the years strengthened relationships and ties with the sources of American neocon thought, broadened the horizon of the themes of our analysis, enriched our work by personal relationships and new ideas. There is no more unfair way to conduct a battle of ideas than to reduce the opponent's positions to a caricature, to fix them in an impossible staticity, as if they did not have the strength to evolve. Seven years have passed since September 11, but the problems posed by that event are still all on the table. And the best answers are still the neoconservative ones; just take them seriously and don't portray them as an old, yellowed photo. ("Parabola neo-con: Chi ci cerca sa dove trovarci," *L'Occidentale*, August 1, 2008.)

The Pontificate of Francis and the Crisis of Globalization

Ethics and Capitalism in *Evangelii Gaudium*: The Neoconservative and Neotraditionalist Reaction

The election on March 13, 2013—after the sudden and unexpected resignation of Benedict XVI—of the new pope "from the other end of the world," the first Latin American pontiff in the history of the church, came to most as a great surprise. Largely unknown outside his own country, the former Cardinal Archbishop of Buenos Aires, Jorge Mario Bergoglio, was studied and analyzed at every step. Like most interested observers, the neocons were initially content to wait and see, though they had concerns about a South American sitting on the chair of Peter.

But the "honeymoon period" ended quickly when Francis published his programmatic manifesto on November 26, 2013: the apostolic exhortation *Evangelii Gaudium*. The document cast sharp doubt on the Catholic neoconservative agenda and criticized its assumptions plainly. It was a shock. After thirty years spent weaving a web of institutional relationships and exercising hegemony within the church, first in the United States and then throughout the West, the shining lights of Catholic neoconservatism were experiencing an unexpected backlash. With the arrival of *Evangelii Gaudium*, the hijacking operation carried out against John Paul II, with the reinterpretation of *Centesimus Annus*, and with Benedict XVI in the name of the defense of the "Christian" West against moral relativism and the Islamic threat, was no longer possible. The points of distance appeared unbridgeable—two in particular.

The first was centrality of ethics in Benedict's pontificate. For Francis, it was, in the scale of priorities, no longer central. This is not to say it was not important, but it would no longer be the decisive factor in the church's stance toward the world. This pope was a Jesuit who, at the age of twenty, was prevented only by his health from seeking an assignment as a missionary to Japan. The church of Francis would be a missionary church. He talked about a church "*in uscita*," a church that goes forth. He was a missionary pope, not a mere guardian of an ecclesial institution deemed firm and immobile. This is a point of the utmost importance, often misunderstood by critics who mistake his approach as a surrender to a progressive spirit. It arises from a desire for simplification that aims to remove obstacles so that it is possible to reach the essential without the pharisaic addition of useless weights and customs that have their legitimacy only through the weight of the years. In *Evangelii Gaudium* Francis wrote:

> I dream of a "missionary option," that is, a missionary impulse capable of transforming everything, so that the Church's customs, ways of doing things, times and schedules, language and structures can be suitably channeled for the evangelization of today's world rather than for her self-preservation. The renewal of structures demanded by pastoral conversion can only be understood in this light: as part of an effort to make them more mission-oriented, to make ordinary pastoral activity on every level more inclusive and open, to inspire in pastoral workers a constant desire to go forth and in this way to elicit a positive response from all those whom Jesus summons to friendship with himself. As John Paul II once said to the Bishops of Oceania: "All renewal in the Church must have mission as its goal if it is not to fall prey to a kind of ecclesial introversion."[1]

"Ecclesial introversion" is a serious pathology, and Francis recognized it at the time of his inauguration. From the 1990s onward, the church had been in constant retreat, fighting in the trenches against secularization and relativism, after having long believed that the fall of Communism would be accompanied by a rebirth of faith in both the East and the West. In this retreat, cemented by new bastions, the church armored itself, preoccupied with its own survival. The image often used by Benedict XVI

---

1. Pope Francis, *Evangelii Gaudium*, November 24, 2013, 27, http://www.vatican.va /content/francesco/en/apost_exhortations/documents/papa-francesco_esortazione-ap _20131124_evangelii-gaudium.html.

of small communities that, like those of St. Benedict, would regenerate the faith also seems to push in that direction.

Francis brought a different perspective. The experience of the Latin American pope was not of the decline of an individualistic faith that characterized old Europe but of a Catholicism that, although beaten by the winds of secularization, still had a place in the lives of everyday people, their families, and society. In the Southern Hemisphere, the church was not retreating but spreading. It was not afraid and closed, like the European church. Alberto Methol Ferré, the Uruguayan intellectual friend of Bergoglio, had recognized this reality in the 1970s. In 1973 he wrote,

> I believe that Latin America is going through a privileged moment in its history. I believe it because it is the moment in which its freedom and its capacity for historical protagonism are at stake. In the decades to come, it either grows or dies. And as goes Latin America, so goes the church. Why is the role of Catholics in Latin America so important? Because Latin America is the great Christian region of the Third World. It is the "most dependent" area of Catholic origin and, at the same time, possesses immense material and cultural resources that give it a "singular mediation" between the dominant modern worlds and the Third World. What the church will do in Latin America will have great repercussions on the entire Third World. It will be the church's greatest advent in the Third World, her most decisive contribution. Furthermore, as Latin America is in a certain sense less distant from "modernity" than the rest of the Third World, it will have a profound effect on the fate of the church of Europe, in the United States, and in the European socialist bloc. Latin America and its church have a great opportunity, and I believe that it is also to some extent an opportunity for the entire global church.[2]

For Methol Ferré,

> An authentic Latin American Catholic Risorgimento is vital for the whole world church. They are the peoples of the Third World in which the church is most rooted. Europe—and its old Latin Christianity—are indelibly part of our origins, of our history. We are not Europe, but yes, perhaps we are among the most European of the Third World, not in spite of our identity and cultural originality but by virtue of it. We are already half of the

---

2. Methol Ferré, "La Chiesa latinoamericana nella dinamica mondiale," 137.

Catholic believers on earth. And everything suggests the importance of the church of Latin America for evangelization, on the threshold of the third millennium. A Latin American Catholic Risorgimento concerns not only us but the whole church. It has repercussions on the path of global history, which is now universal in all its parts.[3]

Methol's prophecy came true with the election of the first Latin American to the papacy. He is a pope who truly expresses the intimate popular-Christian religiosity of Latin America and, precisely for this reason, stands outside the ideological dialectic typical of Catholicism between progressives and reactionaries. A missionary pope is a pope who places himself beyond the right and the left, beyond the ideological-political blocs. In opting for mission and for witness, as stated in the splendid document of the great conference of the Latin American church in Aparecida led by Cardinal Bergoglio in 2007, the pope overturns the Catholic neoconservative model wholly polarized by moral issues.[4] The message and the person of Christ cannot be presupposed in the secularized world. They must come to the fore. The Christian proclamation *existentially* precedes both dogma and morality.

> If we attempt to put all things in a missionary key, this will also affect the way we communicate the message. In today's world of instant communication and occasionally biased media coverage, the message we preach runs a greater risk of being distorted or reduced to some of its secondary aspects. In this way certain issues which are part of the Church's moral teaching are taken out of the context which gives them their meaning. The biggest problem is when the message we preach then seems identified with those secondary aspects which, important as they are, do not in and of themselves convey the heart of Christ's message. We need to be realistic and not assume that our audience understands the full background to what we are saying, or is capable of relating what we say to the very heart of the Gospel which gives it meaning, beauty and attractiveness.

3. Alberto Methol Ferré, "Prologo per Europei" (1983), in Methol Ferré, *Il Risorgimento Cattolico Latinoamericano*, 11–12. [Translator's note: The Risorgimento (literally, "rising again") was an important era of Italian history, a political and social movement of the nineteenth century for the unification of the various small states that made up the Italian peninsula into a single Kingdom of Italy.]

4. Fifth General Conference of the Latin American Episcopate (Aparecida, 2007), "Concluding Document," https://www.celam.org/aparecida/Ingles.pdf.

Pastoral ministry in a missionary style is not obsessed with the disjointed transmission of a multitude of doctrines to be insistently imposed. When we adopt a pastoral goal and a missionary style which would actually reach everyone without exception or exclusion, the message has to concentrate on the essentials, on what is most beautiful, most grand, most appealing and at the same time most necessary. The message is simplified, while losing none of its depth and truth, and thus becomes all the more forceful and convincing.

All revealed truths derive from the same divine source and are to be believed with the same faith, yet some of them are more important for giving direct expression to the heart of the Gospel. In this basic core, what shines forth is *the beauty of the saving love of God made manifest in Jesus Christ who died and rose from the dead.*[5]

This reference to beauty indicates the priority of the aesthetic over the ethical. It is the great lesson of Hans Urs von Balthasar that Bergoglio never forgot.[6] Ethics is persuasive if it arises from the beauty of Christ's love.

When preaching is faithful to the Gospel, the centrality of certain truths is evident and it becomes clear that Christian morality is not a form of stoicism, or self-denial, or merely a practical philosophy or a catalogue of sins and faults. Before all else, the Gospel invites us to respond to the God of love who saves us, to see God in others and to go forth from ourselves to seek the good of others. Under no circumstance can this invitation be obscured! All of the virtues are at the service of this response of love. If this invitation does not radiate forcefully and attractively, the edifice of the Church's moral teaching risks becoming a house of cards, and this is our greatest risk. It would mean that it is not the Gospel which is being preached, but certain doctrinal or moral points based on specific ideological options. The message will run the risk of losing its freshness and will cease to have "the fragrance of the Gospel."[7]

The beauty of Jesus comes first. Grace comes first. In this lies the path for moving beyond the ethical knots that, as we have seen, mark the

---

5. Pope Francis, *Evangelii Gaudium*, 34–36.
6. Borghesi, *The Mind of Pope Francis*, 244–53.
7. Pope Francis, *Evangelii Gaudium*, 39.

Catholic world of recent decades. It is Pope Francis's "revolution."[8] The
Jesuit pope, accused by critics of being a Pelagian, a humanitarian phi-
lanthropist, is, in reality, a staunch supporter of the primacy of grace over
works. In the important 2013 interview given to Fr. Antonio Spadaro for
La Civiltà Cattolica, Francis said:

> We cannot dwell only on issues related to abortion, gay marriage, and the
> use of contraceptive methods. This is not possible. I have not spoken much
> about these things, and I have been reprimanded for that. But when we speak
> about these issues, we have to talk about them in a context. The position of
> the Church, for that matter, is known, and I am a son of the Church, and
> therefore it is unnecessary to talk about these issues all the time.
>
> The dogmatic and moral teachings of the Church are not all equivalent.
> The Church's pastoral ministry cannot be obsessed with the transmission
> of a disjointed multitude of doctrines to be imposed insistently. Proclama-
> tion in a missionary style focuses on the essentials, on the necessary things:
> this is also what fascinates, and is a more attractive proposition, what
> makes the heart burn, as it did for the disciples at Emmaus. We have to
> find a new balance; otherwise even the moral edifice of the Church is likely
> to fall like a house of cards, and risk losing the Gospel's freshness and
> fragrance. The Gospel's proposal must be simpler, profounder, more radi-
> ant. It is from this proposition that the moral consequences then flow.[9]

The missionary stance requires discernment and flexibility, the ability
to evaluate the priority of various moral issues in their given contexts.
This is what the church has done throughout its long history: taking into
account the conditions and circumstances of the times, in the awareness
that the kerygma, that witness, comes first. This is where the neoconservative agenda differs. Its commitment is to opposition to abortion, euthanasia, and gay marriage. The entire life of the church in the world is
reduced to the defense of *three* Christian values that, however important,
do not in fact exhaust the horizon of the church's attention and cannot
determine the scale of its priorities.

8. See Lucio Brunelli, "La rivoluzione placida di Francesco: Una novità di sguardo, in-
nanzitutto," Terre d'America, September 20, 2014, http://www.terredamerica.com/2013
/09/20/la-rivoluzione-placida-di-francesco-una-novita-di-sguardo-innanzitutto/.
9. Pope Francis, *My Door Is Always Open*, 57–58.

By criticizing this approach, the pope attracted criticism from traditionalist sectors and from a significant segment of North American Catholicism. As these sectors saw it, the pope had yielded to moral relativism and the denigration of the church's tradition. These are the premises of the "American schism" described by French author Nicolas Senèze. But what the critics do not see is how deeply rooted in the ecclesial tradition Bergoglio is. They do not understand that within the church, today as in the past, there are different perspectives and priorities that in no way reject or question the deposit of faith. The fact that this is not evident to traditionalists and that they attribute to the pope deviations where none exist cannot be attributed only to the media and to the way in which they often report the words of Francis in a reductive or distorted way. The "distortion" is, at its origin, the weight of an *ideology*, Catholic neo-conservatism, whose weight in the "Western" ecclesial world can hardly be underestimated. The pope is certainly not a conservative. But he is not a "progressive," either, if by progressivism one means the position according to which, according to the spirit of the time, abortion, euthanasia, and other "modern" positions are morally legitimized. That the pope is a critic of progressivism is also openly recognized by Sandro Magister, an author who is certainly not fond of Francis.[10] Which doesn't mean he's a conservative. *He is a missionary and social pope; this is his essential character.*

As Nicolas Senèze writes, "If he can be perceived as a 'progressive,' in several respects Francis can also be considered a 'conservative.' He has never hidden his aversion to the 'crime' of abortion, a 'murder' he insists. . . . Francis actually cannot be confined to the progressive-conservative divide. No more, moreover, than the left-right, he who criticizes both the 'adolescent progressivism' in vogue in Latin America from Chávez to Kirchner and triumphant neoliberalism."[11]

10. Sandro Magister, "Ma Bergoglio non è 'di sinistra,'" Settimo Cielo blog, *L'Espresso*, July 8, 2013: Magister, "Tutti i 'no' di papa Francesco ai progressisti: L'ultimo, fortissimo, è sul fine vita," Settimo Cielo blog, *L'Espresso*, September 28, 2020.

11. Senèze, *Comment l'Amerique veut changer de pape*, 84 in the Italian edition. On Pope Francis's opposition to abortion, see *Evangelii Gaudium* 213: "Among the vulnerable for whom the Church wishes to care with particular love and concern are unborn children, the most defenseless and innocent among us. Nowadays efforts are made to deny them their human dignity and to do with them whatever one pleases, taking their lives and passing laws preventing anyone from standing in the way of this. Frequently, as a way of

For Senèze the controversy over same-sex marriage in Argentina offers an eloquent example of this position.

> At the time, the archbishop of Buenos Aires was perfectly aware of the trap in which power wanted to lead the church by appearing retrograde and against equality. So rather than launching a frontal attack against the government, which he knew would be fruitless, Bergoglio promoted the social inclusion of gays and goes so far as to advocate for them, in contrast to Rome, the alternative of a civil union that does not allow the adoption of children. In this way, marriage would be left intact as the union of a man and a woman, as Catholics understand it. However, the rigorists of the Argentine episcopate did not side with him, opting rather for a battle with the government that was lost from the start . . . and the government did in fact pass its law. It was the only time when, in his role as president of the Argentine bishops' conference, Cardinal Bergoglio was in the minority.[12]

The rigorists and the Puritans are not willing to compromise, consistently rejecting any effort to broaden their list of "nonnegotiable values" to include the overall framework of the values embraced and promoted by Catholic moral and social teaching. Interviewed by Ferruccio de Bortoli in March 2014, the pope said, "I have never understood the expression 'non-negotiable values.' Values are just values. I cannot say that among the fingers of a hand one is less useful than the other. So I don't understand in what sense there can be non-negotiable values. What I had to say on the subject of life, I wrote in the exhortation *Evangelii Gaudium*."[13] It was enough to draw the arrows of the conservatives.

---

ridiculing the Church's effort to defend their lives, attempts are made to present her position as ideological, obscurantist and conservative. Yet this defense of unborn life is closely linked to the defense of each and every other human right. It involves the conviction that a human being is always sacred and inviolable, in any situation and at every stage of development. Human beings are ends in themselves and never a means of resolving other problems. Once this conviction disappears, so do solid and lasting foundations for the defense of human rights, which would always be subject to the passing whims of the powers that be. Reason alone is sufficient to recognize the inviolable value of each single human life, but if we also look at the issue from the standpoint of faith, 'every violation of the personal dignity of the human being cries out in vengeance to God and is an offence against the creator of the individual.'"

12. Senèze, *Comment l'Amerique veut changer de pape*, 84–85 in the Italian edition.

13. Ferruccio de Bortoli, "Benedetto XVI non è una statua: Partecipa alla vita della Chiesa," *Corriere della Sera*, March 5, 2014.

"For these Catholics," Senèze writes,

> the problem is not that Francis is unwilling to engage controversial ethical questions but that he persists in putting such questions within the broader context (too broad, in their opinion) of the church's social teaching on the defense of the dignity of human life, threatened by what the Argentine pope calls the "throwaway culture." . . . It is indeed impressive to see how the pro-life struggle in the United States focuses almost exclusively on the issue of abortion. Yet attempts have been made to assign it a more global vision, such as the creation of the New Pro-Life Movement which, in addition to fighting against abortion, wants to work to oppose euthanasia, violence against women, torture, the death penalty, gun violence, and war—in other words, an approach very close to that of Francis, but one that fails to resonate in the United States.[14]

To repeat: a global perspective that addresses the fight against abortion within the context of an integral defense of the dignity of life against all that threatens it doesn't "resonate" in the United States. Senèze's statement helps us understand why Pope Francis is not understood today in North America and, to a large extent, by the church in the United States. *Neocon ideology, "Catholic Americanism," constitutes an ideological block that prevents the recognition that the magisterium of Pope Francis is, in fact, Catholic.* American Catholics support the life of the unborn—they also support the death penalty, the arms industry, preemptive war, the rejection of the concern for the environment, and capitalism with all its "values." For them, Catholic social teaching is suspect, imbued with Marxist and leftist elements.

And here we come to the second point that divides Pope Francis from the neocons: his stance on capitalism in the era of globalization. This is the real contrasting factor with the ideology of American capitalism. In *Evangelii Gaudium*, Francis has written:

> Just as the commandment "Thou shalt not kill" sets a clear limit in order to safeguard the value of human life, today we also have to say "thou shalt not" to an economy of exclusion and inequality. Such an economy kills. How can it be that it is not a news item when an elderly homeless person dies of exposure, but it is news when the stock market loses two points? This is a case of exclusion. Can we continue to stand by when food is

14. Senèze, *Comment l'Amerique veut changer de pape*, 86 in the Italian edition.

thrown away while people are starving? This is a case of inequality. Today everything comes under the laws of competition and the survival of the fittest, where the powerful feed upon the powerless. As a consequence, masses of people find themselves excluded and marginalized: without work, without possibilities, without any means of escape.

Human beings are themselves considered consumer goods to be used and then discarded. We have created a "throw away" culture which is now spreading. It is no longer simply about exploitation and oppression, but something new. Exclusion ultimately has to do with what it means to be a part of the society in which we live; those excluded are no longer society's underside or its fringes or its disenfranchised—they are no longer even a part of it. The excluded are not the "exploited" but the outcast, the "leftovers."[15]

The distance that separates Francis from the neoconservatives appears truly profound. Faced with such a severe rejection of the neocapitalist model in the era of globalization, the Catholic neoconservative attempt to hijack the papal documents, first through the distorted reading of *Centesimus Annus* and then through the vivisection of *Caritas in Veritate*, no longer appears possible. The neocon world shifted from an attempted alliance with Rome to outright opposition. *The fight against the "populist," "Latin American," "Peronist," "Communist" pope begins here.*[16] With Bergoglio, they believe, Latin American liberation theology with its Marxist orientation has come back into vogue. It matters little that the "theology of the people," the Argentine version of liberation theology, has nothing to do with Marxism and that it rejects revolution and violence. The pope is still a "socialist," a threat to the capitalist order. The Catholic neocons do not know, and of course they do not want to know, that the pope's critique of capitalism is the critique of the "disorder" of a system that, being based on profit alone, is a source of chaos and pain. *Francis recognized this disorder not ideologically but through real events.*

---

15. Pope Francis, *Evangelii Gaudium*, 53.

16. On the opposition to Pope Francis's pontificate by large segments of American capitalism, see Andrea Tornielli and Giacomo Galeazzi, *This Economy Kills: Pope Francis on Capitalism and Social Justice*, trans. Demetrio S. Yokum (Collegeville, MN: Liturgical Press, 2015); Nello Scavo, *I nemici di Francesco* (Milan: Edizioni Piemme, 2015); Borghesi, *The Mind of Pope Francis*, 206–21.

Bergoglio experienced the chaos first of all through his family's memory. At the end of the 1920s, Mario Bergoglio, Jorge's father, had immigrated from northern Italy, together with his father Giovanni and mother Rosa, to Buenos Aires, where three of Giovanni's brothers were waiting for them. In a short time, the Bergoglio family built a construction and paving company in Paraná, northwest of Buenos Aires. The financial stability they established for themselves was abruptly interrupted with the collapse of the New York Stock Exchange on October 24, 1929. The Bergoglios had to sell everything and were left with nothing. They had to start over. Bergoglio's family experienced first-hand, together with millions of other people, the first great crisis of capitalist globalization.

Cardinal Bergoglio experienced such a shock directly during the serious crisis of the Argentine economy at the beginning of the 2000s. When he addressed the topic of the economy in *Evangelii Gaudium*, the pope had in mind "the images of the days of the Argentine economic crisis of December 2001 through January 2002, with the looting of supermarkets, protests and riots in the streets, the thirty-nine dead protesters, the president of the country fleeing the Casa Rosada by helicopter, or the banks' armored trucks that advanced like tanks through the streets of Buenos Aires taking people's savings out of the country. More than seventy years after the economic crisis of 1929, the Argentine economy was in a tailspin after the decade of the neoliberal delirium that coincided with the presidency of Carlos Menem."[17]

Journalist Silvina Pérez recalled:

It was hellishly hot in those summer days in December. Buenos Aires seemed on the verge of exploding. And in fact, it exploded. Many companies closed or went bankrupt, and inflation, accumulated since the devaluation of the peso, was at 80 percent, but wages did not change compared to before the crisis. The nightmare of misery was a fact, and "*Que se vayan todos!*" ["Kick 'em all out!"] was repeated angrily by the population intent on making a clean sweep of a political class responsible for the impoverishment of a rich country. In just one day, Argentines lost their life savings. . . . For months we sailed by sight, the country was in default and stopped paying its foreign debt, and the consequences fell on a society

---

17. Silvina Pérez and Lucetta Scaraffia, *Francesco: Il papa americano* (Milan: Vita e Pensiero, 2017), 54–55.

already hit by the heavy cuts demanded by international credit organizations. The cleaver first hit public workers, then retirees. Finally, the *coup de grace*: the blocking of all current accounts by the then-Minister of the Economy. In those days it was up to the church to reopen the paths of social dialogue.[18]

In an interview in January 2002, Cardinal Bergoglio said of these events,

There has been a real economic-financial terrorism in this time, and it has produced easily recorded effects, such as the increase of the rich, the increase of the poor, and the drastic reduction of the middle class. And other less cyclical effects, such as a disaster in the field of education. At the moment, in the city and in the residential areas around Buenos Aires, there are two million young people who are neither studying nor working. Faced with the barbaric way in which economic globalization took place in Argentina, the church of this country has always referred to the teaching of the magisterium. Our points of reference are, for example, the criteria set out clearly in John Paul II's document *Ecclesia in America*.[19]

Bergoglio's convictions about the "economic-financial terrorism" of "economic globalization" are rooted, then, in the disaster of the Argentine default, brought on by the failure of the liberal model imposed by President Menem and his minister of the economy Domingo Cavallo in the decade from 1989 to 1999. It has nothing to do with liberation theology or "Peronistic" inclinations, but rather a response to the liberal model, the same one exalted by the Austrian school followed by Novak and the Catho-capitalists, which, as history shows, is a failure.[20] *Evangelii Gaud-*

18. Pérez and Scaraffia, *Francesco*, 55.

19. Gianni Valente, "Il volto idolatra dell'economia speculativa: Intervista al cardinale Jorge Mario Bergogio," *30 Giorni* 1 (2002), 29.

20. Pope Francis has said:

The laissez-faire market-centered approach confuses ends and means. Rather than being seen as a source of dignity, work becomes merely a means of production; profit turns into a goal rather than a means to achieving greater goods. From here we can end up subscribing to the tragically mistaken belief that whatever is good for the market is good for society.

I don't criticize the market per se. I decry the all-too-common scenario where ethics and the economy have been decoupled. And I criticize the self-evidently fictitious idea that wealth must be allowed to roam unhindered in order to deliver prosperity *ium* did not enter directly into technical questions about the reasons for this failure. The closest it comes to this is when it criticizes the trickle-down economics that is at the heart of liberal capitalism.

> In this context, some people continue to defend trickle-down theories which assume that economic growth, encouraged by a free market, will inevitably succeed in bringing about greater justice and inclusiveness in the world. This opinion, which has never been confirmed by the facts, expresses a crude and naïve trust in the goodness of those wielding economic power and in the sacralized workings of the prevailing economic system. Meanwhile, the excluded are still waiting. To sustain a lifestyle which excludes others, or to sustain enthusiasm for that selfish ideal, a globalization of indifference has developed. Almost without being aware of it, we end up being incapable of feeling compassion at the outcry of the poor, weeping for other people's pain, and feeling a need to help them, as though all this were someone else's responsibility and not our own. The culture of prosperity deadens us; we are thrilled if the market offers us something new to purchase. In the meantime all those lives stunted for lack of opportunity seem a mere spectacle; they fail to move us.[21]

Here Francis rejects the central point of the neoconservative economic doctrine: the idea that the market is capable of self-regulation by an internal logic. This is the economic theodicy used by Novak, Weigel, and Neuhaus, to legitimize the "ethical" superiority of the capitalist system. It is not a matter of secondary importance. The entire intellectual structure of Novak's *The Spirit of Democratic Capitalism* is based, in fact, on the "doctrine of involuntary consequences." It is thanks to these "consequences" that the market can, in contrast to individual interests, support the "common good." If that postulate is false—as the pope insists that it is—then the theoretical framework that justifies the Catho-capitalist position fails. If it is false, Catholic Americanism is deprived of its material basis and shown to be what it is: the ideological form of bourgeois-American Christianity.

---

for all. The refutation of that idea is all around us: left to their own devices, markets have generated vast inequality and huge ecological damage. Once capital becomes an idol that presides over a socioeconomic system, it enslaves us, sets us at odds with each other, excludes the poor, and endangers the planet we all share. (Pope Francis, *Let Us Dream*, 109–10)

21. Pope Francis, *Evangelii Gaudium*, 54.

Aware of the threat that this criticism represented, Michael Novak did not fail to respond to the apostolic exhortation. In a December 2013 article published by *National Review*, he began, "Reading the new exhortation by Pope Francis after the wildly misleading presentations of it by the *Guardian* and Reuters (both from the left side of the U.K. press), and reading it with an American ear for language, I was at first amazed at how partisan and empirically unfounded were five or six of its sentences."[22] According to Novak, "About six of his swipes are so highly partisan and biased that they seem outside this pope's normal tranquility and generosity of spirit. Exactly these partisan phrases were naturally leapt upon by media outlets such as Reuters and the *Guardian*. Among these are 'trickle-down theories,' 'invisible hand,' 'idolatry of money,' 'inequality,' and trust in the state 'charged with vigilance for the common good.'"[23]

Francis's criticisms of the capitalist system were, for Novak, a problem: "Ever since Max Weber, Catholic social thought has been blamed for much of the poverty in many Catholic nations. Pope Francis inadvertently adds evidence for Weber's thesis."[24] The exhortation undermines Novak's attempt to position himself as the Catholic Max Weber.

One point, in particular, could not be allowed to stand: the pope's criticism of trickle-down economics. Novak wrote:

> Allow me here to focus on the flaws in only one of the pope's too-hasty claims: his careless mention of "trickle-down theories." Actually, the fault here seems to have been exacerbated by a poor translation, as seen in the stark differences between the Vatican's official English version and the pope's original Spanish. The Spanish: "*En este contexto, algunos todavía defienden las teorías del 'derrame,' que suponen que todo crecimiento económico, favorecido por la libertad de mercado, logra provocar por sí mismo mayor equidad e inclusión social en el mundo.*" Now compare the unfortunate English version: "In this context, some people continue to defend trickle-down theories which assume that economic growth, encouraged by a free market, will inevitably succeed in bringing about greater justice and inclusiveness in the world."

22. Michael Novak, "Agreeing with Pope Francis," *National Review*, December 7, 2013, https://www.nationalreview.com/2013/12/agreeing-pope-francis-michael-novak/.

23. Novak, "Agreeing with Pope Francis."

24. Novak, "Agreeing with Pope Francis."

Note first that "trickle-down" nowhere appears in the original Spanish, as it would have done if the pope had meant to invoke the battle-cry of the American Democrats against the American Republicans. Professional translators of Spanish say the correct translation of derrame is "spillover" or "overflow." Instead, the English translation introduces both a sharply different meaning and a harsh new tone into this passage. Only those hostile to capitalism and Reagan's successful reforms, and to the policies of Republicans in general after the downward mobility of the Carter years, use the derisive expression "trickle-down," intended to caricature what actually happened under Reagan, namely, dramatic upward mobility.

Those who emphasize capitalism's successes in raising the poor out of poverty do not use that term. They see the defining classical movement of capitalist economies as upward for the poor: higher employment rates, higher wages, measurable outbursts of personal initiative and new enter-prises, unparalleled opportunities for upward mobility among the poor, immigrants moving out of poverty in less than ten years, the working-class "proletariat" becoming solid members of the middle class who can afford to own their own homes and support the higher education of their children.

There is no empirical evidence, *Evangelii Gaudium* says, for trust in such economic outcomes. It is "instead a crude and naïve trust in the goodness of those wielding economic power and in the sacralized workings of the prevailing economic system." In Argentina and other static systems with no upward mobility, this comment might be understandable. In na-tions with generations of reliable upward mobility, it is not true at all.[25]

Beyond the clumsy attempt to distinguish between the Spanish *der-rame* and the English *trickle-down*, Novak grasped the crucial point, the fact that he and his neoconservative friends would never succeed in fashioning an Americanist version of the South American pope. They were faced with a pope who could not be coopted. All that remained was to acknowledge this and to warn public opinion of the threat represented by the Argentine pontiff.

To oppose that threat, the neoconservative movement, with its dual religious and secular soul, would join forces with Catholic conservatism, both American and European, which had stratified since the 1990s. Hence the strange alliance between conservative liberals and Catholic reaction-aries hostile to the Second Vatican Council that would constitute the

25. Novak, "Agreeing with Pope Francis."

shock wave against the Francis pontificate. Conservative liberals and Catholic traditionalists—diametrically opposed on the topic of the value of modernity—combined forces in the ethical battle against relativism and in unquestioning fidelity to the Western-capitalist model. Both groups saw Bergoglio as the adversary, the corrupter of the church, and a threat to the political-economic order.

And at the forefront of criticism of Francis in Italy was Marcello Pera, the most illustrious ally of Catholic neoconservatism. Pope Benedict's coauthor quickly became one of Pope Francis's most ardent adversaries. For Pera, there was only one tactic to discredit the pope: to demonstrate his "break" with respect to previous popes and to the entire tradition of the church. In a 2016 interview, Pera declared, "We are facing an epochal and profound turning point. The pope is orienting Christianity toward social doctrine, therefore toward a worldly doctrine."[26] For the founder of the Magna Carta Foundation, "Both John Paul II and Benedict XVI gave their mission a strong Western emphasis. They had constantly referred to Europe, and there was an evident Western perspective, with our continent seen as the cradle of Western values. Francis, on the other hand, has a purely South American vision. He does not understand the European crisis in which we are immersed. He puts all responsibility on political institutions, on nation-states, on capitalism. No other path is contemplated."[27] The neocon judgment was clear: Francis was a South American imbued with an anti-Western culture.

Pera continued,

Francis is strongly influenced by Marxism. The idea of turning to the poor is something we have already seen, especially if I think of what was said in the 1960s and 70s, when it was preached that Marxism was nothing more than a rib of Christianity. I lived through that historical phase, and I think I can say that this pope shares that idea. After all, it shows in the priorities he has placed at the top of his agenda, namely, the issues of social justice. Is Christianity still a religion of salvation, or has it, rather, become a religion of social justice? Is it a religion that seeks *beatitude*, or does it aim for *felicitas*? *Beatitudo* refers to an otherworldly dimension; *felicitas* is nothing more than the correction of the injustices present in the world. The former seeks the construction of the city of God, the latter is directed

---

26. Matteo Matzuzzi, "'Il Papa sta secolarizzando la Chiesa': Intervista a Marcello Pera," *Il Foglio*, November 22, 2016.

27. Matzuzzi, "'Il Papa sta secolarizzando la Chiesa.'"

to the city of man. In short, they are very distinct things. I have the impression that we are moving toward *felicitas*; otherwise we would not understand this constant criticism of state and institutional structures, of capitalism as the origin of all current evils.[28]

The reasoning of the philosopher Pera was truly unique. The Augustinian distinction between the two cities was used to neutralize any criticism of the capitalist system. Thus "Augustinian capitalism" forbade any criticism of the *civitas mundi*, a kingdom in which sin resolves into harmony without the need for grace. It is a Pelagian Augustinianism that Pera used casually against the "Marxist" pope. He has repeated these theses over the years without a shadow of a doubt. In a July 2017 interview—after confessing, "Frankly, I don't understand this pope, what he says is beyond any rational understanding"—Pera reiterated,

I can offer only one answer: the pope does it because he hates the West. He aspires to destroy it and does everything to achieve this end. Just as he aspires to destroy the Christian tradition, Christianity as it has taken shape in history. . . . And his vision is the South American Peronist vigilantism [*giustizialismo*], which has nothing to do with the Western tradition of political freedoms and its Christian matrix. The pope's Christianity is of a different nature. And it is political Christianity, in its entirety. . . .

The pope reflects all the South American prejudices toward North America, toward the market, freedoms, capitalism. It would have been like that even if Obama had remained in the US presidency, but there is no doubt that these ideas of the pope are welded today, in a dangerous mix, to the anti-Trump sentiment widespread in Europe. . . . Definitely. Bergoglio is little or not at all interested in Christianity as a doctrine, in the theological aspect. And this is undoubtedly a novelty. This pope took Christianity and turned it into politics. His claims are [only] apparently based on Scripture; in reality they are strongly secular. Bergoglio is not concerned with the salvation of souls but only with safety and social well-being.

And this is a preliminary fact. If we then enter into the merits of the things he says, one cannot fail to observe with concern that his statements risk unleashing an uncontrollable political crisis and religious crisis. From the first point of view, he suggests to our states to commit suicide; he invites Europe to no longer be itself. From the second point of view, I cannot fail to observe that a hidden schism is taking place in the Catholic world and

28. Matzuzzi, "'Il Papa sta secolarizzando la Chiesa.'"

that it is pursued by Bergoglio with obstinacy and determination and, by his collaborators, even with malice.[29]

And so Bergoglio is anti-Christian and anticapitalist—indeed, anti-Christian *because* he is anticapitalist. He is a Latin American Catho-Marxist who hates the West, America, and the market.

> I mean that Pope Francis is of South American culture and that the Jesuits' contribution to South American political civilization has been less than that of Protestants to North American liberalism and democracy. Other than dictatorships and military coups, I don't remember much else in South America. This difference between Protestantism and Catholicism should be studied and pondered. There is a historical fact: when the one first professed democracy, the other was still stuck in theocracy.[30]

Pera, the leading intellectual for Cardinal Ruini's cultural project, became, in the first decade of the 2000s, one of the strongest opponents of the pope. A devout atheist who advocates living "as if God existed," Pera elevates himself to the pope's theology professor, teaching Francis how and what to believe. This is a curious situation that has few precedents—and he enjoys the full support of traditionalist Catholicism, which sees the "devout atheists" as the masters of authentic "Catholic" thought, the one not marred by the miasma of modernism and progressivism.

In this leadership role exercised by unbelievers over Catholics, Pera is not alone. Other secular leaders of the Ruinian cultural project stand out in this role.[31] Among them is Ernesto Galli della Loggia, who from

---

29. Corrado Ocone, "Bergoglio vuole fare politica: Il Vangelo non c'entra nulla: Intervista a Marcello Pera," *Il Mattino*, July 9, 2017.

30. "Dio esiste, ma Bergoglio non lo vede più: Ormai siamo vicini allo scisma: Intervista a Marcello Pera," *La Gazzetta di Lucca*, November 12, 2020.

31. Among them are Angelo Panebianco and Sergio Belardinelli, authors of the book *All'alba di un mondo nuovo* (At the dawn of a new world) (Bologna: Il Mulino, 2019). For Belardinelli, the problem of Francis's pontificate lies in equating social values with "nonnegotiable" ones. Bergoglio's universalist vision is also accused of neglecting the "Christian" identity of Europe. Among the critics of Francis's pontificate close to the Ruinian "cultural project," we should also mention Sandro Magister and his blog Settimo Cielo, which is translated into various languages. Magister's position, in line with the neocon perspective, should not be confused with the traditionalist orientation marked by the rejection of the Second Vatican Council.

the columns of the *Corriere della Sera* repeats ideas already widely expressed by Pera, ideas that fully correspond to the Catholic neoconservative model that Galli della Loggia had already perfectly interpreted on the occasion of the war in Iraq in 2013. Like Pera, Galli della Loggia criticizes Bergoglio for being the cause of "a break with the tradition of the papal magisterium."[32] It is a break, we are to believe, dependent on Francis's ideological standpoint, for which "religious" discourse falls into the background and becomes marginal.

"In Bergoglio's teaching," Galli writes,

> the Gospel message and the Catholic *depositum fidei* tend to be placed in the background until it vanishes. This is evidenced by the widespread absence in that same teaching, for example, of any exhortation to the need for repentance and conversion or to discover the Christian meaning of life and death, or the truth of transcendence, a constitutive element of every religion. Thus in the end that teaching, devoid of a significant religious content, remains just an ideological teaching, an ideology with a populist-communitarian-anticapitalist background, not unlike others in circulation, especially in the southern hemisphere of the world.[33]

For Galli della Loggia:

> What is striking here is the substantial abandonment of that "social doctrine of the Church" that had held the field from Leo XIII to John Paul II and that was characterized by its always reaffirmed position as the center between liberal capitalism and socialist statism. Equally clear is the substantial abandonment of another element typical of pontifical pastoral ministry: namely, that humanistic universalism so central to the main conciliar resolutions. Instead of all this, Bergoglio's teaching dominates, together with a marked disregard toward the cultural history of the West and an always mentioned but very clear hostility toward capitalism and the United States, a strong sympathy for the dimension of spontaneous initiative from below and for popular self-organization, the consequent aversion to everything that smacks of institutionalized, official, formal, as well as the general sharing of the expectations and choices made by each

---

32. Ernesto Galli della Loggia, "Una Chiesa poco politica," *Corriere della Sera*, May 9, 2020.

33. Galli della Loggia, "Una Chiesa poco politica."

marginal group, and finally the hope of a sort of natural-communitarian economy with an egalitarian basis.[34]

The accusations that resound from the liberal side are always the same: the pope is not Western enough, not capitalist enough, not pro-American enough. In other words, he fails to accept the structure of world power that constitutes, for the neoconservatives, the guiding star of all reasoning. This is expressed perhaps most clearly by one of the most zealous opponents of the "Bergoglio threat," Loris Zanatta, enlightened defender and apologist of the liberal-capitalist order. In his recent book, with the significant title *Il populismo gesuita: Perón, Fidel, Bergoglio*, Zanatta, in full agreement with Pera's assertions, places South American populism in line with the Catholic tradition as understood by the Society of Jesus, the same that would inspire the political orientation of Juan Perón, Fidel Castro, and Jorge Mario Bergoglio.[35] Zanatta writes:

> Bergoglio's ideal world is a poor Arcadia sheltered from "social sin"—the "populist Jesuit" Arcadia. Bergoglio did not reach this place like so many priests of his generation, by following the revolutionary Marxist path, invoking the "class struggle" and the "death of capital." He arrived there on the wings of Peronism, which, with its "preventive revolution" based on the "collaboration of the classes," allowed the "Catholic nation" to defeat liberalism in the most modern country in Latin America. That had been Perón's great achievement: restoring the people to their Christian "culture," saving them from the centuries-old sirens. Therefore Bergoglio never pushed the aversion for capitalism to the extremes of the Marxists. He never completely disavowed private property, commercial enterprise, individual initiative. As long as they had a "social function," as long as the state fulfilled the moral function of "resource distributor." Hence the widespread image in Europe of a "socialist democratic" pope, an advocate of an "ethical and responsible" market system, extraneous to the anticapitalist fury of the "Jesuit populist" regimes. Yet these very "Jesuit populists" are his political and intellectual "family." Beyond tenuous concessions to the mercantile economy, Bergoglio does not hybridize socialism and lib-

---

34. Galli della Loggia, "Una Chiesa poco politica." Galli della Loggia repeated these ideas in "Il Papa, il sentimento religioso e il richiamo agli 'ultimi,'" *Corriere della Sera*, May 19, 2020. In full agreement is Stefano Fontana, "Galli della Loggia e il pontificato ideologico: Ha ragione," *La Nuova Bussola Quotidiana*, May 11, 2020.

35. Loris Zanatta, *Il populismo gesuita: Perón, Fidel, Bergoglio* (Bari: Laterza, 2020).

eralism as socialist democrats do. For him, "capitalism" is not a complex and changing historical phenomenon, at times a harbinger of progress and civilization, at times of barbarism and exploitation, depending on the historical and institutional context. It is the incarnation of evil, from which emanates "the stench of the devil's dung." Thus emerges the humus of Hispanic Christianity which, far from hybridizing with the fruits of the Enlightenment, cultivates the dream of canceling them to reestablish the Kingdom, where no trace of the enemy will remain.[36]

In his deliberate simplification and reduction of Bergoglio to Jesuit-Peronist populism, Zanatta produces a caricature. In his depiction of an antimodern Bergoglio, Zanatta demonstrates that he is unaware of the role of the Second Vatican Council in Bergoglio's formation and, together with him, the formation of Alberto Methol Ferré. His acknowledgments that Bergoglio "indeed claims the respect for the individual who 'disagrees,'" and that "he praises 'freedom' and 'democracy' in the United States,"[37] are only wrinkles in the dress sewn onto the pope, minor details destined to be lost in the portrait being painted of Bergoglio as a Latin American enemy of the West.[38]

What Zanatta, like Pera and Galli della Loggia, carefully avoids saying is that, in reality, *the pope's social vision is fully consistent with that of Catholic social teaching.* Francis did not "break" with the social doctrine; the vision he brings is no different from that offered in the great encyclicals of his predecessors. *This is the point on which Zanatta and Francis's liberal critics are silent.* Their strategy lies in presenting the pope's social vision as derived from his Argentine context rather than organically rooted in the social tradition of the church. The "break" strategy was first used by Novak, Weigel, and Neuhaus, to assert the "novelty" of *Centesimus*

---

36. Zanatta, *Il populismo gesuita*, 129–30.

37. Zanatta, *Il populismo gesuita*, 120, 124.

38. Zanatta's assertions, already proposed by him in articles that preceded his 2020 volume, gave rise to a discussion with the Vatican expert Riccardo Cristiano. See Cristiano, "'Bergoglio peronista': per il Mulino è un peccato l'empatia umana," *Reset*, June 22, 2016; Zanatta, "Le mie critiche a Bergoglio e ai guasti del peronismo," *Reset*, June 27, 2016; Cristiano, "Così l'empatia di Francesco ha riportato la Chiesa nella storia," *Reset*, June 29, 2016. Cristiano has published two books on Pope Francis, *Bergoglio, sfida globale: Il Papa delle periferie tra famiglia, giustizia sociale e modernità* (Rome: Castelvecchi, 2015) and *Bergoglio o barbarie: Francesco davanti al disordine mondiale* (Rome: Castelvecchi, 2020).

Annus with respect to the entire social tradition of the church. With *Evangelii Gaudium*, the same method is employed to achieve a diametrically opposite result. Here, too, we are to believe that we are faced with a novelty that radically breaks with the previous tradition of the church.

In reality, if Bergoglio's position seems new, it is only because the church, after 1989, has gradually put aside its social teaching, concentrating only on the defense of certain "nonnegotiable" values. Hence the bewilderment of a part of the Catholic world, mostly residing in the rich part of the planet, when faced with Francis's straightforward, strong, and realistic language. With Bergoglio, the man who sits on the Chair of Peter is a pope of the peripheries, of the Latin American metropolises surrounded by the great shanty towns, of the continent plagued by so many injustices and miseries. The voice that resounds in Francis's magisterium and that the church, faithful to Christ, cannot deny is the voice of the poor.

But it is a voice that is decidedly out of tune in the world of Catholic conservatism. It is in disharmony with the liberal line in both economic and ethical matters. As one of that line's most distinguished representatives, Ettore Gotti Tedeschi, the Italian economist, banker, and former president of the Vatican Bank, writes: "The Lord appreciates a rich man who has worked hard more than an envious and slovenly poor man. Pauperism is a serious mistake from both an economic and a cultural point of view. It never teaches that with rights come responsibilities. With welfare, which is one of the most colossal economic and educational mistakes, it pampers people rather than helps them to grow. If you want to harm a person, make sure he gets everything easily and give him cheap handouts. He will never grow."[39]

Gotti Tedeschi—whose works include a book on Catholicism and the global economy that opens with a preface by Cardinal Tarcisio Bertone,[40] Pope Benedict XVI's secretary of state—is a prolific author with a single consistent message: wealth and capitalism do not contrast with the ethics of the gospels but, rather, form an indissoluble alliance.[41] It aligns with

---

39. Bruno Volpe, "Gesù non contesta la ricchezza, solo il cattivo uso del denaro: Intervista a Ettore Gotti Tedeschi," *La Fede Quotidiana*, November 25, 2020.

40. Ettore Gotti Tedeschi and Rino Camilleri, *Denaro e paradiso: I cattolici e l'economia globale: Con un commento all'Enciclica* Caritas in veritate (Turin: Lindau, 2010).

41. See Ettore Gotti Tedeschi, *Denaro e paradiso: L'economia globale e il mondo cattolico* (Casale Monferrato: Piemme, 2004); Gotti Tedeschi, *Elogio della finanza* (Soveria Mannelli:

Novak's model perfectly. Consistent with his position on the economy, Gotti Tedeschi is in the front row among the vocal critics of Francis's pontificate. He is among the signatories of the "filial correction" sent to the pope on *Amoris Laetitia* and is also a member of Opus Dei, the prelature whose founder, St. José María Escrivá de Balaguer, was a firm supporter of the pope, whoever he was.[42] And he is not the only prominent Opus Dei member who opposes Bergoglio. We also find the Vatican expert Aldo Maria Valli, author of several books critical of Francis.[43] Like Gotti Tedeschi, Valli is also an exponent of the alliance between traditionalism and capitalism. In a 2016 article on "the (forgotten) Catholic roots of the free market," Valli wrote that "for a long time the Catholic roots of the market economy appeared dangerous and even subversive in the eyes of those who, on the contrary, preferred to favor an alliance of the Gospel with Marx."[44] He continued, wondering,

> Now, is it really true that Jesus condemns the possession of wealth? Catholics who have espoused the cause of statism, against private property, think so. But authors like the late scholastics remind us that this is not the most correct reading. The authentic interpretation of the Gospel is different: Jesus condemns not those who produce and possess goods, but those who put goods above everything and consider them more important even than God himself. The problem is not goods, but attachment to goods. Let's not forget that Jesus praises the rich man Zacchaeus and enters his house when the chief tax collector (who collected taxes on behalf of the Roman Empire) promises to donate half of his assets to the poor and to give back "four times as much" if he had defrauded someone. Nor should we forget that Jesus

---

Rubbettino, 2009); Gotti Tedeschi, *Amare Dio e fare soldi: Massime di economia divina* (Verona: Fede & cultura, 2014); Gotti Tedeschi, *Dio è meritocratico: Manuale per la salvaguardia della fede cattolica* (Cesena: Giubilei Regnani, 2017). In his 2004 interview book with Camilleri, Gotti Tedeschi makes clear that his points of reference are Michael Novak, Robert Sirico, Dario Antiseri, Flavio Felice, Friedrich Hayek, and Samuel Huntington.

42. See Andrea Tornielli, "Il banchiere Gotti Tedeschi (con altri 61) accusa il papa di 7 eresie," *Vatican Insider*, September 25, 2017.

43. Aldo Maria Valli, *266: Jorge Mario Bergoglio Franciscus P.P.* (Macerata: Liberilibri, 2016); Valli, *Come la Chiesa finì* (Macerata: Liberilibri, 2017); Valli and Aurelio Porfiri, *Sradicati: Dialoghi sulla Chiesa liquida* (Rome: Chorabooks, 2018).

44. Aldo Maria Valli, "Le (dimenticate) radici cattoliche della libertà di mercato," personal blog, May 3, 2016, https://www.aldomariavalli.it/2016/05/03/le-dimenticate-radici-cattoliche-della-liberta-di-mercato/.

chooses his friends and followers in general among the wealthy (Peter, Andrew, John, and James are fishermen and have a kind of cooperative; Philip and Bartholomew own land, as well as Judas and the other James; Matthew is a tax collector) and that he himself lived for thirty years with his mother Mary and father Joseph, a carpenter, working in the family shop.[45]

Of course, Valli's examples of the "wealthy" apostles make one smile a little. But Catho-capitalism is relentless. Needless to say, his opponent is once again the pope. In a 2017 article, Valli writes that "toward the free market, Francis is, at the very least, suspicious and very far from Catholic liberalism. Rather, one sees clear evidence in him of the influence of the Peronism known and experienced in Argentina, that 'third way' between capitalism and Communism to which Bergoglio alludes when, using a typically Peronist expression (as in the speech he addressed to the Italian Confederation of Workers' Unions), he says that the ideal is a 'social market economy.'"[46] To counter the pope's "Peronism," Valli refers to an article by Martin Rhonheimer, a prominent figure among the professors of the Opus Dei–led Pontifical University of the Holy Cross in Rome.

A helpful alternative understanding of the role of the entrepreneur can be found in the latest issue of the journal *Studi cattolici* (n. 680, October 2017), edited by Cesare Cavalleri. This is the article "Il lavoro del capitale" [The work of capital], in which Martin Rhonheimer, Catholic priest, professor of ethics and political philosophy at the Pontifical University of the Holy Cross in Rome and founding president of the Austrian Institute of Economics and Social Philosophy in Vienna, demonstrates how much the Catholic distrust toward entrepreneurial activity, which has never really ceased, is senseless. It is true, writes Rhonheimer, that John Paul II, in both *Sollicitudo Rei Socialis* (1987) and *Centesimus Annus* (1991), recognizes the importance of entrepreneurial action to overcome the drama of poverty, but with Francis the ancient distrust, which is more precisely a misunderstanding of entrepreneurial dynamics, has appeared again.

The good entrepreneur, explains Rhonheimer, is not motivated by the intention of creating jobs or promoting the common good. His purpose is to put products on the market that sell. But it is precisely in this way that, in practice, he creates work and promotes the common good. Profit,

45. Valli, "Le (dimenticate) radici cattoliche della libertà di mercato."

46. Aldo Maria Valli, "In difesa del profitto," personal blog, October 23, 2017, https://www.aldomariavalli.it/2017/10/23/in-difesa-del-profitto/.

work, and the common good are connected, not opposed. One who seeks profitability creates profit, and profit creates jobs. In addition to that, the pursuit of profit through efficiency generates competition, and competition generates innovation, and here, too, there are important social benefits. "The existence of a profit signals that production and consumer needs coincide. A search for profit based on entrepreneurial rationality, and not on greedy irrationality, is therefore at the service of the common good, and as a rule high entrepreneurial profits are a sign of great creation of added value."[47]

The position of Valli, a supporter of Archbishop Carlo Maria Viganò, highlights the singular combination of religious neotraditionalism and capitalism. Unlike the old traditionalists, who were medievalists and radically antimodern, the new ones are antiliberal in ethics and liberal in economics. With this, they differentiate themselves from the American and even Italian Catholic neoconservatives, who are firm supporters of the value of modern freedoms and the Second Vatican Council. The common elements that remain are the celebration of the capitalist model and the total aversion to Pope Francis. Liberal traditionalism is thus the hircocervus—the mythological beast that is half-goat and half-deer—that arises from the metamorphosis of the neocon ideology that dominated American Catholicism for twenty years, from the 1990s to the first decade of the 2000s. It is economically liberal, because in its absolute opposition to Marxism it must reject anything "social" in nature, every aspect of "solidarity." And thus it has fully embraced that Hobbesian anthropology that, dialectically, ends up overthrowing itself in the panacea of generalized well-being. Among the proponents of liberal Catholic traditionalism in Italy there are various prominent blogs, all strongly critical of the "Peronist" and "progressive" pope. Included among them are traditionalist historian Roberto de Mattei's Corrispondenza Romana, Riccardo Cascioli's La Nuova Bussola Quotidiana, and Marco Tosatti's Stilum Curiae.[48] It is a very active universe with many landing points, each characterized by an economic theology on the one hand and a political theology

---

47. Valli, "In difesa del profitto."

48. Among these, La Nuova Bussola Quotidiana stands out for its combination of traditionalism and Catholic neoconservatism. From 2012 to 2018, George Weigel was an especially frequent reference point, as were Robert Sirico and, naturally, Michael Novak. See Stefano Magni, "Michael Novak, il filosofo della libertà," La Nuova Bussola Quotidiana, February 18, 2017.

on the other. It engages readers in a process of double-ideologization that, like a solid mental block, eliminates any possibility of understanding the pontificate of Francis.

A Soulless Technocracy: The Ecological Question in *Laudato Si'*

The encyclical *Laudato Si'*, on caring for the planet understood as the common home of humanity, was published by Pope Francis on May 24, 2015.[49] It is not an encyclical against Donald Trump for the simple reason that the occupant of the White House at the time was still Barack Obama, a president who had invested considerable effort on the environmental issue. Unlike him, his successor, from the moment he took office on January 20, 2017, seemed set on demonstrating an absolute disinterest in the environment, supporting industrial and commercial interests in every way possible. On June 1, 2017, the United States withdrew from the Paris climate treaty, a process that went into effect on November 4, 2020. The changes that the Trump administration introduced during the years of his presidency were substantial.

In 2012, Obama had imposed consumption limits on automobiles, to be achieved by 2026, to increase efficiency and reduce gasoline consumption and polluting emissions. The Trump administration, following the demands of oil companies and car manufacturers, has weakened this rule by raising the consumption threshold. Protective measures against mercury emissions from coal-fired power plants were withdrawn. Power plants will no longer have the obligation imposed by the Obama administration to reduce this type of pollution, which is particularly serious for public health. Trump has replaced the Obama-era clean power plan, aimed at limiting carbon emissions from power plants, with a new, more malleable version, which allows individual states to set their own rules. He canceled the obligation for companies involved in the extraction of oil and natural gas to

---

49. See Marco Dotti, "Papa Francesco: la svolta ecologica convince gli ambientalisti," *Vita*, June 18, 2015. Supporting the pope's teaching, Michael Löwy, "Pontifex maximus versus Kapitalismus: Laudato si', une encyclique anti-systémique," *Revista Helius* 2, no. 1 (2019), 4–21. Criticisms come from materialist authors for whom nature has its "order" through the natural-selection criteria inherent to it. See Antonello La Vergata, "Considerazioni sull'enciclica di Papa Francesco *Laudato si'*," *Atti Soc. Nat. Mat. Modena* 148 (2017), 353–68.

report methane emissions. He has undermined a law dating back to the Clinton administration aimed at limiting emissions from major industrial polluters and a law proposed by Obama designed to reduce air pollution in national parks. He also proposed to modify the current appeal procedure to contest the pollution permits issued by the EPA, effectively weakening the ability of individuals and communities to protect themselves. Particularly sensitive to the demands of the oil lobby, Trump has reopened oil exploration in the Arctic that had been halted by Obama . . . and has eliminated the obligation for the owners of Gulf oil rigs to demonstrate that they can cover the costs of removal of disused platforms. He has also reduced the size of two national parks in Utah by about eight thousand square kilometers, to encourage the exploitation of mineral resources and hydrocarbons. He eliminated a law that required mines to prove they could pay to clean up future pollution and approved construction of the Dakota Access pipeline near the Standing Rock Sioux Reservation.[50]

The list could go on. According to the *New York Times*, Trump abolished or canceled more than sixty environmental regulations.[51] The president's positions were soon reflected in conservative American Catholicism, the same one that opposes Pope Francis as an "anticapitalist" South American. The decline of the Catholic neoconservative ideology does not change the cards on the table from this point of view. Catholic Americanism followed the wave of power, remaining focused on the two canonical points: culture war and Catho-capitalism. Trump, the president opposed to abortion, became the point of reference for the new season for the neoconservatives who by this point might more accurately be called "oldconservatives." From this point of view, Francis's *Laudato Si'* could only appear as an outdated document of the Obama era, yet another bit of evidence of the green, ecological, progressive soul of Pope Bergoglio. Trumpian Catholics agreed with their president in denying any validity to environmental concerns. They laughed at young Greta Thunberg, the Swedish activist for sustainable development and against climate change. Economy and finance come first; the planet can self-regulate on its own.

50. Lorenzo Brenna, "Come Trump sta eliminando l'eredità ambientale di Obama," *Lifegate*, May 27, 2020, https://www.lifegate.it/trump-eliminando-leggi-ambientali-obama.
51. Nadja Popovich, Livia Albreck-Ripka, and Kendra Pierre-Louis, "The Trump Administration Is Reversing Nearly 100 Environmental Rules. Here's the Full List," *New York Times*, November 10, 2020.

As a result, *Laudato Si'*, like *Evangelii Gaudium* before it, aroused considerable debate upon its release in 2015.[52]

The objections and criticisms followed two directions. First, the papal document represented the pope's step into terrain where he didn't belong, an area (ecology) that did not fall within the competence of theology. On the part of the pope, this was an operation guided solely by tactical needs, by the convenience of riding the green wave that crossed the peoples of the planet. This criticism came from circles of religious conservatism that dismiss environmental concerns as typical of today's progressivism. According to them, the Roman pontiff, instead of focusing on the evangelization of peoples and the church, had become lost in the protection of plants and oceans. The pope was concerned with the world and not with Christ. These critics obviously had forgotten how each of the latest popes, from John XXIII onward, had dedicated time and attention to the theme of peace, social justice, the development of peoples, and work. This is Catholic social teaching, into which *Laudato Si'* fit quite naturally.[53] The care of the natural world, inseparable from the destiny of human life, is part of the theology of creation to which the second chapter of the encyclical is dedicated. The document takes its title from a line of praise to God in St. Francis of Assisi's "Canticle of the Sun," which, of course, bears no naive ecological ideology but a firm theological vision. It is also no coincidence that the encyclical ends with a hymn to the Holy Trinity that is decidedly not pantheistic.

The second line of criticism aimed at the content of the document. Many, especially the more radical sectors of liberal capitalism, did not like the pope's criticism of environmental exploitation by an economic model based solely on the law of profit. Samuel Gregg, of Sirico's Acton Institute, wrote, "While most of the text's reflections upon public policy issues focus on the environment, a subterranean theme that becomes decidedly visible from time-to-time is the encyclical's deeply negative view of free markets. This would confirm that this pontificate's reaction

52. On the American critics of *Laudato Si'*, see Scavo, *I nemici di Francesco*, 64–77.

53. In a 2019 *La Stampa* interview, in response to a question about the 2019 Synod of Bishops for the Pan-Amazon region, the pope said, "It [the synod] is the child of *Laudato Si'*. One who has not read it will not understand the Amazonian synod. *Laudato Si'* is not a 'green' encyclical; it is a social encyclical based on a 'green' reality, care for creation." Domenico Agasso, Jr., "Papa Francesco: 'Il sovranismo mi spaventa, porta alle guerre,'" *La Stampa*, August 9, 2019.

to respectful questions asked about the adequacy of the economic analysis contained in Francis's 2013 Apostolic Exhortation *Evangelii Gaudium* has been to simply recycle (no pun intended) some of that document's demonstrably flawed arguments concerning the market economy's nature and effects."[54]

Gregg continued,

> *Laudato Si'* also emphasizes that the Church doesn't have a monopoly of wisdom on the prudential dimension of environmental and economic questions. Yet the encyclical's use of phrases such as "deified market" (56) and "magical conception of the market" (190); its unsupported association of moral relativism with Adam Smith's "invisible hand" (123); its relentless linkage of the market with materialism and consumerism (neither of which have had any difficulty flourishing in non-market economies); its failure to critique the left-populist regimes that have brought economic destruction and increased poverty to countries such as Argentina and Venezuela; and its attribution of suspicious motives to those who favor markets, runs contrary to this appeal for open and respectful debate.[55]

Gregg's concerns are clear: what simply cannot be tolerated about the encyclical's teaching is not its concern for the environment but rather its criticism of capitalism, the same critique already offered in *Evangelii Gaudium*. The same reservation was expressed by the Australian priest Paul Anthony McGavin in an article posted on Sandro Magister's blog:

> "Laudato si'" clearly has a Bergoglio hand (for example, the most cited non-ecclesial text is "The End of the Modern World" by Romano Guardini, on whose writings Bergoglio commenced doctoral studies)—but evidence of lack of integration suggests more than one ghost writer. What quite stands out in the document is its Latin American culture (reading the nations of Central and South Americas that arose from Iberian Catholic imperialism as "Latin America"). Broadly speaking, Latin America is notable internationally for economic backwardness and opportunistic behaviors that prevail under weak governance regimes.[56]

---

54. Samuel Gregg, "Laudato Si': Well Intentioned, Economically Flawed," *The American Spectator*, June 19, 2015, https://spectator.org/laudato-si-well-intentioned-economically-flawed/.

55. Gregg, "Laudato Si."

56. Paul Anthony McGavin, "What's Wrong with 'Laudato si,'?" Settimo Cielo blog, *L'Espresso*, February 9, 2016, http://chiesa.espresso.repubblica.it/articolo/1351224.html.

What critics deny the pope, in the first place, is the way he orients Catholic social teaching along the North-South global axis, as in the time of Paul VI, after the decades of East-West conflict. That's what Gregg says when he writes:

> Then there is the encyclical's use of "global north and south" language to describe some of the global economy's dynamics (51). This terminology has been used occasionally by popes in the recent past. But it also reflects the conceptual apparatus of what was called dependency theory: the notion that resources—especially natural resources—flow from a "periphery" of poor countries to a "core" of rich states, thereby benefiting the wealthy at the poor's expense. . . .
>
> This understanding of the global economy, much of which was formulated by Latin American economists in the 1950s, has long been discredited. Not even many center-left economists are willing to defend it.[57]

As in the case of *Evangelii Gaudium*, what the Catholic neocapitalists attempt is to reduce the papal position to a Marxist variant (the theory of dependence), a "Southernist" vision of the economy. Environmental considerations take a back seat here. To this perspective is added the one according to which economic development cannot be hindered by environmental considerations. The reason is simple: the ecological question is a concern of the left and the greens. *Therefore it can only be an ideological question to be rejected.*

Francis's critics forget here the great address delivered by Benedict XVI to the German Reichstag on September 22, 2011. He said on that occasion,

> I would say that the emergence of the ecological movement in German politics since the 1970s, while it has not exactly flung open the windows, nevertheless was and continues to be a cry for fresh air which must not be ignored or pushed aside, just because too much of it is seen to be irrational. Young people had come to realize that something is wrong in our relationship with nature, that matter is not just raw material for us to shape at will, but that the earth has a dignity of its own and that we must follow its directives. In saying this, I am clearly not promoting any particular political party—nothing could be further from my mind. If something is

---

57. Gregg, "Laudato Si'."

wrong in our relationship with reality, then we must all reflect seriously on the whole situation and we are all prompted to question the very foundations of our culture. Allow me to dwell a little longer on this point. The importance of ecology is no longer disputed. We must listen to the language of nature and we must answer accordingly.[58]

Given the context in which the address was delivered, it was one of great importance. Claudia Roth, the president of the German political party known as the Greens, commented at the time:

Benedict XVI, in his vision of protection of creation, which rejects an over-exploitation of the planet, has a vision common to ours. I am also interested in the issues that he shares with us Greens in the field of social policy. I am thinking, for example, of solidarity with the weak, of responsibility toward the less affluent sections of society, of the victims of violence and environmental disasters, of the protection of refugees, and above all of the pacifism expressed in recent years by the Vatican. From all these points of view, I see the pope not only as an interlocutor but as a potential partner![59]

Pope Benedict's speech demonstrated that the ecological question is not an "ideological" one but rather constitutes a capital point of the church's social teaching.[60] John Paul II had affirmed the same thing more than a decade earlier, in his 1999 apostolic exhortation *Ecclesia in America*:

---

58. Pope Benedict XVI, "The Listening Heart: Reflections on the Foundations of Law," September 22, 2011, http://www.vatican.va/content/benedict-xvi/en/speeches/2011/september/documents/hf_ben-xvi_spe_20110922_reichstag-berlin.html.

59. F. Noli, "Tra il Papa e i verdi Tedeschi: Intervista a Claudia Roth," *Globalist*, September 24, 2011.

60. Francis has said, "*Laudato Si'* is not a green encyclical. It's a social encyclical. The green and the social go hand in hand. The fate of creation is tied to the fate of all humanity" (Pope Francis, *Let Us Dream*, 32). In the same volume, the Pope reveals his awareness of the importance of the problem of the environment starting from the meeting of the bishops of Latin America in Aparecida, Brazil, in 2007 (30–32). For Francis, "It's an awareness, not an ideology. There are green movements that turn the ecological experience into ideology, but ecological awareness is just that: awareness, not ideology. It's being conscious of what's at stake in the fate of humanity" (31–32). The Aparecida document treated the ecological problem in paragraphs 83–87, in the section titled, "Biodiversity, Ecology, the Amazon, and the Antarctic" (Fifth General Conference of the Latin American Episcopate, "Concluding Document").

In this area [ecology] too, so relevant today, the action of believers is more important than ever. Alongside legislative and governmental bodies, all people of good will must work to ensure the effective protection of the environment, understood as a gift from God. How much ecological abuse and destruction there is in many parts of America! It is enough to think of the uncontrolled emission of harmful gases or the dramatic phenomenon of forest fires, sometimes deliberately set by people driven by selfish interest. Devastations such as these could lead to the desertification of many parts of America, with the inevitable consequences of hunger and misery. This is an especially urgent problem in the forests of Amazonia, an immense territory extending into different countries: from Brazil to Guyana, Surinam, Venezuela, Colombia, Ecuador, Peru and Bolivia. This is one of the world's most precious natural regions because of its bio-diversity which makes it vital for the environmental balance of the entire planet.[61]

John Paul II's teaching removes all credibility from critics of Francis's "ecologism." These critics reject any suggestion that the teachings are founded in a concern for human well-being, and they absolve industry of any responsibility for the use and pollution of land, water, and air, all out of concern that the capitalist model may be embraced without qualification. Hence the reaction to the papal document which, on the contrary, addresses planetary inequality[62] in the exploitation of primary resources and in the distribution of environmental degradation and solid waste to the poorest countries in the world—the garbage countries. Pope Francis writes: "The warming caused by huge consumption on the part of some rich countries has repercussions on the poorest areas of the world, especially Africa, where a rise in temperature, together with drought, has proved devastating for farming. There is also the damage caused by the export of solid waste and toxic liquids to developing countries, and by the pollution produced by companies which operate in less developed countries in ways they could never do at home, in the countries in which they raise their capital."[63]

This process, in which economic dependence translates into a profound change in environmental conditions, is not adequately understood due to the lack of a culture willing to fully address the problem. In deciphering the crisis, Francis says, the positions oscillate between two opposite

61. Pope John Paul II, *Ecclesia in America*, 25.
62. Pope Francis, *Laudato Si'*, 48.
63. Pope Francis, *Laudato Si'*, 51.

polarities: "At one extreme, we find those who doggedly uphold the myth of progress and tell us that ecological problems will solve themselves simply with the application of new technology and without any need for ethical considerations or deep change. At the other extreme are those who view men and women and all their interventions as no more than a threat, jeopardizing the global ecosystem, and consequently the presence of human beings on the planet should be reduced and all forms of intervention prohibited."[64]

This latter position becomes, in its critique of the anthropic principle, a pantheism, a mysticism of nature that implies an equivalence, in terms of value, between humanity and other living species. For Francis, it would be a mistake "to put all living beings on the same level [or] to deprive human beings of their unique worth and the tremendous responsibility it entails. Nor does it imply a divinization of the earth which would prevent us from working on it and protecting it in its fragility."[65] The antihumanist ecology is profoundly contradictory. He writes, "A sense of deep communion with the rest of nature cannot be real if our hearts lack tenderness, compassion and concern for our fellow human beings. It is clearly inconsistent to combat trafficking in endangered species while remaining completely indifferent to human trafficking, unconcerned about the poor, or undertaking to destroy another human being deemed unwanted."[66]

The ecology promoted by *Laudato Si'* is deeply humanistic. The drama of environmental degradation with the upheaval of climatic processes that characterizes the present moment consists precisely in the fact that it can lead to the extinction of humanity. Like an announced nuclear catastrophe, according to the pope, we are facing "a breaking point,"[67] a point of no return. To avoid this, a new awareness of the relevant processes and their interconnection is required.

"Everything is related"[68]: this conviction is repeated several times in the text of the encyclical. It is not a "holistic" phrase, expressing some kind of pantheistic vision, but the application of the model of polarity that is the foundation of Bergoglio's thought.

---

64. Pope Francis, *Laudato Si'*, 60.
65. Pope Francis, *Laudato Si'*, 90.
66. Pope Francis, *Laudato Si'*, 91.
67. Pope Francis, *Laudato Si'*, 61.
68. Pope Francis, *Laudato Si'*, 92.

This synthetic consideration requires, in order to address the ecological question, an understanding of the connection between economics, finance, politics, and the technocratic model. The third chapter of *Laudato Si'*, entitled "The Human Roots of the Ecological Crisis," is dedicated precisely to the hegemony of this model. This is not a new idea on the part of the pope. The emergence of a positivistic, technocratic mentality accompanying the process of post-Marxist globalization was already a fixed point of Bergoglio's thought and that of one of his intellectual reference points, the Uruguayan Alberto Methol Ferré, in the years when he was bishop (and then cardinal) in Buenos Aires. As Pope Francis said in an address to the European Parliament in 2014,

> To our dismay we see technical and economic questions dominating political debate, to the detriment of genuine concern for human beings. Men and women risk being reduced to mere cogs in a machine that treats them as items of consumption to be exploited, with the result that—as is so tragically apparent—whenever a human life no longer proves useful for that machine, it is discarded with few qualms, as in the case of the sick, of the terminally ill, the elderly who are abandoned and uncared for, and children who are killed in the womb.
>
> This is the great mistake made "when technology is allowed to take over"; the result is a "confusion between ends and means." It is the inevitable consequence of a "throwaway culture" and an uncontrolled consumerism. Upholding the dignity of the person means instead acknowledging the value of human life, which is freely given us and hence cannot be an object of trade or commerce.[69]

The technocratic model that guides today's economy is combined, in the era of globalization, with *an individualistic and relativistic philosophy*. A positivistic neo-empiricism, which undergirds the post-1989 culture, is *the meeting point between technocracy and relativism*.

Laudato Si' teaches that the global hegemony of the technocratic model, accompanied by ethical relativism, means that "humanity has entered a new era in which our technical prowess has brought us to a

69. Pope Francis, "Address to the European Parliament," November 25, 2014, http://www.vatican.va/content/francesco/en/speeches/2014/november/documents/papa-francesco_20141125_strasburgo-parlamento-europeo.html.

crossroads."[70] On the one hand, there are the great aesthetic and progress possibilities offered by technology.

> Technoscience, when well directed, can produce important means of improving the quality of human life, from useful domestic appliances to great transportation systems, bridges, buildings and public spaces. It can also produce art and enable men and women immersed in the material world to "leap" into the world of beauty. Who can deny the beauty of an aircraft or a skyscraper? Valuable works of art and music now make use of new technologies. So, in the beauty intended by the one who uses new technical instruments and in the contemplation of such beauty, a quantum leap occurs, resulting in a fulfilment which is uniquely human.[71]

On the other hand, technoscience constitutes a formidable challenge for human responsibility. "Never has humanity had such power over itself, yet nothing ensures that it will be used wisely, particularly when we consider how it is currently being used."[72] It is not possible to ignore the dangers represented by nuclear energy, the use of biotechnologies, control of systems by computers, and DNA experimentation. In his evaluation of the present time, Pope Francis takes into account the reflections of an author important in his own intellectual formation, Romano Guardini.

In his book *The End of the Modern World* and its essay "Power and Responsibility," the Italian-German author described the degradation and exploitation of nature by the industrialization of technology in a way not unlike the reflections of Martin Heidegger. However, he did not indulge in archaic utopias but realistically questioned humanity's ability to control the power it gained through technical progress. *Power over one's power is the fundamental anthropological question of our time.*[73] It is a problem complicated by the fact that the modern era demonstrates that it is unable, in its "autonomy," to maintain the values that come from its Christian heritage. The parasitic use of those values, cut from the roots of faith, proves impossible, as Nietzsche's work documents. It is this situation that makes humanity's relationship with power and technology today problematic.

---

70. Pope Francis, *Laudato Si'*, 102.
71. Pope Francis, *Laudato Si'*, 103.
72. Pope Francis, *Laudato Si'*, 104.
73. See Borghesi, *Romano Guardini: Dialettica e antropologia*, 197–236.

In his 1989 article "Necessità di un'antropologia politica" (The necessity of a political anthropology), then–Fr. Bergoglio observes that no one adheres any longer to the belief in progress that was typical of the Enlightenment. As Guardini highlighted in his book *The End of the Modern World*, the three *absoluta*—nature, subject, and culture—have disappeared. It is a fact, writes Bergoglio, that *"the three elements typical of Modernity (self-subsistent nature, the autonomous subject-personality, and the creative culture starting from its own norms) have lost their referential validity."*[74] The consequence, he says, citing the Spanish philosopher Alfonso López Quintás, is that "the person of today feels absurdly free, a freedom that, in large part, is abandonment. . . . The fact that creation can generate pride goes unnoticed, and this causes an imbalance between the power one has over things and the power one has over power."[75]

There is a disproportion between technical power and the ethical development of those who use it. For this reason, "in the development of an anthropology that does not become a return to ignorance, the question of control over power moves within the fullness-form tension, which avoids chaos and formalism. The challenge of anthropology is to shape and place a limit on the unlimited fullness of the technique of power."[76] Here Bergoglio quotes Guardini directly:

> The wildernesses of nature have long been under the control of man; nature as it exists round and about us obeys its master. Nature now, however, has emerged once again into history from within the very depths of culture itself. Nature is rising up in that very form which subdued the wilderness—in the form of power itself. All the abysses of primeval ages yawn before man, all the wild choking growth of the long-dead forests press forward from this second wilderness, all the monsters of the desert wastes, all the horrors of darkness are once more upon man. He stands again before chaos.[77]

74. Jorge Mario Bergoglio, "Necessità di un'antropologia politica: Un problema pastorale," *Stromata*, January-June 1989, It. trans. in Jorge Mario Bergoglio–Pope Francis, *Pastorale sociale*, M. Gallo, ed. (Milan: Jaca Book, 2015), 293.

75. Bergoglio, "Necessità di un'antropologia politica," 293. The citation is of Alfonso López Quintás, "Pasión de verdad y dialectica en Romano Guardini," afterword to Romano Guardini, *El ocaso de la edad moderna* (Madrid: Ediciones Guadarrama, 1958), 171.

76. Bergoglio, "Necessità di un'antropologia politica," 298n24.

77. Romano Guardini, *The End of the Modern World*, trans. Joseph Theman and Herbert Burke (Wilmington, DE: ISI Books, 1998), 91–92. The citation is in Bergoglio, "Necessità di un'antropologia politica," 298.

It is therefore necessary to control this new manmade chaos. Speaking at a 2003 conference on the social teaching of John Paul II, then–Cardinal Bergoglio, regarding the understanding of work in John Paul's thought, said:

> The Pope reiterates this concept from the perspective of the very essence of humanity, the essence from which the mission of "dominating the earth" springs and which involves the free choice of being a collaborator of the Creator. Here the prophecy of Romano Guardini in his book *The End of the Modern World* is implicitly reflected. "Power and Responsibility" (1950) identified the fundamental reason for the paradigm shift that was taking place more and more widely in our modern world. Guardini saw as a characteristic feature of our civilization today the fact that power was transforming itself more and more into something anonymous. And from there, as if from a root, all the dangers and injustices we suffer from today arise. And the antidote that he proposed consisted in nothing other than making us all, each of us in solidarity, responsible for power. It is precisely here that John Paul II's vision of human work is inserted as the place where humanity freely opts for the use of power as a service and collaboration in God's creative work for the good of his brothers.[78]

The Guardinian reading on the relationship between technology and power in the postmodern era will become important again when Bergoglio, as pope, writes his encyclical letter *Laudato Si'*. That document cites *The End of the Modern World* five times. Guardini offered a broad picture of the mentality and currents that move postmodern times, marked, on the one hand, by an immeasurable power thanks to technical-scientific progress and, on the other, by the lack of an ethics capable of governing such power.[79] *Humanity today does not have power over its own power.* Technique, as a tool, becomes the engine of a process that seems no longer to have a recognizable subject. According to the pope, the eclipse of the subject, revealing the lack of a moral position capable of supporting the centrality of the human person, explains "the globalization of the technocratic model." The universalization of the technical model, raised to an absolute value, is the cause of widespread reductionism, the strength of the functionalist mentality, to the point that "the idea of

---

78. Jorge Mario Bergoglio, "'Duc in altum': il pensiero sociale di Giovanni Paolo II," in Jorge Mario Bergoglio–Pope Francis, *Nei tuoi occhi è la mia parola: Omelie e discorsi di Buenos Aires 1999–2013* (Milan: Rizzoli, 2016), 229.

79. See Borghesi, *Romano Guardini: Dialettica e antropologia*, 197–236.

promoting a different cultural paradigm and employing technology as a mere instrument is nowadays inconceivable. The technological paradigm has become so dominant that it would be difficult to do without its resources and even more difficult to utilize them without being dominated by their internal logic."[80]

The technocratic model constitutes the "logic" that guides the economy, finance, and politics. Francis cites Guardini, for whom technology "moves forward in the final analysis neither for profit nor for the well-being of the human race," that "in the most radical sense of the term power is its motive—a lordship over all."[81] Technique is dominion, and nothing, from today's perspective, seems to escape this law. Everything that should have the dignity of an end—humanity, nature—becomes a means. Means become ends and ends become means. *The technocratic model leads to the ethical inversion of the world.* This inversion is supported by the fact that "the specialization which belongs to technology makes it difficult to see the larger picture."[82] The reduction of reality to the set of technical problems "often leads to a loss of appreciation for the whole, for the relationships between things."[83] What is lost is the relationship between "philosophy and social ethics."[84] In this way the environmental problem appears as a variable, an accident of the journey, a byproduct of other problems. The essential, vital connection between humanity and the environment—not only as physical space but, more deeply, as the place of humanity's living, of humanity's feeling at home, in a vital link with nature that surrounds—is lost. For this reason, according to Francis,

> Ecological culture cannot be reduced to a series of urgent and partial responses to the immediate problems of pollution, environmental decay and the depletion of natural resources. There needs to be a distinctive way of looking at things, a way of thinking, policies, an educational program, a lifestyle and a spirituality which together generate resistance to the assault of the technocratic paradigm. Otherwise, even the best ecological initiatives can find themselves caught up in the same globalized logic. To seek only a technical remedy to each environmental problem which comes up

---

80. Pope Francis, *Laudato Si'*, 108.
81. Cited in Pope Francis, *Laudato Si'*, 108.
82. Pope Francis, *Laudato Si'*, 110.
83. Pope Francis, *Laudato Si'*, 110.
84. Pope Francis, *Laudato Si'*, 110.

is to separate what is in reality interconnected and to mask the true and deepest problems of the global system.[85]

Laudato Si' therefore does not limit itself to a critical diagnosis of today's ecological problem. It identifies the cause of the environmental crisis: a loss of the ethical-humanistic sense that has resulted from the establishment of the technocratic model worldwide. With respect to this hegemony, the encyclical calls for moral "resistance." The theology of redemption cannot ignore the theology of creation at a time when dominant technology, separated from any ethical purpose, risks making humanity's home unlivable forever. We need a "bold cultural revolution,"[86] a change of perspective that lets us rethink the conceptual orientation that has guided European modernity, a humanism without bounds, incapable of understanding or respecting its own limits. "Modern anthropocentrism has paradoxically ended up prizing technical thought over reality, since 'the technological mind sees nature as an insensate order, as a cold body of facts, as a mere "given," as an object of utility, as raw material to be hammered into useful shape; it views the cosmos similarly as a mere "space" into which objects can be thrown with complete indifference.'"[87]

Due to the "excessive anthropocentrism"[88] that is typical of modernity, Francis writes, "[o]ften, what was handed on was a Promethean vision of mastery over the world, which gave the impression that the protection of nature was something that only the faint-hearted cared about."[89] This "excess" does not make necessary, as some currents of radical ecology suggest, the reduction of the human presence on earth, nor does it imply neo-Malthusian programs based on abortion and reduction of births.[90]

---

85. Pope Francis, *Laudato Si'*, 111.

86. Pope Francis, *Laudato Si'*, 114.

87. Pope Francis, *Laudato Si'*, 115. The quotation is from Guardini, *The End of the Modern Age*.

88. Pope Francis, *Laudato Si'*, 116.

89. Pope Francis, *Laudato Si'*, 116.

90. "Since everything is interrelated, concern for the protection of nature is also incompatible with the justification of abortion. How can we genuinely teach the importance of concern for other vulnerable beings, however troublesome or inconvenient they may be, if we fail to protect a human embryo, even when its presence is uncomfortable and creates difficulties? 'If personal and social sensitivity towards the acceptance of the new life is lost, then other forms of acceptance that are valuable for society also wither away.'" Pope Francis, *Laudato Si'*, 120.

"A misguided anthropocentrism need not necessarily yield to 'biocentrism,' for that would entail adding yet another imbalance, failing to solve present problems and adding new ones."[91]

Reflecting the model of polarity at the center of Bergoglio's thought, he continues, "We need to develop a new synthesis capable of overcoming the false arguments of recent centuries."[92] It is important to note that in this sentence, where the English translation of the encyclical uses the word *arguments*, the Italian version uses *dialettiche*, the Spanish *dialécticas*, and the Latin *dialecticas*: dialectics. The new synthesis the pope calls for means *the overcoming of the false dialectic between humanity and nature*. The relational model at the heart of *Laudato Si'* stands beyond the antithesis between anthropic excess and biocentric excess. The anthropological primacy of humanity over nature requires respect for "humanity's home," for the habitat, for the natural world. It is not possible to separate humanity and humanity's quality of life from its environmental context. Its uprooting is a consequence of the technocratic model that, in its turn, presupposes a disembodied self, without a fixed abode, the nomadic person forced by the neocapitalist market for both the elites and the masses into internal and international immigration. The nomadic condition finds its confirmation in the moral relativism that characterizes the era of globalization.

> When human beings place themselves at the center, they give absolute priority to immediate convenience and all else becomes relative. Hence we should not be surprised to find, in conjunction with the omnipresent technocratic paradigm and the cult of unlimited human power, the rise of a relativism which sees everything as irrelevant unless it serves one's own immediate interests. There is a logic in all this whereby different attitudes can feed on one another, leading to environmental degradation and social decay.[93]

The technocratic model is accompanied by the culture of relativism. The combination of positivism and relativism is characteristic of the era of globalization. This is an important statement that refutes the accusations of those who accuse the pope of yielding to relativistic culture.

91. Pope Francis, *Laudato Si'*, 118.
92. Pope Francis, *Laudato Si'*, 121.
93. Pope Francis, *Laudato Si'*, 122.

The culture of relativism is the same disorder which drives one person to take advantage of another, to treat others as mere objects, imposing forced labor on them or enslaving them to pay their debts. The same kind of thinking leads to the sexual exploitation of children and abandonment of the elderly who no longer serve our interests. It is also the mindset of those who say: Let us allow the invisible forces of the market to regulate the economy, and consider their impact on society and nature as collateral damage. In the absence of objective truths or sound principles other than the satisfaction of our own desires and immediate needs, what limits can be placed on human trafficking, organized crime, the drug trade, commerce in blood diamonds and the fur of endangered species? Is it not the same relativistic logic which justifies buying the organs of the poor for resale or use in experimentation, or eliminating children because they are not what their parents wanted?[94]

So how do we get ourselves out? How do we get out of a culture of relativism that fully legitimizes the economic-technocratic model, the primary cause of the environmental disaster? *Laudato Si'* offers skepticism about a purely technical solution, derived from economics.

Here too, it should always be kept in mind that "environmental protection cannot be assured solely on the basis of financial calculations of costs and benefits. The environment is one of those goods that cannot be adequately safeguarded or promoted by market forces." Once more, we need to reject a magical conception of the market, which would suggest that problems can be solved simply by an increase in the profits of companies or individuals. Is it realistic to hope that those who are obsessed with maximizing profits will stop to reflect on the environmental damage which they will leave behind for future generations? Where profits alone count, there can be no thinking about the rhythms of nature, its phases of decay and regeneration, or the complexity of ecosystems which may be gravely upset by human intervention. Moreover, biodiversity is considered at most a deposit of economic resources available for exploitation, with no serious thought for the real value of things, their significance for persons and cultures, or the concerns and needs of the poor.[95]

94. Pope Francis, *Laudato Si'*, 123.
95. Pope Francis, *Laudato Si'*, 190.

The economy, guided by the principle of profit maximization, is unable to avoid "an instrumental way of reasoning."[96] *Laudato Si'* responds to the criticism of positivism by Max Horkheimer and the Frankfurt school.[97] The alternative that the encyclical proposes, with respect to the hegemony of technical-economic positivism, is two-part: the recovery of the primacy of politics over the economy and the reprioritizing of the aesthetic model over the functionalist one. "Politics must not be subject to the economy, nor should the economy be subject to the dictates of an efficiency-driven paradigm of technocracy."[98]

To this end, a policy is needed that is capable of "a new, integral and interdisciplinary approach"[99] to problems, one that includes a synthetic notion of "common good" in which human ecology has an authentic place.[100] This policy must be guided by an anthropology and a social philosophy governed by the four principles noted in both *Evangelii Gaudium* and *Laudato Si'*: "realities are more important than ideas,"[101] "the whole is greater than the part,"[102] "time is greater than space,"[103] "unity is greater than conflict."[104] An integral politics must place the human person—including the person's habitat—at the center. Dominion of the world includes care for the world. The exploitation of the land has limits beyond which the destruction of the environment is irreversible. This implies moving beyond the dominant ethical vision to gain a new image of the human.

The drama of the present moment is made worse by the lack of awareness that the restoration of the environment requires the restoration of the person. The persistence of the myth of progress, which paradoxically renders liberal conservatives enemies of ecology, leads us to think that solutions to environmental problems will magically appear, that the atmosphere and the ecosystem of the planet can tolerate everything, that there is no limit, that climate change is physiological. Technocratic pro-

96. Pope Francis, *Laudato Si'*, 195.

97. See Max Horkheimer, *Eclipse of Reason* (New York: Oxford University Press, 1947).

98. Pope Francis, *Laudato Si'*, 189.

99. Pope Francis, *Laudato Si'*, 197.

100. On the notion of the common good, see Pope Francis, *Laudato Si'*, 156–59.

101. Pope Francis, *Laudato Si'*, 110.

102. Pope Francis, *Laudato Si'*, 141.

103. Pope Francis, *Laudato Si'*, 178.

104. Pope Francis, *Laudato Si'*, 198. On the meaning of the principles in Bergoglio's polar model or system, see Borghesi, *The Mind of Pope Francis*, 107–22.

gressivism thus conceals economic-financial interests and prevents the anthropological problem from being considered. For Francis, "there can be no renewal of our relationship with nature without a renewal of humanity itself. There can be no ecology without an adequate anthropology."[105]

This means that respect for natural conditions implies, first of all, a new relationality that makes it possible to overcome the technocratic mentality and ideology. "If the present ecological crisis is one small sign of the ethical, cultural and spiritual crisis of modernity, we cannot presume to heal our relationship with nature and the environment without healing all fundamental human relationships."[106] The way forward for such a restoration is a rediscovering of beauty, an aesthetic revolution. Attentive to the lesson of the great theologian Hans Urs von Balthasar, the author of the monumental *Glory of the Lord*, Pope Francis declares, citing John Paul II, "In this regard, 'the relationship between a good aesthetic education and the maintenance of a healthy environment cannot be overlooked.' By learning to see and appreciate beauty, we learn to reject self-interested pragmatism. If someone has not learned to stop and admire something beautiful, we should not be surprised if he or she treats everything as an object to be used and abused without scruple."[107]

An aesthetic revolution would allow an escape from the technocratic model. Beauty indicates a higher functionality than the restricted, instrumental one that is governed solely by the law of income and earnings. On the one hand, beauty opens up to the sense of mystery, of thanksgiving, as can be seen in St. Francis of Assisi's "Canticle of Brother Sun," and on the other hand it opens us to authentic human relationships with one another and with nature. With use, there is also respect; with dominion, also gratitude. A different logic comes into play here that downsizes the technocratic mindset and makes it possible to place technology and economics at the service of a politics of the common good. It is at the service of a project that can reconcile city and countryside, the North and the South, the center of the metropolis and the miserable, polluted, dangerous peripheries. In *Laudato Si'*, the pope takes up again a passage he originally offered in *Evangelii Gaudium*: "How beautiful those cities which overcome paralyzing mistrust, integrate those who are different

---

105. Pope Francis, *Laudato Si'*, 118.
106. Pope Francis, *Laudato Si'*, 119.
107. Pope Francis, *Laudato Si'*, 215.

and make this very integration a new factor of development! How attractive are those cities which, even in their architectural design, are full of spaces which connect, relate and favor the recognition of others!"[108]

Beauty favors integration, relationship, recognition. Technique can make a powerful contribution, unheard of in the past, to such beauty. To this end, it is necessary to start from experiences that bring together groups of people who share a particular region. We need *a communitarian environmental revolution.*

> Nevertheless, self-improvement on the part of individuals will not by itself remedy the extremely complex situation facing our world today. Isolated individuals can lose their ability and freedom to escape the utilitarian mindset, and end up prey to an unethical consumerism bereft of social or ecological awareness. Social problems must be addressed by community networks and not simply by the sum of individual good deeds. This task "will make such tremendous demands of man that he could never achieve it by individual initiative or even by the united effort of men bred in an individualistic way. The work of dominating the world calls for a union of skills and a unity of achievement that can only grow from quite a different attitude." The ecological conversion needed to bring about lasting change is also a community conversion.[109]

It is in this context that the church has an important contribution to offer. As Massimo Faggioli has observed,

> Francis is a radical social Catholic. He defends a way of life and a social system that is threatened by what he calls in the encyclical *Laudato si'* "the technocratic paradigm."
>
> He is also a progressive Catholic, in the sense that he has no nostalgia for an idealized past. Yet there is an anti-modern mindset in him typical of Catholic thinkers of the 1930s (the decade he was born), such as Romano Guardini whom he quotes more than once in *Laudato si'*.
>
> The fact that some progressive Catholics are reluctant to abolish the established Church model is connected to the role the Church plays within the "technocratic paradigm" (to use the pope's phrase). For instance, the established Church is one of the few remaining bastions against the de-

---

108. Pope Francis, *Evangelii Gaudium*, 210, and *Laudato Si'*, 152.

109. Pope Francis, *Laudato Si'*, 219. The quotation is from Guardini, *The End of the Modern World*.

struction of the welfare state, "turbo capitalism" and the radical individu-
alization of human life.[110]

Polarity versus Polarization: *Fratelli Tutti*: A New *Pacem in Terris*

Five years after *Laudato Si'*, on October 3, 2020, Francis released *Fratelli Tutti*, an encyclical letter "On Fraternity and Social Friendship." In spirit, it is a continuation of the Abu Dhabi declaration, a document on human fraternity signed jointly by the pope and Grand Imam Ahmad AlTayyeb the previous year.[111] Traditionalists mostly didn't read the encyclical; they stopped at the title. For the Catholic right, *fraternity* is an equivocal term, reminiscent of the French Revolution and leftist utopias. Their reactions were harsh. One that stood out was that of Ettore Gotti Tedeschi. This was not surprising; the former head of the Vatican Bank never missed an opportunity to pummel the pope. Gotti Tedeschi is a proud champion of capitalism, professes an unshakable faith in the free market, and is, at the same time, a rigorist in the defense of "nonnegotiable values." Increasing the birth rate is the only solution he sees for healing the cracks of capitalism; otherwise, the poor must simply trust in the generosity of the rich. Gotti Tedeschi offers his little lesson of irony without bothering to give any attention to the content of the text that he may not even have read.

> Recalling the values of St. Thomas More's utopia (placed there by the author with evident satire), I approached the due reading of the encyclical with the critical spirit of those who find themselves having to interpret utopias proposed as television commercials. Five hundred years after the publication of *Utopia* (1516), the world and the church have changed a little, but what is significant in this context is that until yesterday the church had to deal only with consciences and not with economics and politics, while today— this encyclical is an example—it must deal with economics and politics and not so much with consciences. But since economics is not a science, when used politically for ideological reasons, it invents socio-economic utopias.

---

110. Massimo Faggioli, "The Established Church Dilemma," *La Croix International*, February 18, 2016, https://international.la-croix.com/news/world/the-established-church-dilemma/2655.

111. "Document on Human Fraternity for World Peace and Living Together," February 4, 2019, https://www.vatican.va/content/francesco/en/travels/2019/outside/documents/papa-francesco_20190204_documento-fratellanza-umana.html.

But if these utopias are sponsored by the Moral Authority and become the magisterium of the church, they risk being transformed into "heresies." That *Fratelli Tutti* could risk suffering this fate seems to me suspicious. It comes across as a television commercial, complete with testimonials from those who inspired it. Apart from St. Francis (who is used here, rather than imitated), the testimonials are from prestigious personalities who have fought for civil rights against oppression: Desmond Tutu, Gandhi, Martin Luther King. And they have already been used for commercials: we remember the Telecom commercials where Gandhi was used as a peacemaker or the Fiat-Chrysler commercials with Martin Luther King in the Atlanta sermon. Here they are chosen as witnesses of solidarity, brotherhood, equality, peace.[112]

Gotti Tedeschi refers here to the notable figures that the encyclical points to as models of fraternity. He avoids mentioning the last one, Charles de Foucauld, perhaps because he is a Catholic (and beatified) and his presence was not convenient to Gotti Tedeschi's thesis. Whatever the misplaced irony, the criticism demonstrated the mediocrity of Francis's critics.[113]

---

112. Ettore Gotti Tedeschi, "L'Enciclica 'Fratelli Tutti' più che a san Francesco sembra ispirarsi a san Tommaso Moro (Utopia)," Stilum Curiae blog, October 9, 2020, https://www.marcotosatti.com/2020/10/09/fratelli-tutti-non-san-francesco-ma-utopia-di-tommaso-moro/.

113. We also note Riccardo Cascioli, editor of La Nuova Bussola Quotidiana, who wrote in his online magazine:

For Pope Francis, the ultimate goal of every person, Christians in spirit, is to build universal fraternity; human reason alone is enough to conceive it and recognize the tools necessary to make it happen. And religions, all without distinction, must contribute to this because it is for this purpose, all without distinction, they are called. For St. John Paul II, however, only Christ was an exhaustive answer to the questions of humanity and of peoples; the whole world is under his power, and only He has "the words of eternal life." The vision that Pope Francis expresses in *Fratelli Tutti* is not an articulation of that certainty expressed by Saint John Paul II; it is clearly another thing. It is quite in tune with the thinking that inspires *Our Global Neighborhood,* the Report of the UN Commission on Global Governance, published in 1995, which outlines a global ethic for a peaceful and fraternal world. The inspiration and founding values of this global ethics are clearly comparable to those expressed in *Fratelli Tutti.* It is a socialist and utopian manifesto that claims to include every "country, race, religion, culture, language, lifestyle." (Riccardo Cascioli, "*Fratelli Tutti*: visione opposta a Giovanni Paolo II," La Nuova Bussola Quotidiana, October 6, 2020)

Cascioli's criticisms of Pope Francis are identical to those levelled at Pope John Paul II on October 27, 1986, on the occasion of the great meeting for the cause of peace with

Among these was also Archbishop Viganò, who was concerned above all by the affirmation that "we, the believers of the different religions, know that our witness to God benefits our societies."[114] This proposition, according to the pope's inquisitor, "is erroneous and heretical, because it places the divine revelation of the living and true God on the same level as 'prostitution,' as Sacred Scripture calls false religions. Claiming that the presence of false religions is 'good for our societies' is equally heretical, because it not only offends the Majesty of God, but also legitimizes the action of dissidents, attributing to it a merit rather than responsibility for the damnation of souls and for the wars of religion waged against the church of Christ by heretics, Mohammedans, and idolaters."[115]

Viganò insisted that *Fratelli Tutti*, by recognizing the value of religions, denies "the sovereign rights of Jesus Christ," commits the sin of indifferentism, and repeats the erroneous teaching of Vatican II, the ecumenical council that Viganò rejects wholly. Two documents of the council are unacceptable for the archbishop: *Nostra Aetate*, on dialogue with non-Christian religions, and *Dignitatis Humanae*, on religious freedom. "The reference to the conciliar document *Nostra Aetate* is the confirmation of the ideological connection of Bergoglian heretical thought with the premises set by Vatican II. In false religions there is nothing true and holy 'ex se,' since any elements of truth that they may retain are in any case usurped and used to conceal the error and make it more harmful. No respect can be accorded to false religions, whose precepts and doctrines must be rejected and rejected in their entirety."[116]

Viganò evidently has in mind the confessional states of the past, those of the sixteenth and seventeenth centuries in particular, where Catholics or Protestants were guaranteed civil rights denied to others. "Religious freedom for believers of all religions is not a human right but an abuse lacking any theological foundation or even any philosophical or logical foundation. This concept of religious freedom—which replaces the freedom of the one Religion, the 'freedom of the Catholic Religion to exercise

---

representatives of various Christian confessions and world religions. Then, too, the custodians of orthodoxy did not fail to accuse the pope of syncretism and a break with tradition.

114. Pope Francis, *Fratelli Tutti*, 274.

115. Marco Tosatti, "Viganò e l'Enciclica: la fratellanza contro Dio è blasfema," Stilum Curiae blog, October 7, 2020.

116. Tosatti, "Viganò e l'Enciclica."

its mission,' and the 'freedom of the faithful to join the Catholic Church without hindrance from the State,' with the license to join any creed, regardless of its credibility and belief (which must be believed)—is heretical and irreconcilable with the immutable doctrine of the church. Human beings have no right to make mistakes."[117]

Viganò's criticisms belong, obviously, to reactionary traditionalism, which, in its visionary and apocalyptic extremism, places itself outside the church. His comments involve the rejection not only of Pope Francis but of all his predecessors from John XXIII onward. It is the whole church that, from the council onward, would have derogated from orthodoxy. Only the archbishop remains to defend the right doctrine.

The criticisms of *Fratelli Tutti* come, then, from different fronts. They range from the capitalist conservatism of Gotti Tedeschi to the reactionary position of Viganò to the pure liberalism embodied by Loris Zanatta. According to the latter, "the pope always writes the same things, for which I always criticize him."[118] Bergoglio, an antiliberal, is close to Rousseau. Zanatta, ultraliberal, declares himself the ideal disciple of Karl Popper, like Marcello Pera. He loves the individual, difference; he abhors harmony and all that is communal. For Zanatta, it is not that Bergoglio is a Communist but rather that Communism is, in its roots, Christian. "Enough with this story of the Communist pope; it is the Latin Communism of America and Europe that is a Christian utopia, a pre-liberal idea of Christianity. More than Marx, his father is the Counter-Reformation. Therefore Catho-Communism is the hegemonic trait of our culture."[119] For Zanatta's pure Anglo-Saxon liberalism, every Catholic is potentially a Catho-Communist and Bergoglio is no exception.

But there are two basic criticisms that, in mocking and disrespectful language, the illustrious professor addresses to the encyclical and its author. The first is that the pope is a "populist" and the criticisms of populism offered in *Fratelli Tutti* are only a diversion. "It matters little that the encyclical gives an arrogant lecture on 'populism' by trivializing the concept: its distinction between 'popularism' and 'populism' is a worn-out lexical trick."[120] Only the professor has the competence to deal with the question; the pope does not. The second criticism concerns the "Man-

117. Tosatti, "Viganò e l'Enciclica."
118. Loris Zanatta, "Manifesto populista," *Il Foglio*, October 17, 2020.
119. Zanatta, "Manifesto populista."
120. Zanatta, "Manifesto populista."

ichean" soul behind the encyclical: "The pope's sacralized idea of the people transforms the political dialectic of democracies into the religious war of populisms. Other than 'all brothers'!"[121] Thus in Zanatta's eyes, an encyclical created with the intention of reconciling a world divided by irremediable dialectics is in fact a Manichean document.[122]

The short sampling noted here indicates the nature of the criticism, which either stops at the title or generally avoids confronting the ideas offered by the text, highlighting only particular details. What is, it must be asked, the purpose of the encyclical? If *Evangelii Gaudium* is the manifesto of the pontificate and *Laudato Si'* the text on ecology and technocracy, *Fratelli Tutti* is the new *Pacem in Terris*, the encyclical that, like that of John XXIII, invites a divided and torn world to rediscover the spirit of fraternity and harmony. As the Italian journalist Luigi Accattoli wrote in his blog: "*Fratelli Tutti* arrives fifty-seven years after Pope Roncalli's *Pacem in Terris*, which was also addressed to 'all men of good will' . . . and offers the same call to unity of the human family—John XXIII to a world stuck in the enmity of the Cold War, Francis to a world torn apart by nationalisms and sovereignties, a third world war being conducted in little pieces."[123]

The observation could not be more correct. It allows us to situate the document in its correct perspective, which is not that of a philanthropic and optimistic irenicism but, rather, of a realism that does not give up hope. The context is one of shattered dreams.

> For decades, it seemed that the world had learned a lesson from its many wars and disasters and was slowly moving towards various forms of integration. For example, there was the dream of a united Europe, capable of acknowledging its shared roots and rejoicing in its rich diversity. We think

121. Zanatta, "Manifesto populista."

122. Previously Aldo Maria Valli took a position identical to Zanatta's. "It seems clear enough," Valli wrote, "that the notion of people in Bergoglio is romantic, so much so that the pope tends to perceive in the 'pueblo' a moral and cultural superiority. From this point of view, Zanatta argues, we can speak of a Manichean vision: on the one hand the people, always good and in any case virtuous, on the other the unjust and exploitative oligarchies. A simplification that, according to the professor, is typical of populisms, which always need an external enemy to justify themselves." Valli, "Il 'pueblo' secondo Francesco," Aldo Maria Valli blog, October 4, 2017. On Zanatta's article, see Guido Puccio, "Per una critica al manifesto contro 'Fratelli tutti,'" politicainsieme.com, October 10, 2020.

123. Luigi Accattoli, "Mia conferenza da remoto sull'enciclica 'Fratelli tutti'" (added in the comment section), Il blog di Luigi Accattoli, October 15, 2020, http://www.luigiaccattoli .it/blog/mia-conferenza-da-remoto-sullenciclica-fratelli-tutti/.

of "the firm conviction of the founders of the European Union, who envisioned a future based on the capacity to work together in bridging divisions and in fostering peace and fellowship between all the peoples of this continent." There was also a growing desire for integration in Latin America, and several steps were taken in this direction. In some countries and regions, attempts at reconciliation and rapprochement proved fruitful, while others showed great promise.

Our own days, however, seem to be showing signs of a certain regression. Ancient conflicts thought long buried are breaking out anew, while instances of a myopic, extremist, resentful and aggressive nationalism are on the rise. In some countries, a concept of popular and national unity influenced by various ideologies is creating new forms of selfishness and a loss of the social sense under the guise of defending national interests.[124]

It is this observation—and the pope's concern over a world that is dangerously shattered, from Europe to the United Nations; marked by profound economic-political antagonisms between America, China, Russia, Turkey; torn apart by populist and religious antagonisms—that inspired the encyclical's name. The church, troubled by this drift, by the crumbling of the international order since September 11, 2001, cannot stand by and watch. Hence Francis's idea of extending the design of the great Abu Dhabi event in 2019 to the whole world: "I offer this social Encyclical as a modest contribution to continued reflection, in the hope that in the face of present-day attempts to eliminate or ignore others, we may prove capable of responding with a new vision of fraternity and social friendship that will not remain at the level of words. Although I have written it from the Christian convictions that inspire and sustain me, I have sought to make this reflection an invitation to dialogue among all people of good will."[125] This is not a utopia but an idea rooted in the Gospel.

The Church esteems the ways in which God works in other religions, and "rejects nothing of what is true and holy in these religions. She has a high regard for their manner of life and conduct, their precepts and doctrines which . . . often reflect a ray of that truth which enlightens all men and women." Yet we Christians are very much aware that "if the music of the Gospel ceases to resonate in our very being, we will lose the joy born of

---

124. Pope Francis, *Fratelli Tutti*, 10–11.
125. Pope Francis, *Fratelli Tutti*, 6.

compassion, the tender love born of trust, the capacity for reconciliation that has its source in our knowledge that we have been forgiven and sent forth. If the music of the Gospel ceases to sound in our homes, our public squares, our workplaces, our political and financial life, then we will no longer hear the strains that challenge us to defend the dignity of every man and woman." Others drink from other sources. For us the wellspring of human dignity and fraternity is in the Gospel of Jesus Christ. From it, there arises, "for Christian thought and for the action of the Church, the primacy given to relationship, to the encounter with the sacred mystery of the other, to universal communion with the entire human family, as a vocation of all."[126]

Francis is clear, in *Fratelli Tutti*, about the Christian nature of his message. The entire second chapter, from which the model of fraternity comes, is taken from the Gospel parable of the Good Samaritan. Paragraph 273 quotes at length what Francis calls the "memorable statement" from Pope John Paul II's *Centesimus Annus*:

> If there is no transcendent truth, in obedience to which man achieves his full identity, then there is no sure principle for guaranteeing just relations between people. Their self-interest as a class, group or nation would inevitably set them in opposition to one another. If one does not acknowledge transcendent truth, then the force of power takes over, and each person tends to make full use of the means at his disposal in order to impose his own interests or his own opinion, with no regard for the rights of others. . . . The root of modern totalitarianism is to be found in the denial of the transcendent dignity of the human person who, as the visible image of the invisible God, is therefore by his very nature the subject of rights that no one may violate—no individual, group, class, nation or state. Not even the majority of the social body may violate these rights, by going against the minority.[127]

Fratelli Tutti starts from the ethical and anthropological consequences of the Christian presence in history, capable of enhancing every seed of true humanity present in the religious traditions of peoples, drawing them toward a commitment to peace and fraternity. It is a dream that, in

---

126. Pope Francis, *Fratelli Tutti*, 277.
127. Pope Francis, *Fratelli Tutti*, 273, quoting Pope John Paul II, *Centesimus Annus*, 44.

the face of the prevailing theological-political Manichaeism, consciously goes against the tide. The accusations against the pope of supporting the powers of the world are, from this point of view, laughable. Zanatta recognizes this in his own way when he writes: "If they were smarter, instead of making fools of themselves by portraying the pope as the globalist Antichrist, the sovereigntists would give him their license: like them, he defends the 'culture' of the 'people' from 'corruption.' It's just that he invokes a different 'people' than theirs."[128]

Bergoglio's is certainly not the sovereigntist conception of the people, and yet it is not globalist in the sense of globalization. In *Fratelli Tutti*, he writes:

> "Opening up to the world" is an expression that has been co-opted by the economic and financial sector and is now used exclusively of openness to foreign interests or to the freedom of economic powers to invest without obstacles or complications in all countries. Local conflicts and disregard for the common good are exploited by the global economy in order to impose a single cultural model. This culture unifies the world, but divides persons and nations, for "as society becomes ever more globalized, it makes us neighbors, but does not make us brothers." We are more alone than ever in an increasingly standardized and depersonalized world that promotes individual interests and weakens the communitarian dimension of life. Indeed, there are markets where individuals become mere consumers or bystanders. As a rule, the advance of this kind of globalism strengthens the identity of the more powerful, who can protect themselves, but it tends to diminish the identity of the weaker and poorer regions, making them more vulnerable and dependent. In this way, political life becomes increasingly fragile in the face of transnational economic powers that operate with the principle of "divide and conquer."[129]

Francis is not a globalist, as many of his opponents portray him, but neither is he the sovereigntist-populist opposed by the Catholic neoconservatives and liberals. The dialectic between globalization and populism is the necessary outcome of the struggle between two abstract poles,

---

128. Zanatta, "Manifesto populista."

129. Pope Francis, *Fratelli Tutti*, 12. [Translator's note: Here I have corrected the Vatican's English translation, rendering the Italian verb *massificato* as "standardized and depersonalized" rather than "massified." (The Vatican website offers no Latin-language *editio typica* of the document for reference.)]

between two opposing sides whose very identities are grounded in their mutual antagonism. To understand Bergoglio's actual position—an effort from which his critics spare themselves—it is necessary to go to the sources of his thought, sources whose presence is felt throughout all of his documents. In *Evangelii Gaudium*, Francis writes:

> Progress in building a people in peace, justice and fraternity depends on four principles related to constant tensions present in every social reality. These derive from the pillars of the Church's social doctrine, which serve as "primary and fundamental parameters of reference for interpreting and evaluating social phenomena." In their light I would now like to set forth these four specific principles which can guide the development of life in society and the building of a people where differences are harmonized within a shared pursuit. I do so out of the conviction that their application can be a genuine path to peace within each nation and in the entire world.[130]

These four principles state: time is superior to space; unity prevails over conflict: realities are more important than ideas; the whole is superior to the part. Of them, two—the second and the fourth—have a prominent place in *Fratelli Tutti*. Both revolve around the theme of "communion amid disagreement":[131]

> In this way it becomes possible to build communion amid disagreement, but this can only be achieved by those great persons who are willing to go beyond the surface of the conflict and to see others in their deepest dignity. This requires acknowledging a principle indispensable to the building of friendship in society: namely, that *unity is greater than conflict*. Solidarity, in its deepest and most challenging sense, thus becomes a way of making history in a life setting where conflicts, tensions and oppositions can achieve a diversified and life-giving unity. This is not to opt for a kind of syncretism, or for the absorption of one into the other, but rather for a resolution which takes place on a higher plane and preserves what is valid and useful on both sides.[132]

Here resounds, unequivocally, the lesson of Romano Guardini, the subject of the future pope's 1986 doctoral thesis in Frankfurt. Guardini's

---

130. Pope Francis, *Evangelii Gaudium*, 221.
131. Pope Francis, *Evangelii Gaudium*, 228.
132. Pope Francis, *Evangelii Gaudium*, 221 (emphasis mine).

polar anthropology, explained in his 1925 book *Der Gegensatz: Versuche zu einer Philosophie der Lebendig-Konkreten* (Opposition: attempts in a philosophy of the living and concrete), is at the center of Bergoglio's philosophical-theological thought. The pope explains this in an interview with Fr. Spadaro:

> Opposition opens a path, a way forward. Speaking generally, I have to say that I love oppositions. Romano Guardini helped me with his book *Der Gegensatz*, which was important to me. He spoke of a polar opposition in which the two opposites are not annulled. One pole does not destroy the other. There is no contradiction and no identity. For him, opposition is resolved at a higher level. In such a solution, however, the polar tension remains. The tension remains; it is not cancelled out. The limits are overcome, not negated. Oppositions are helpful. Human life is structured in an oppositional form. And we see this happening now in the church as well. The tensions are not necessarily resolved and ironed out; they are not like contradictions.[133]

Life is opposition, and opposition is fruitful. For this reason,

> Here our model is not the sphere, which is no greater than its parts, where every point is equidistant from the center, and there are no differences between them. Instead, it is the polyhedron, which reflects the convergence of all its parts, each of which preserves its distinctiveness. Pastoral and political activity alike seek to gather in this polyhedron the best of each. There is a place for the poor and their culture, their aspirations and their potential. Even people who can be considered dubious on account of their errors have something to offer which must not be overlooked. It is the convergence of peoples who, within the universal order, maintain their own individuality; it is the sum total of persons within a society which pursues the common good, which truly has a place for everyone.[134]

The image of the polyhedron is at the center of *Fratelli Tutti*'s conceptual framework. It corrects the perspective of

---

133. Antonio Spadaro, "Le orme di un pastore: Una conversazione con Papa Francesco," introduction to Jorge Mario Bergoglio–Pope Francis, *Nei tuoi è occhi la mia parola: Omelie e discorsi di Buenos Aires 1999–2013* (Milan: Rizzoli, 2016), xix.

134. Pope Francis, *Evangelii Gaudium*, 236.

an authoritarian and abstract universalism, devised or planned by a small group and presented as an ideal for the sake of levelling, dominating and plundering. One model of globalization in fact "consciously aims at a one-dimensional uniformity and seeks to eliminate all differences and traditions in a superficial quest for unity. . . . If a certain kind of globalization claims to make everyone uniform, to level everyone out, that globalization destroys the rich gifts and uniqueness of each person and each people." This false universalism ends up depriving the world of its various colors, its beauty and, ultimately, its humanity. For "the future is not monochrome; if we are courageous, we can contemplate it in all the variety and diversity of what each individual person has to offer. How much our human family needs to learn to live together in harmony and peace, without all of us having to be the same!"[135]

For Francis,

Just as there can be no dialogue with "others" without a sense of our own identity, so there can be no openness between peoples except on the basis of love for one's own land, one's own people, one's own cultural roots. I cannot truly encounter another unless I stand on firm foundations, for it is on the basis of these that I can accept the gift the other brings and in turn offer an authentic gift of my own. I can welcome others who are different, and value the unique contribution they have to make, only if I am firmly rooted in my own people and culture. Everyone loves and cares for his or her native land and village, just as they love and care for their home and are personally responsible for its upkeep. The common good likewise requires that we protect and love our native land. Otherwise, the consequences of a disaster in one country will end up affecting the entire planet. All this brings out the positive meaning of the right to property: I care for and cultivate something that I possess, in such a way that it can contribute to the good of all.[136]

Rootedness, belonging, and ownership are not evil. They configure the identity and personality, the character of individuals and peoples. However, they cannot withdraw and celebrate themselves in an alleged absoluteness. Because "universal does not necessarily mean bland, uniform and standardized, based on a single prevailing cultural model, for this

135. Pope Francis, *Fratelli Tutti*, 100.
136. Pope Francis, *Fratelli Tutti*, 143.

will ultimately lead to the loss of a rich palette of shades and colors, and result in utter monotony," it is clear that the right approach is "a polyhedron, in which the value of each individual is respected, where '*the whole is greater than the part, but it is also greater than the sum of its parts.*'"[137] This is the fourth principle that governs Francis's social doctrine. The polyhedron represents a model of integration between the particular and the universal where the totality is made up of the parts and does not dissolve them in their specificity. This idea of totality corrects the localistic drift, the particularism that rejects all integration, ethnic and ideological nationalism.

> There is a kind of "local" narcissism unrelated to a healthy love of one's own people and culture. It is born of a certain insecurity and fear of the other that leads to rejection and the desire to erect walls for self-defense. Yet it is impossible to be "local" in a healthy way without being sincerely open to the universal, without feeling challenged by what is happening in other places, without openness to enrichment by other cultures, and without solidarity and concern for the tragedies affecting other peoples. A "local narcissism" instead frets over a limited number of ideas, customs and forms of security; incapable of admiring the vast potential and beauty offered by the larger world, it lacks an authentic and generous spirit of solidarity. Life on the local level thus becomes less and less welcoming, people less open to complementarity. Its possibilities for development narrow; it grows weary and infirm. A healthy culture, on the other hand, is open and welcoming by its very nature; indeed, "a culture without universal values is not truly a culture."[138]

Faced with one-sided perspectives destined to sink into false polarizations, the model offered by Francis is one of integration and synthesis.

> In fact, a healthy openness never threatens one's own identity. A living culture, enriched by elements from other places, does not import a mere carbon copy of those new elements, but integrates them in its own unique way. The result is a new synthesis that is ultimately beneficial to all, since the original culture itself ends up being nourished. That is why I have urged indigenous peoples to cherish their roots and their ancestral cultures. At

---

137. Pope Francis, *Fratelli Tutti*, 144–45 (emphasis mine). See also *Fratelli Tutti*, 215.
138. Pope Francis, *Fratelli Tutti*, 146.

the same time, though, I have wanted to stress that I have no intention of proposing "a completely enclosed, a-historic, static 'indigenism' that would reject any kind of blending (*mestizaje*)." For "our own cultural identity is strengthened and enriched as a result of dialogue with those unlike ourselves. Nor is our authentic identity preserved by an impoverished isolation." The world grows and is filled with new beauty, thanks to the successive syntheses produced between cultures that are open and free of any form of cultural imposition.[139]

The true dialectic is the antinomic one, according to which opposites relate to one another in a polar tension, not an exclusionary, Manichean one.

It should be kept in mind that "an innate tension exists between globalization and localization. We need to pay attention to the global so as to avoid narrowness and banality. Yet we also need to look to the local, which keeps our feet on the ground. Together, the two prevent us from falling into one of two extremes. In the first, people get caught up in an abstract, globalized universe. . . . In the other, they turn into a museum of local folklore, a world apart, doomed to doing the same things over and over, incapable of being challenged by novelty or appreciating the beauty which God bestows beyond their borders." We need to have a global outlook to save ourselves from petty provincialism. When our house stops being a home and starts to become an enclosure, a cell, then the global comes to our rescue, like a "final cause" that draws us towards our fulfilment. At the same time, though, the local has to be eagerly embraced, for it possesses something that the global does not: it is capable of being a leaven, of bringing enrichment, of sparking mechanisms of subsidiarity. Universal fraternity and social friendship are thus two inseparable and equally vital poles in every society. To separate them would be to disfigure each and to create a dangerous polarization.[140]

Bergoglio's social philosophy is based on the idea of polarity. As long as this model is ignored or misunderstood, wild accusations about the globalist or populist pope are destined to continue. Polarity is the formula for peace, just as polarizations are the way of conflict. It is the formula of dialogue that always moves in the antinomy between identity and difference.

139. Pope Francis, *Fratelli Tutti*, 148.
140. Pope Francis, *Fratelli Tutti*, 142.

This is the same model proposed by the pope in his address to the Council of Europe in Strasbourg on November 25, 2014.

> The history of Europe might lead us to think somewhat naïvely of the continent as *bipolar*, or at most *tripolar* (as in the ancient conception of Rome-Byzantium-Moscow), and thus to interpret the present and to look to the future on the basis of this schema, which is a simplification born of pretentions to power.
>
> But this is not the case today, and we can legitimately speak of a "multipolar" Europe. Its tensions—whether constructive or divisive—are situated between multiple cultural, religious and political poles. Europe today confronts the challenge of "globalizing," but in a creative way, this multipolarity. Nor are cultures necessarily identified with individual countries: some countries have a variety of cultures and some cultures are expressed in a variety of countries. The same holds true for political, religious, and social aggregations.
>
> Creatively globalizing multipolarity, and I wish to stress this creativity, calls for striving to create a constructive harmony, one free of those pretensions to power which, while appearing from a pragmatic standpoint to make things easier, end up destroying the cultural and religious distinctiveness of peoples.
>
> To speak of European multipolarity is to speak of peoples which are born, grow and look to the future. The task of globalizing Europe's multipolarity cannot be conceived by appealing to the image of a sphere—in which all is equal and ordered, but proves reductive inasmuch as every point is equidistant from the center—but rather, by the image of a *polyhedron*, in which the harmonic unity of the whole preserves the particularity of each of the parts. Today Europe is multipolar in its relationships and its intentions; it is impossible to imagine or to build Europe without fully taking into account this *multipolar* reality.[141]

Multipolar globalization implies the process of integration between the particular and the universal—nations, states, peoples. These poles are dissociated today because the tension of the moment is the empty universalism of the market in conflict with the ideological communitarianism of peoples who feel threatened in their identity and in their culture.

---

141. Pope Francis, "Address to the Council of Europe," November 25, 2014, http://www.vatican.va/content/francesco/en/speeches/2014/november/documents/papa-francesco_20141125_strasburgo-consiglio-europa.html.

In the first case we see a philosophy of individualism that "does not make us more free, more equal, more fraternal. The mere sum of individual interests is not capable of generating a better world for the whole human family."[142] In the second case we run into a deformation of the category of *people*.

It is in Francis's correction of this deformation, in the fifth chapter of *Fratelli Tutti*, on "A Better Kind of Politics," that Francis's position becomes extraordinarily relevant. In dense and extremely rich paragraphs, the pope criticizes the two dominant models: the liberalism of the era of globalization and its populist reaction. This is where the attention of commentators, especially critics, should have been, but for the most part it was lost along the way. One of the accusations of both the Catholic neoconservatives and the exponents of liberal culture against the Argentine pope is that he is a "populist." The pope responds to these criticisms with *Fratelli Tutti* and his opposition to "an unhealthy 'populism.'"[143]

> In recent years, the words "populism" and "populist" have invaded the communications media and everyday conversation. As a result, they have lost whatever value they might have had, and have become another source of polarization in an already divided society. Efforts are made to classify entire peoples, groups, societies and governments as "populist" or not. Nowadays it has become impossible for someone to express a view on any subject without being categorized one way or the other, either to be unfairly discredited or to be praised to the skies. . . .
>
> Closed populist groups distort the word "people," since they are not talking about a true people. The concept of "people" is in fact open-ended. A living and dynamic people, a people with a future, is one constantly open to a new synthesis through its ability to welcome differences. In this way, it does not deny its proper identity, but is open to being mobilized, challenged, broadened and enriched by others, and thus to further growth and development.[144]

Due to the misunderstanding created by populist ideology, the very concept of *people* risks becoming meaningless. "The attempt to see populism

---

142. Pope Francis, *Fratelli Tutti*, 105.

143. Pope Francis, *Fratelli Tutti*, 159. The critique of populism, as distinct from a correct popularism, comes back in Pope Francis, *Let Us Dream*, 97–103.

144. Pope Francis, *Fratelli Tutti*, 156, 160.

as a key for interpreting social reality is problematic in another way: it disregards the legitimate meaning of the word 'people.' Any effort to remove this concept from common parlance could lead to the elimination of the very notion of democracy as 'government by the people.'"[145] It is therefore necessary to clarify what is meant by *people*. To answer, Francis returns to a definition he had used in the past. "'People' is not a logical category, nor is it a mystical category, if by that we mean that everything the people does is good, or that the people is an 'angelic' reality."[146] The people are not "pure" or perfect, as they are in the caricature that Zanatta attributes to Bergoglio. This is the romantic version of populism, certainly not Francis's, who in *Fratelli Tutti* responds, in turn, to the deformed version of the concept of *people* that marks the liberal vision.

> The concept of a "people," which naturally entails a positive view of community and cultural bonds, is usually rejected by individualistic liberal approaches, which view society as merely the sum of coexisting interests. One speaks of respect for freedom, but without roots in a shared narrative; in certain contexts, those who defend the rights of the most vulnerable members of society tend to be criticized as populists. The notion of a people is considered an abstract construct, something that does not really exist. But this is to create a needless dichotomy. Neither the notion of "people" nor that of "neighbor" can be considered purely abstract or romantic, in such a way that social organization, science and civic institutions can be rejected or treated with contempt.[147]

The category of *people* is *neither purely mythical nor purely romantic.* Francis is responding here to his critics, to those for whom the "Argentine" pope is a Peronist-populist. To clarify the question conceptually, he resorts to an essay by Paul Ricoeur, "The *Socius* and the Neighbor," included in his book *History and Truth*, where the great French philosopher writes, "Private life cannot exist unless it is protected by public order. A domestic hearth has no real warmth unless it is safeguarded by law, by a state of tranquility founded on law, and enjoys a minimum of wellbeing ensured by the division of labor, commercial exchange, social justice and

---

145. Pope Francis, *Fratelli Tutti*, 157.
146. In Spadaro, "Le orme di un pastore," xv.
147. Pope Francis, *Fratelli Tutti*, 163.

political citizenship."[148] Legality and ethics, morality and law, people and democratic institutions are the two poles of an antinomy. If Bergoglio's emphasis falls on the first pole, it is because the moral life of a people is a fundamental condition for its legality, and what is under discussion today, also following the moral relativism that the encyclical discusses extensively, is precisely the sense of belonging.[149]

Populisms represent the politically dangerous ideological deformation of a need that, in a society of lonely people, is no longer satisfied. This is what Zygmunt Bauman described with the notion of "liquid society."

---

148. Paul Ricoeur, *Histoire et verité* (Paris: Éditions du Seuil, 1967), 122, in Pope Francis, *Fratelli Tutti*, 164. (Eng. trans: *History and Truth*, trans. Charles A. Kelbley [Evanston, IL: Northwestern University Press, 2007].) Francis refers to Ricoeur's work previously, regarding the difference between "neighbors" and "associates" or "partners," in *Fratelli Tutti*, 102.

149. Francis writes,

The solution is not relativism. Under the guise of tolerance, relativism ultimately leaves the interpretation of moral values to those in power, to be defined as they see fit. "In the absence of objective truths or sound principles other than the satisfaction of our own desires and immediate need . . . we should not think that political efforts or the force of law will be sufficient. . . . When the culture itself is corrupt, and objective truth and universally valid principles are no longer upheld, then laws can only be seen as arbitrary impositions or obstacles to be avoided." . . . What is now happening, and drawing us into a perverse and barren way of thinking, is the reduction of ethics and politics to physics. Good and evil no longer exist in themselves; there is only a calculus of benefits and burdens. As a result of the displacement of moral reasoning, the law is no longer seen as reflecting a fundamental notion of justice but as mirroring notions currently in vogue. Breakdown ensues: everything is "leveled down" by a superficial bartered consensus. In the end, the law of the strongest prevails. (*Fratelli Tutti*, 206, 210 [internal quotation from *Laudato Si'*, 123])

Criticizing moral relativism, the document arrives at the affirmation, by reason, of "non-negotiable" values (n. 211).

That every human being possesses an inalienable dignity is a truth that corresponds to human nature apart from all cultural change. For this reason, human beings have the same inviolable dignity in every age of history and no one can consider himself or herself authorized by particular situations to deny this conviction or to act against it. The intellect can investigate the reality of things through reflection, experience and dialogue, and come to recognize in that reality, which transcends it, the basis of certain universal moral demands. . . . To agnostics, this foundation could prove sufficient to confer a solid and stable universal validity on basic and *non-negotiable* ethical principles that could serve to prevent further catastrophes. (*Fratelli Tutti*, 213–14 [emphasis mine])

Faced with a "liquid world," liberal capitalism is silent. Or, as in the case of Zanatta, it celebrates its individualistic attitude, the distance between people, the sovereign egoism of Max Stirner as though they were virtues. At the foundation of this satisfaction there is an unshakable trust in the ability of the economic "order" to turn the wheels of human passions in the direction of general well-being. It is at this level that Francis's critique of technocratic liberalism is aimed. *It is a theological criticism.* Liberal capitalism, in its classic Enlightenment version, ignores the reality of what Scripture calls "concupiscence." It believes in an autonomous natural order in which weakness and sin are irrelevant. Bergoglio's critique of "pure" capitalism does not depend on liberation theology or his being a Latin American "populist," but on a sound theological principle, the same that motivated David Schindler's criticisms of Michael Novak.

> My criticism of the technocratic paradigm involves more than simply thinking that if we control its excesses everything will be fine. The bigger risk does not come from specific objects, material realities or institutions, but from the way that they are used. It has to do with human weakness, the proclivity to selfishness that is part of what the Christian tradition refers to as "concupiscence": the human inclination to be concerned only with myself, my group, my own petty interests. Concupiscence is not a flaw limited to our own day. It has been present from the beginning of humanity, and has simply changed and taken on different forms down the ages, using whatever means each moment of history can provide. Concupiscence, however, can be overcome with the help of God.
>
> Education and upbringing, concern for others, a well-integrated view of life and spiritual growth: all these are essential for quality human relationships and for enabling society itself to react against injustices, aberrations and abuses of economic, technological, political and media power. Some liberal approaches ignore this factor of human weakness; they envisage a world that follows a determined order and is capable by itself of ensuring a bright future and providing solutions for every problem.[150]

Bergoglio's critique of capitalism is a critique of perfectionist liberalism, heir to the classical Enlightenment. It is a liberalism based on the economic theodicy of the market, trusting that reason triumphs over selfishness through the mechanism of "involuntary consequences." It is

---

150. Pope Francis, *Fratelli Tutti*, 166–67.

the optimistic liberalism criticized by the liberal Catholic Antonio Rosmini. In *Fratelli Tutti* the postulate of liberal economic theology—what Francis calls the "dogma of neoliberal faith"—is criticized starting from the democratic primacy of politics and ethics over economics.

> The marketplace, by itself, cannot resolve every problem, however much we are asked to believe this dogma of neoliberal faith. Whatever the challenge, this impoverished and repetitive school of thought always offers the same recipes. Neoliberalism simply reproduces itself by resorting to the magic theories of "spillover" or "trickle"—without using the name—as the only solution to societal problems. There is little appreciation of the fact that the alleged "spillover" does not resolve the inequality that gives rise to new forms of violence threatening the fabric of society. It is imperative to have a proactive economic policy directed at "promoting an economy that favors productive diversity and business creativity" and makes it possible for jobs to be created and not cut. Financial speculation fundamentally aimed at quick profit continues to wreak havoc. Indeed, "without internal forms of solidarity and mutual trust, the market cannot completely fulfil its proper economic function. And today this trust has ceased to exist." The story did not end the way it was meant to, and the dogmatic formulae of prevailing economic theory proved not to be infallible. The fragility of world systems in the face of the pandemic has demonstrated that not everything can be resolved by market freedom. It has also shown that, in addition to recovering a sound political life that is not subject to the dictates of finance, "we must put human dignity back at the center and on that pillar build the alternative social structures we need."[151]

This is one of the most direct passages of the encyclical, and it didn't fail to arouse the consternation of liberals and Catho-capitalists. As *Evangelii Gaudium* before it, it strikes at the heart of neoliberal optimism: the concept of "spillover," or as it is commonly referred to in English, trickle-down. *History, Francis says, is not over.* The allusion is clearly toward Francis Fukuyama's book, *The End of History and the Last Man*, published in 1992, a true manifesto of the era of globalization. At that time, Western neocapitalism, having triumphed over Communism, promised the end of history, that is, the end of conflicts and the advent of generalized

---

151. Pope Francis, *Fratelli Tutti*, 168.

prosperity.[152] In the years since then, humanity has had the war in the Balkans, 9/11, the wars in Iraq, Libya, Syria, the madness of ISIS, the exodus of millions of refugees, endless immigration, the financial crisis of 2008 and economic stagnation, the increase in social inequalities, the growing conflict between the great powers, the COVID-19 pandemic, and the multiple perils of the Trump administration. History is far from over, and it has revealed, repeatedly, the utopianism of economic theodicy. *Fratelli Tutti*, far from being a utopia, represents the rejection of utopia, the one that dominated the world scene after the fall of the Berlin Wall.

The "Great Americans": A Renewed Dialogue between the Church and the United States

Between the publication of *Laudato Si'* and *Fratelli Tutti*, Pope Francis made a pastoral visit to the United States in September 2015. The one whom critics defined as a "Latin American" pope was received with great enthusiasm by the American people and authorities. The visit was a success. With his simple style and simple words, the pope knew how to touch the right chords, avoiding the exploitation and politicization of his visit. The American journey was one of the most important and most difficult of his pontificate. Francis knew that he was not understood by a large part of the church and the public in the United States. His stance on

---

152. The "end of history" is more realistically understood as what *Fratelli Tutti* calls "the end of historical consciousness," one of the results of the "spherical" homogenization of victorious neocapitalism:

> As a result, there is a growing loss of the sense of history, which leads to even further breakup. A kind of "deconstructionism," whereby human freedom claims to create everything starting from zero, is making headway in today's culture. The one thing it leaves in its wake is the drive to limitless consumption and expressions of empty individualism. Concern about this led me to offer the young some advice. "If someone tells young people to ignore their history, to reject the experiences of their elders, to look down on the past and to look forward to a future that he himself holds out, doesn't it then become easy to draw them along so that they only do what he tells them? He needs the young to be shallow, uprooted and distrustful, so that they can trust only in his promises and act according to his plans. That is how various ideologies operate: they destroy (or deconstruct) all differences so that they can reign unopposed. To do so, however, they need young people who have no use for history, who spurn the spiritual and human riches inherited from past generations, and are ignorant of everything that came before them." (*Fratelli Tutti*, 13)

capitalism, care for the environment, concern for the poor and immigrants, and insistence on placing "nonnegotiable" values in a broader moral context were largely not understood. Yet the pope managed to build a bridge and establish a real dialogue with North America. He was not the anti-American, the populist of the South that American and European conservatives and liberals would like to make him out to be. He contrasted South America with North not according to the vulgate of populism, but in order to unite the two parts of a single continent.[153] Again the law of polarity distinguishes in order to unite.

This was a geopolitical perspective that was not easy to understand. His election, wrote the Italian journalist Massimo Franco, meant a shift

> from a German, twenty-four-carat, pro-US pope to a pontiff who, not recognizing his own empire, implicitly tended not to recognize any; who did not dwell on the now anachronistic borders of the Cold War, nor the division between East and West that had dominated relations between the West and the Soviet Union for half a century. An exponent of the Southern hemisphere of the world, of an 'extreme West' that was actually something else: a sort of alternative West to the known one, a southern West, and one not especially fond of a 'North' that was all capitalism, competition, and worship of wealth.[154]

153. Pope John Paul II made the same effort in the opening of his 1999 apostolic exhortation, *Ecclesia in America*:

> In Santo Domingo, when I first proposed a Special Assembly of the Synod, I remarked that "on the threshold of the third Christian millennium and at a time when many walls and ideological barriers have fallen, the Church feels absolutely duty-bound to bring into still deeper spiritual union the peoples who compose this great continent and also, prompted by the religious mission which is proper to the Church, to stir among these peoples a spirit of solidarity." I asked that the Special Assembly of the Synod of Bishops reflect on America as a single entity, by reason of all that is common to the peoples of the continent, including their shared Christian identity and their genuine attempt to strengthen the bonds of solidarity and communion between the different forms of the continent's rich cultural heritage. The decision to speak of "America" in the singular was an attempt to express not only the unity which in some way already exists, but also to point to that closer bond which the peoples of the continent seek and which the Church wishes to foster as part of her own mission, as she works to promote the communion of all in the Lord. (*Ecclesia in America*, 5)

154. Massimo Franco, *Imperi paralleli: Vaticano e Stati Uniti: due secoli di alleanza e conflitto* (Milan: Mondadori, 2015), 250.

During the 2015 trip, this orientation of the pope, this awareness of the "southwestern periphery," was particularly clear. Francis stopped first in Cuba, in Havana, before continuing on to the United States. Less than a year earlier, in December 2014, President Obama and Raúl Castro had reestablished diplomatic relations between Havana and Washington, thanks in part to Vatican mediation. Cuba was particularly dear to the pope. Franco wrote,

> There are at least three reasons. The first is that the Catholic Church never left the Caribbean island during the years of the Communist regime. Although persecuted and imprisoned, the Catholic minority, with the Cuban episcopate, held up. And "the Castro regime was the only one of all the world's Communist countries never to expel the pope's apostolic nuncio," recalled the former "historical" director of *La Civiltà Cattolica*, Gianpaolo Salvini; it even engaged in a simulacrum of dialogue. Among other things, the Vatican has always criticized the US embargo, considering it an excuse unintentionally provided to the dictatorship to cover up its mistakes and misdeeds.
>
> The second reason is Bergoglio's Latin American origin. One of his goals is to restore religious freedom throughout Latin America. Obama hailed the reopening of the channels with Cuba by saying in Spanish: "We are all Americans." Francis would say "We are all Christians," and Cuba is perceived by him as part of Christian Latin America. He reaped the seeds planted by his predecessors, John Paul II and Benedict XVI, who had visited the island repeatedly.[155]

Francis could reap those seeds because, in the eyes of Cubans, he did not present himself as a pro-Western and pro-Yankee pontiff. He appeared as a true "mediator," the one who could bring down "Latin America's Berlin Wall." As Massimo Franco wrote, "Such a collapse could inaugurate a détente throughout Latin America and give substance to that 'great homeland' that Francis sees as one of the geopolitical objectives of his papacy. Healing the Cuban wound means leaving behind decades in which the continent has suffered under the conflict between dictatorial regimes, often supported by the US in an anti-Communist function, and regimes influenced by Marxism. It's a fracture that has reverberated on the South

---

155. Franco, *Imperi paralleli*, 256. For a chronicle of the role of Vatican diplomacy toward Cuba, see Ivan Danyliuk, "La diplomazia Vaticana nel processo di uscita di Cuba dall'isolamento dal 1991 al 2015," *Oikonomia*, June 2020.

American Catholic Church, creating painful internal contrasts."[156] It was a big plan—one that was interrupted by the freezing of relations between Havana and Washington by the Trump administration.[157]

In 2015, then, the pope's Cuban stop came in the context of a détente in progress. Massimo Faggioli wrote at the time,

> The trip to Cuba for Pope Francis expresses a geopolitical and spiritual vision of America that is typical of the pontiff, but not totally new for the Catholic Church: that of the unity of the continent. This vision belongs to the Latin American heritage of Pope Bergoglio, who does not see in the United States a nation entrusted with a divine mission, as the "exceptionalism" dear to Americanist rhetoric (from which even US Catholicism is not immune) prefers. But the unitary vision of the continent is in contrast with the recent history of American Christianity, including Catholic, which has loosened many of the bonds that united the churches of the United States and the countries south of the artificial border between Mexico and the United States until the 1980s. In other words, Francis's choice to visit Cuba before arriving in the United States was the first message to an American Catholic Church whose leaders (clerical and otherwise) have become, in the last thirty years, more Americanist, more patriotic, and more conservative, and have narrowed the historical gap between Roman Catholicism and the mainstream.[158]

In addition to this first message, there was a second, this one addressed to bishops guided by a culture war mindset, a stance that was decidedly pro-life, meaning antiabortion, but removed from the context of broader social questions. But the disinterest in the social question went beyond Republican Catholics. It also concerned those of Democratic orientation. As Faggioli wrote,

> The relationship between Pope Francis and the American political class was a dialogue without real interlocutors. The case of Obama—a Christian who worked early in his career for Catholic social services in the Chicago of Cardinal Bernardin, an icon of progressive postconciliar Catholicism in the United States—is distinctive. But in the American political class, the old-school "social Catholics" (the generation of Ted Kennedy and Joe Biden) have practically disappeared, replaced by Democrat Catholics for

---

156. Franco, *Imperi paralleli*, 257.

157. On the contribution of Pope Francis to the détente between the United States and Cuba, see Scavo, *I nemici di Francesco*, 117–139.

158. Massimo Faggioli, "Bergoglio e le Americhe," *Italianieuropi*, December 16, 2015.

whom Catholicism is essentially a matter of family inheritance and not of religious or spiritual (and certainly not intellectual) practice, or by Republican Catholics inspired (at least publicly) by a religious devotion of past times but who embrace a political and social message that totally conflicts with the magisterium of Pope Francis on questions of economic and social ethics. Until now, the antiabortion platform has been the only article of political faith that, for conservative American Christianity and Catholicism, can be expressed in the public square.[159]

Despite the absence of interlocutors, the pope managed to find a way to make his mind known. Hence the success of the trip, which illustrates that the papal message avoids the ideological Manichaeism of which he is accused. "If in general terms [the pastoral visit to the United States] marked the introduction of a unitary vision of the continent in contrast to the recent history of American Christianity, with regard to the specificities of the American context, it allowed the pontiff to speak directly to American Catholics, bypassing the filter of the bishops—who are largely hostile to the new pope—and to promote the return to the North American Catholic scene of the great tradition of social Catholicism, supplanted in recent decades by pro-life, antiabortion battles and support for neoliberal economic culture."[160]

This "return" found expression in the two most significant moments of Francis's time in the United States. The first came on September 23, in an address by the pope to the American bishops. In it, as in the following day's address to Congress, the pope was keen to declare himself a son of America, of "all" America.

> I speak to you as the Bishop of Rome, called by God in old age, and from a land which is also American, to watch over the unity of the universal Church and to encourage in charity the journey of all the particular Churches toward ever greater knowledge, faith and love of Christ. Reading over your names, looking at your faces, knowing the extent of your churchmanship and conscious of the devotion which you have always shown for the Successor of Peter, I must tell you that I do not feel a stranger in your midst. I am a native of a land which is also vast, with great open ranges, a land which, like your own, received the faith from itinerant missionaries. I too know how hard it is to sow the Gospel among people from different

159. Faggioli, "Bergoglio e le Americhe."
160. Faggioli, "Bergoglio e le Americhe."

worlds, with hearts often hardened by the trials of a lengthy journey. Nor am I unaware of the efforts made over the years to build up the Church amid the prairies, mountains, cities and suburbs of a frequently inhospitable land, where frontiers are always provisional and easy answers do not always work. What does work is the combination of the epic struggle of the pioneers and the homely wisdom and endurance of the settlers. As one of your poets has put it, "strong and tireless wings" combined with the wisdom of one who "knows the mountains."[161]

It was a poetic and compelling opening. He was not a European or Asian who was visiting for the first time; he was a son of the same land who came from the most European and most "Western" capital of Latin America: Buenos Aires. He was a child of the Hispanic world that was a fundamental component of the United States's multipolar and multiethnic society, a Hispanic world that, though ignored by the nation's WASP historiography, held a prominent place in the very origins of the nation. Cities like San Francisco, Los Angeles, and San Diego owe their beginnings to Franciscan missionaries from Spain. Among these, a leading role was played by the friar Junípero Serra (1713–1784), whom Francis canonized in Washington, DC, on September 23. On that occasion, the pope remembered him as

one of those witnesses who testified to the joy of the Gospel in these lands, Father Junípero Serra. He was the embodiment of "a Church which goes forth," a Church which sets out to bring everywhere the reconciling tenderness of God. Junípero Serra left his native land and its way of life. He was excited about blazing trails, going forth to meet many people, learning and valuing their particular customs and ways of life. He learned how to bring to birth and nurture God's life in the faces of everyone he met; he made them his brothers and sisters. Junípero sought to defend the dignity of the native community, to protect it from those who had mistreated and abused it.[162]

Francis's decision to canonize Serra was not accidental. It was fully part of that project of reunification of the continent and of integration between

---

161. Pope Francis, "Meeting with the Bishops of the United States of America," September 23, 2015, https://www.vatican.va/content/francesco/en/speeches/2015/september /documents/papa-francesco_20150923_usa-vescovi.html. (The poem from which the pope quoted is Edgar Lee Masters's "Alexander Throckmorton" in *Spoon River Anthology*.)

162. Pope Francis, "Homily, Holy Mass and Canonization of Blessed Fr. Junípero Serra," September 23, 2015, https://www.vatican.va/content/francesco/en/homilies/2015 /documents/papa-francesco_20150923_usa-omelia-washington-dc.html.

the various components of North America. This required the inclusion of the Hispanic component in American history. Writes Massimo Franco:

> Francis's decision to canonize Friar Junípero Serra, an eighteenth-century Franciscan considered "the apostle of America," in Washington on September 23, 2015, meant rediscovering the roots of an American Catholicism that arrived in California before the great migrations of Irish, Italians, and Poles to the Atlantic coast; and in some way reconnecting this story to immigration from Latin American countries in recent decades. It is a sort of historical reminder that recognizes the very strong Hispanic presence in the North American continent, even prior to the British colonization. "Long before the arrival of the Mayflower and the foundation of the thirteen colonies on the Atlantic coast, there is a long history of Hispanic, Catholic, and missionary presence that begins in 1565 with the foundation of St. Augustine, the oldest point of occupation in the US," Guzmán Carriquiry recalled. He listed Florida, Louisiana, Texas, and Santa Fe as places and place names that make this influence clear.[163]

The canonization of Fr. Junípero Serra, whose statue stands in the US Capitol, had an inclusive symbolic value. It illustrated well what Francis meant when he told the American bishops that he did not feel like a foreigner. Latin Americans, Hispanic-Latinos/as, are part of the history of the United States. The relevance to current events was clear, and the

---

163. Franco, *Imperi paralleli*, 266–267. Guzmán Carriquiry Lecour, to whom Franco refers, is a Uruguayan lawyer, journalist, and professor. The words he cites here are from his address, "Fray Junípero Serra, apóstol de la California: Testimonio del santitad," Pontifical North American College, Rome, May 2, 2015. According to Franco,

> it was President John Fitzgerald Kennedy himself, in his book *A Nation of Immigrants*, who emphasized the removal of an entire phase of US history in the Southern states. "Unfortunately," wrote Kennedy, "there are too many Americans who believe that America was discovered in 1620 . . . and they forget the formidable adventure that took place in the sixteenth and early seventeenth centuries in the South and Southeast of the United States." It was a story written by the victors and for the victors, according to many Latin Americans. And it gave rise, in their opinion, to anti-Catholic prejudices in times of religious conflict and anti-Hispanic prejudices in times of struggle for European and world hegemony. "Prejudices that are slow to die," because a series of Californian lobbies sought to cast heavy shadows on that story. Junípero Serra, on the other hand, is considered an integral part of the forgotten Catholic missionary epic: this is why the state of California had a statue of him installed in the United States Capitol's National Statuary Hall, in Washington, DC, in 1931. (*Imperi paralleli*, 267)

pope made no attempt to hide it. This helps explain the disappointment engendered by the Trump administration's interruption of relations with Cuba, insistence on the construction of a wall between the United States and Mexico, and controversial immigration policies, all of which largely annulled the fruits of Francis's journey to America.

When he met with the American bishops during the trip, he did so in the context of a church troubled by the abuse crisis and the winds of secularization. For Francis, "The 'style' of our mission" must be one of "[stepping] back, away from the center," "not . . . concerned only with our concerns," to "[fleeing] the temptation of narcissism."[164] It was a matter of moving beyond a warrior mentality in which the notion of the enemy always plays an outsized role. He told them,

> Bishops need to be lucidly aware of the battle between light and darkness being fought in this world. Woe to us, however, if we make of the cross a banner of worldly struggles and fail to realize that the price of lasting victory is allowing ourselves to be wounded and consumed (Phil 2:1-11).
>
> We all know the anguish felt by the first Eleven, huddled together, assailed and overwhelmed by the fear of sheep scattered because the shepherd had been struck. But we also know that we have been given a spirit of courage and not of timidity. So we cannot let ourselves be paralyzed by fear.
>
> I know that you face many challenges, and that the field in which you sow is unyielding and that there is always the temptation to give in to fear, to lick one's wounds, to think back on bygone times and to devise harsh responses to fierce opposition.
>
> And yet we are promoters of the culture of encounter. We are living sacraments of the embrace between God's riches and our poverty. We are witnesses of the abasement and the condescension of God who anticipates in love our every response.
>
> Dialogue is our method, not as a shrewd strategy but out of fidelity to the One who never wearies of visiting the marketplace, even at the eleventh hour, to propose his offer of love (Mt 20:1-16).
>
> The path ahead, then, is dialogue among yourselves, dialogue in your presbyterates, dialogue with lay persons, dialogue with families, dialogue with society. I cannot ever tire of encouraging you to dialogue fearlessly.[165]

164. Pope Francis, "Meeting with the Bishops of the United States of America."
165. Pope Francis, "Meeting with the Bishops of the United States of America."

An approach marked by dialogue, however, does not mean ignoring "essential aspects of the Church's mission" such as defense of "the innocent victims of abortion, children who die of hunger or from bombings, immigrants who drown in the search for a better tomorrow, the elderly or the sick who are considered a burden, the victims of terrorism, wars, violence and drug trafficking, the environment devastated by man's predatory relationship with nature—at stake in all of this is the gift of God, of which we are noble stewards but not masters. It is wrong, then, to look the other way or to remain silent."[166]

The pope thus demonstrated that he did not reject the moral agenda that drives the US episcopate. Among the "essential aspects" to be protected were "the innocent victims of abortion." These were not words that he spoke lightly, simply a formula to satisfy the desire of the bishops. During his American trip, Francis was aware of the reactions of the US church to the Affordable Care Act, the law signed by President Obama in 2010 to extend health insurance to a substantial part of the population that had lacked access to it—in the minds of the bishops an excellent law, if not for rules that obliged employers to pay for policies that included costs for contraceptives. Those who did not were forced to pay high fines. For Catholic health facilities, this meant, in the opinion of some, a choice between the serious violation of the principle of freedom of conscience or the risk of ending their work. "Obamacare," as it was known, together with Obama's extremely liberal stance on abortion, established a deep gap between the US bishops and the presidency. By 2015, when Francis visited the United States, the waters had not calmed down at all.

The pope addressed the issue first of all with the President himself, in his meeting in the White House.

> Mr. President, together with their fellow citizens, American Catholics are committed to building a society which is truly tolerant and inclusive, to safeguarding the rights of individuals and communities, and to rejecting every form of unjust discrimination. With countless other people of good will, they are likewise concerned that efforts to build a just and wisely ordered society respect their deepest concerns and their right to religious liberty. That freedom remains one of America's most precious possessions. And, as my brothers, the United States Bishops, have reminded us, all are

166. Pope Francis, "Meeting with the Bishops of the United States of America."

called to be vigilant, precisely as good citizens, to preserve and defend that freedom from everything that would threaten or compromise it.[167]

The pope, together with "my brothers, the United States Bishops," reminded the president to ensure that the rights connected with religious freedom were respected. The appeal was clear in its meaning. Nonetheless, as often happens with Francis, the words are followed by gestures. On Wednesday, September 24, after the meeting with Obama, the pope made an unscheduled stop to visit the Little Sisters of the Poor in their nursing home near the Catholic University of America in Washington. The visit was high in symbolic significance. The Little Sisters were litigants in an appeal to the Supreme Court on the lawfulness of the Obamacare mandate.[168] The pope noted the significance of his visit on the return flight from Philadelphia.

> I can't foresee every possible case of conscientious objection. But yes, I can say conscientious objection is a right, and enters into every human right. It is a right, and if a person does now allow for conscientious objection, he or she is denying a right. Every legal system should provide for conscientious objection because it is a right, a human right. Otherwise, we would end up selecting between rights: "this right is good, this one less so." It is a human right. I am always moved when I read, and I have read it many times, when I read the "Chanson de Roland," when there were all these Moors lined up before the baptismal font, and they had to choose between baptism and the sword. They had to choose. They weren't permitted conscientious objection. It's a right and if we want to have peace, we have to respect all rights.[169]

The papal position was clear and in support of the legal actions brought by the American episcopate against Obamacare. On conscientious objection

167. Pope Francis, "Address of the Holy Father," September 23, 2015, https://www .vatican.va/content/francesco/en/speeches/2015/september/documents/papa -francesco_20150923_usa-benvenuto.html.

168. See Sarah Pulliam Bailey and Abby Ohlheiser, "Pope Francis Meets with Little Sisters of the Poor, Nuns Involved in an Obamacare Lawsuit," *Washington Post*, September 24, 2015. On the legal actions of the Sisters, see Elena Molinari, "Riforma sanitaria Usa" 'Noi, piccole suore contro il gigante Obama,'" *Avvenire*, January 6, 2014; Andrea Gagliarducci, "Stati Uniti, le Piccole Sorelle dei Poveri segnano un punto per l'obiezione di coscienza," ACI Stampa, July 14, 2020.

169. Pope Francis, "In-flight Press Conference," September 27, 2015, https://www .vatican.va/content/francesco/en/speeches/2015/september/documents/papa -francesco_20150927_usa-conferenza-stampa.html.

and the fight against the Obama administration's stance on abortion, the pope's agenda did not differ from that of the bishops. It simply broadened it, starting from an overall vision of the "common good" that was not limited to certain "nonnegotiable" values. It was an organic perspective that offered a way to go beyond the dialectic between progressives and conservatives, Democrats and Republicans, that divides the American church. It resembled the efforts of Cardinal Joseph L. Bernardin (1928–1996), archbishop of Chicago and president of the US bishops' conference, who, in an address at Georgetown University on September 9, 1996, shortly before his death, said:

> In proposing the consistent ethic over a decade ago, my purpose was to help create a dialogue about the full range of threats to life which modern society poses. I recognize the difference between the obligation to care for life and that to defend life against attack. I recognize that the moral failure to care for life adequately is different than the moral crime of taking an innocent life. But I was convinced—and still am firmly convinced—that the overriding moral need in our society is to cultivate a conviction that we must face *all* the major threats to life, not only one or two.[170]

Bernardin said that in his 1995 encyclical *Evangelium Vitae*, Pope John Paul II

> identified three issues—abortion, capital punishment, and euthanasia—in his sweeping critique of what he described as a creeping "culture of death." Here again, even within the Catholic tradition these three issues have not been simply collapsed into one question. Capital punishment has not been regarded in the past as "unjust killing" in the way abortion and euthanasia have been. But the power of the papal argument is that it helps us to see that, today, different times of taking life should be systematically related. Faced with a need to build a societal consensus that respects life, Catholic teaching has clearly moved to restrict the state's right to take life, even in instances previously approved.[171]

For this reason, the cardinal said,

---

170. Joseph L. Bernardin, "Reflections on the Public Life and Witness of the Church in U.S. Society and Culture," in *The Seamless Garment: Writings on the Consistent Ethic of Life*, Thomas A. Nairn, ed. (Maryknoll, NY: Orbis, 2008), 296. Video of the entire address is available at https://www.c-span.org/video/?74873-1/church-america.

171. Bernardin, "Reflections on the Public Life and Witness," 296.

After two decades of struggle over abortion, our society and our Church now face a double challenge to *defend* life even as we continue to pursue ways to *care* for and *nurture* it. I remain convinced that our witness will be more effective, more persuasive, and better equipped to address the moral challenge we face, if we witness to life across the spectrum of life from conception until natural death, calling our society to see the connection between caring for life and defending it.[172]

Taking a similar approach, Pope Francis was aware that in his relations with Obama, they could find agreement and harmony on some issues and not on others. He declined to adopt a Manichean stance of total opposition. In this respect, his approach differed from that of many members of the US episcopate, firm in their *damnatio* of Obama.[173] The

---

172. Bernardin, "Reflections on the Public Life and Witness," 297. On Cardinal Bernardin, see Gianfranco Brunelli, "Joseph L. Bernardin 1928–1996: Vita e morte di un vescovo americano," *Il Regno*, November 15, 1996.

173. The pope's approach was similar to that of theologian Cardinal Georges Cottier, OP, expressed after reading the address delivered by Obama at the University of Notre Dame on May 17, 2009. See Georges Cottier, "La politica, la morale e il peccato originale," *30 Giorni* 5 (2009), 32–37. Cottier's article prompted the criticism of the Archbishop of Denver. See Charles J. Chaput, "L'ascia del vescovo pellerossa," *Il Foglio*, October 6, 2009. On the honorary degree conferred upon Obama by Notre Dame, Sandro Magister wrote,

> the most drastic protests came from the leaders of neoconservative Catholic thought: Michael Novak, George Weigel, Deal Hudson. Their protest was aimed above all against the Vatican and *L'Osservatore Romano*, accused of excessive indulgence of Obama in spite of his bioethical positions contrary to the doctrine of the Church. . . . In *National Review*, George Weigel wrote that *L'Osservatore Romano* does not necessarily express the positions of the Holy See at all times but has nonetheless shown, from the way in which the matter has proceeded, the presence in the Vatican of a strong pro-Obama current, as well as "a sorry ignorance of recent American history" and of the attack carried out by the new president on the doctrine of the church in matters of life. Michael Novak, in the Italian daily newspaper *Liberal*, also accused *L'Osservatore Romano* of failing to understand the American reality, with the result that "it has placed itself alongside the abortionists and against the marginalized minority of practicing Catholics." The popes who have called abortion an "intrinsic evil" are as if they had spoken in vain: "We asked for bread and Rome gave us stones." (Sandro Magister, "Obama laureato a Notre Dame: Ma i vescovi gli rifanno l'esame," Settimo Cielo blog, *L'Espresso*, May 26, 2009)

The neoconservatives once again moved in a dissonant line with that of the Vatican. The articles referred to by Magister are: Michael Novak, "Osservatore traditore?," *Liberal*, May 23, 2009; George Weigel, "Parsing the Vatican Newspaper: It Doesn't Always Speak for the Pope," *National Review*, May 21, 2009.

challenge that the pope offered to the American political world was that of the *common good*: one cannot be against abortion if one is in favor of capital punishment, and, vice versa, one who legitimizes abortion cannot defend the dignity of those facing the death penalty. The values of both the right and the left are self-contradictory.

The category of the common good constitutes a key point of Bergoglio's thought. It plays an important role in Francis's most important speech during the US visit, the one delivered on Capitol Hill on September 24, before the plenary assembly of the United States Congress, a first in history for a Roman pontiff. This speech is a masterpiece, a fact that ought not be taken for granted.

Addressing "this Joint Session of Congress in 'the land of the free and the home of the brave,'" the pope began by declaring himself "a son of this great continent."[174] He addressed the representatives of the American people and, through them, "the entire people of the United States." The category of *people* thus comes to the fore—not an amorphous, indistinct people, but a living reality that finds its expression in those who contribute to forming the spirit of the common ethos.

> I wish to dialogue with all of you, and I would like to do so through the historical memory of your people.
>
> My visit takes place at a time when men and women of good will are marking the anniversaries of several great Americans. The complexities of history and the reality of human weakness notwithstanding, these men and women, for all their many differences and limitations, were able by hard work and self-sacrifice—some at the cost of their lives—to build a better future. They shaped fundamental values which will endure forever in the spirit of the American people. A people with this spirit can live through many crises, tensions and conflicts, while always finding the resources to move forward, and to do so with dignity. These men and women offer us a way of seeing and interpreting reality. In honoring their memory, we are inspired, even amid conflicts, and in the here and now of each day, to draw upon our deepest cultural reserves.[175]

174. Pope Francis, "Visit to the Joint Session of the United States Congress," September 24, 2015, https://www.vatican.va/content/francesco/en/speeches/2015/september /documents/papa-francesco_20150924_usa-us-congress.html.

175. Pope Francis, "Visit to the Joint Session of the United States Congress."

Here Francis employs a hermeneutic methodology learned and used from the time he was Jesuit provincial in Argentina. The "greats" of a people are not those Hegel would recognize as cosmic-historical figures. They are the symbols of goodness, justice, and dedication in whom others can see their own lives and values reflected. They represent the concrete universal, the point of synthesis between the ideal and life. In 1976, speaking of the heroes and martyrs of the Society of Jesus, Bergoglio wrote:

> I prefer to illustrate the symbols through which the Society of Jesus has expressed its mission, its vision of reality, its possibilities of action. They are symbols who have shaped its men; symbols of ardor and total fidelity, such as Blessed Roque; symbols of the patience that founds a people, like Florián Paucke; symbols of the scientific approach and of the value given to American innovation, such as Sánchez Labrador and Dobrizhoffer; symbols of original philosophical thought, such as Domingo Muriel; symbols of fruitful continuity, even after the expulsion of the Society, in the Indians who mourned its absence, in the ideas that founded the patriotic revolutions, and even in the courage of that woman who continued to preach the Exercises and whom our people know as Mother Antula.[176]

Similarly, speaking to Congress, Bergoglio referred to the "symbols" of the American people: "I would like to mention four of these Americans: Abraham Lincoln, Martin Luther King, Dorothy Day and Thomas Merton."[177] Unlike *Fratelli Tutti*, which also includes Gandhi among the "symbols," here the names he mentions all belong to Christians. Each of them is recalled as representative of an ideal that shaped the character of the United States. "This year marks the one hundred and fiftieth anniversary of the assassination of President Abraham Lincoln, the guardian of liberty, who labored tirelessly that 'this nation, under God, [might] have a new birth of freedom.' Building a future of freedom requires love of the common good and cooperation in a spirit of subsidiarity and solidarity."[178]

Lincoln devoted himself to unity and to freedom. He is the father of American democracy who paid with his life for his dedication to the good

---

176. Jorge Mario Bergoglio, *Fede e giustizia nell'apostolato dei gesuiti* (Buenos Aires: CLAS, 1976); it. trans. in Jorge Mario Bergoglio–Pope Francis, *Pastorale sociale*, 247–248.

177. Pope Francis, "Visit to the Joint Session of the United States Congress."

178. Pope Francis, "Visit to the Joint Session of the United States Congress."

of all. Francis referred to him, before the members of Congress, also to criticize the political-religious Manichaeism that marked the present hour.

> Our world is increasingly a place of violent conflict, hatred and brutal atrocities, committed even in the name of God and of religion. We know that no religion is immune from forms of individual delusion or ideological extremism. This means that we must be especially attentive to every type of fundamentalism, whether religious or of any other kind. A delicate balance is required to combat violence perpetrated in the name of a religion, an ideology or an economic system, while also safeguarding religious freedom, intellectual freedom and individual freedoms. But there is another temptation which we must especially guard against: the simplistic reductionism which sees only good or evil; or, if you will, the righteous and sinners. The contemporary world, with its open wounds which affect so many of our brothers and sisters, demands that we confront every form of polarization which would divide it into these two camps. We know that in the attempt to be freed of the enemy without, we can be tempted to feed the enemy within. To imitate the hatred and violence of tyrants and murderers is the best way to take their place. That is something which you, as a people, reject.[179]

Here we see ideas that would reappear five years later in *Fratelli Tutti*: the critique of religious fundamentalism, political theology, Manichean "polarizations" that divide everything in society, politics, and faith into either friends or enemies. True politics is not based on such opposition but on concern for the common good. This is the essence of democracy. "If politics must truly be at the service of the human person, it follows that it cannot be a slave to the economy and finance. Politics is, instead, an expression of our compelling need to live as one, in order to build as one the greatest common good: that of a community which sacrifices particular interests in order to share, in justice and peace, its goods, its interests, its social life."[180]

179. Pope Francis, "Visit to the Joint Session of the United States Congress." In *Let Us Dream*, Francis clarifies the use of the category of the "internal enemy" in his speech to Congress: "I spoke of the 'enemy within' because polarization also has a spiritual root. Polarization is amplified and exacerbated by some media and politicians, but it is born in the heart. When we are in a polarized environment, we must be aware of the bad spirit which enters into division and creates a downward spiral of accusation and counteraccusation. An ancient term for the devil is the Great Accuser." Pope Francis, *Let Us Dream*, 77.

180. Pope Francis, "Visit to the Joint Session of the United States Congress."

Then, following his reference to Lincoln, Francis called to mind Martin Luther King, Jr.

> I think of the march which Martin Luther King led from Selma to Montgomery fifty years ago as part of the campaign to fulfill his "dream" of full civil and political rights for African Americans. That dream continues to inspire us all. I am happy that America continues to be, for many, a land of "dreams." Dreams which lead to action, to participation, to commitment. Dreams which awaken what is deepest and truest in the life of a people.
>
> In recent centuries, millions of people came to this land to pursue their dream of building a future in freedom. We, the people of this continent, are not fearful of foreigners, because most of us were once foreigners. I say this to you as the son of immigrants, knowing that so many of you are also descended from immigrants.[181]

Francis also recalls King—together with Gandhi, Desmond Tutu, and Charles de Foucauld—in the closing paragraphs of *Fratelli Tutti*. He is the symbol of integration between white people and black people, another dream that was paid for at the cost of life. The pope suggested to Congress that the same dream must motivate the welcoming of immigrants into that great immigrant population that is the United States of America.

The pope then mentioned a third exemplary figure, this one a woman: Dorothy Day. "In these times when social concerns are so important, I cannot fail to mention the Servant of God Dorothy Day, who founded the Catholic Worker Movement. Her social activism, her passion for justice and for the cause of the oppressed, were inspired by the Gospel, her faith, and the example of the saints."[182] Here the "symbol" regards the fight against poverty and for a more supportive economy. Certainly less well-known than Lincoln and King, Day was described well by Giulia Galeotti in a beautiful article published in *L'Osservatore Romano* in 2020:

> She was poor among the poor ("Going on site to see what happens is not enough. It is not even enough to help the organizers, to give what you have for assistance, or even to live your life in voluntary poverty to conform to them. One has to live with them and share their sufferings"); a woman of peace in a world at war; a bulwark for workers, both men and women, and

---

181. Pope Francis, "Visit to the Joint Session of the United States Congress."
182. Pope Francis, "Visit to the Joint Session of the United States Congress."

their material and spiritual well-being; a woman of picket lines and protests who endured imprisonment for it; a lay woman in a church led by clergy; a woman of mind, of prayer, but also of action ("I think I've spent my life trying to make things work better, to change them at least a little"). In all this, Day was truly a woman of our time, experienced by her with great anxiety, anticipating many of the issues that later exploded in public agendas, including the church.[183]

The final figure offered by the pope to members of Congress was that of a monk, just as the final one in *Fratelli Tutti* would be a monk, though a different one. In this case, it was Thomas Merton.

A century ago, at the beginning of the Great War, which Pope Benedict XV termed a "pointless slaughter," another notable American was born: the Cistercian monk Thomas Merton. He remains a source of spiritual inspiration and a guide for many people. . . . Merton was above all a man of prayer, a thinker who challenged the certitudes of his time and opened new horizons for souls and for the Church. He was also a man of dialogue, a promoter of peace between peoples and religions. . . .

Being at the service of dialogue and peace also means being truly determined to minimize and, in the long term, to end the many armed conflicts throughout our world. Here we have to ask ourselves: Why are deadly weapons being sold to those who plan to inflict untold suffering on individuals and society? Sadly, the answer, as we all know, is simply for money: money that is drenched in blood, often innocent blood. In the face of this shameful and culpable silence, it is our duty to confront the problem and to stop the arms trade.[184]

Merton is referred to here as the "symbol" of peace and dialogue. The author of *The Seven Storey Mountain* (1948),[185] he was, starting from the Cuban missile crisis and then during the Vietnam War, a passionate

---

183. Giulia Galeotti, "Così radicale, così necessaria: Quarant'anni fa moriva Dorothy Day," *L'Osservatore Romano*, November 24, 2020. On the Catholic Worker movement, see William D. Miller, *A Harsh and Dreadful Love: Dorothy Day and the Catholic Worker Movement* (Milwaukee: Marquette University Press, 1973, 2005).

184. Pope Francis, "Visit to the Joint Session of the United States Congress."

185. Thomas Merton, *The Seven Storey Mountain: An Autobiography of Faith* (Boston: Mariner Books, 1999).

advocate of peace.[186] His name is offered by the pope to illustrate a criticism—certainly not very welcome by many in the United States—of the unjustified power of the arms industry.

These four, whom the pope calls "four representatives of the American people," thus exemplify four virtues, "four dreams," that constitute the noblest face of America: freedom and democracy as care for the common good; integration and the rejection of discrimination; solidarity and the struggle against poverty; dialogue and the rejection of war. Four representatives: "Three sons and a daughter of this land, four individuals and four dreams: Lincoln, liberty; Martin Luther King, liberty in plurality and non-exclusion; Dorothy Day, social justice and the rights of persons; and Thomas Merton, the capacity for dialogue and openness to God."[187] The four ideals of "the spirit of the American people"—freedom, equal rights, justice and equity for all, dialogue—take shape in four "heroes" who make America great.

We are a long way here from Michael Novak's *The Spirit of Democratic Capitalism*. The four American "symbols" all fought for the common good, for equality and justice. They fought for people, not for the priority of a structure. Francis went to the heart of the American *ethos*, not the Weberian-capitalist one represented by Wall Street, but the one represented by the "Christian" heart of America.

186. See Thomas Merton, *Passion for Peace: Reflections on War and Nonviolence*, William H. Shannon, ed. (Spring Valley, NY: Crossroad Publishing Company, 2006).
187. Pope Francis, "Visit to the Joint Session of the United States Congress."

A Church That Goes Forth and a Field Hospital

The Missionary Face of the Church

Away from the Center and Toward the Peripheries of the World and of Life

As we have seen in chapter 2, the Catholic neoconservative critique of *Evangelii Gaudium* was fundamentally an effort to use Christianity to legitimize the superiority of the Western economic system rather than to judge it. Catho-capitalism could tolerate minor "ethical" corrections but not a critique of the system that questioned the movement's basic postulate: the cooperation between private selfishness and the common good. In his reservations about the neocapitalist model, Bergoglio represented for Michael Novak the typical Latin American, hostile to the North American Protestant ethos. Long before he expressed this in his 2013 *National Review* article "Agreeing with Pope Francis," Novak had expounded his thesis on the subject in chapter 18 of *The Spirit of Democratic Capitalism*. Here he emphasized how "Latin Americans do not value the same moral qualities North Americans do. The two cultures see the world quite differently."[1]

A student of the Weber school, Novak traced the differences between the United States and Latin America to two irreducible worldviews. The common Christian roots, rather than providing points of contact, offered

---

1. Novak, *The Spirit of Democratic Capitalism*, 302.

insurmountable walls. This vision, with its "expansive" Westernism, sounded a lot like what would be expressed by Samuel Huntington in his 1996 book *The Clash of Civilizations and the Remaking of World Order*. It is therefore not surprising that when Novak disagreed with the thesis of *Evangelii Gaudium*, his inclination was to attribute the differences to the polarization between North and South. Bergoglio was the man of the South, a Latin American who did not have the conceptual categories to understand the economic-political culture of the North. This was the Anglo-Saxon liberal culture's typical critique. In reality, Bergoglio was quite familiar with the neocapitalism promoted by the liberals. He had seen its effects in Argentina, which the neoliberal economic policy of Domingo Cavallo, during the presidencies of Carlos Menem and Fernando de la Rúa (1989–2001), had plunged into chaos and misery. The Argentine crisis and the world crisis of 2008, triggered by the collapse of the American investment bank Lehman Brothers, are both illustrations of the validity of the criticism of the neoliberal model that *Evangelii Gaudium* offers.

On the contrary, Bergoglio responds to Novak's conception, according to which a correct vision of the world can only be reached starting from the center (that is, from the North), that to understand reality, not only its lights but also its shadows, one must look at it from the periphery. One does not understand the tragedies and dramas, the cracks and wounds, if one remains inside the "sphere," the soap bubble of the skyscrapers of New York and London. Bergoglio drew the category of "periphery" from an Argentine thinker he highly esteemed: Amelia Lezcano Podetti (1928–1979), professor of modern philosophy at the Salvador University and the National University of La Plata in Buenos Aires. Podetti was one of the best-known intellectual figures in Argentina in the 1970s. As Pope Francis recalled in 2017, "The thought of Amelia Podetti, the dean of philosophy at the university, a specialist in Hegel who died young, influenced me. It is from her that I received the intuition regarding the 'peripheries.' She worked a lot on this."[2]

In addition to Podetti, Bergoglio also found the notion of "periphery" in the work of Alberto Methol Ferré. At the end of the 1970s, Methol had hoped the great conference of the Latin American church in Puebla in

---

2. Pope Francis, audio recording of January 3, 2017. See Borghesi, *The Mind of Pope Francis*, 32–33. On the figure and work of Amelia Podetti, see esp. 28–36.

1979 would be followed by a "Latin American Catholic Risorgimento," where the South of the world found its expression in the universal church and Latin American Catholicism passed from the "periphery" to the "center."

> In the history of the church there is . . . a particular dynamic of "centers" (spiritual, intellectual, artistic) and "peripheries"—centers that radiate and thus guide the rest of the church (such as Alexandria and Antioch in antiquity or the Franco-German churches at the Second Vatican Council) and that in turn generate new centers in the periphery, which will replace them. This is a dialectic charged with tension, a singular "ecclesial geopolitics" of renewals, because ecclesial centers and peripheries always have their concreteness in historical "space-time."[3]

Bergoglio drew these ideas of Podetti and Methol Ferré together, giving rise to a dense and original idea of the notion of "periphery."[4] This was not simply a matter of the church of the South taking on a role as a model for the church of the North. Thus posed, the question could appear as a problem of hegemony and power. Nor is it an anticipation of a purely sociological development, though it certainly takes into account the social configuration of the world in the era of globalization. As Pasquale Ferrara aptly writes:

> It would be superficial to want to trace the roots of Francis's discourse on the peripheries to some typically Latin American antecedents and in particular to the theory of *dependencia* that intellectuals like Andre Gunder Frank, Samir Amin, and Fernando Henrique Cardoso developed in the 1970s and 1980s. For these thinkers, underdevelopment is caused by a global division of labor governed by industrialized countries, which assign the "third world" the role of reserve of basic products (agricultural, forestry, extractive) but keep it removed from the circuit of innovation and development.
>
> Similarly, the resonance of the concept of periphery in Pope Francis with Immanuel Wallerstein's theory of the "world economy," which divides the globe into central, semi-peripheral, and peripheral areas—with the resulting growing tensions producing political and social instability, causing a global crisis and revolutionary change—is only apparent.

---

3. Alberto Methol Ferré, "Prologo per Europei," 12.
4. See Andrea Riccardi, *Periferie: Crisi e novità per la Chiesa* (Milan: Jaca Book, 2016).

Francis's vision of the peripheries is broader and perhaps more realistic. On the one hand, the periphery is not only an economic and historical reality. . . ; it also implies a symbolic characterization in the distribution of world power. On the other hand, it is a structural anomaly in the integrative perspective of the world, which is not reabsorbed by the global process, threatening to solidify and make permanent the conditions of exclusion and marginalization of a large part of the world population.[5]

According to Ferrara,

Closer to Bergoglio's conceptualization is the category of *expulsion*, as articulated by [the Dutch-American sociologist] Saskia Sassen. It explains a plurality of situations, such as the impoverishment of the middle class in rich countries, the eviction of millions of small farmers in poor countries due to the massive purchase of land by foreign investors, the destructive industrial practices of the biosphere, the increase of the prison population in Western countries as a method of managing the "social surplus," the multiplication of refugee camps. For Sassen, the mass expulsion that is taking place on a large scale signals a systemic transformation of global capitalism.

Having said this, it should be noted that Pope Francis's vision is not dichotomous or dialectizing, as in the neo-Marxist conceptions of the contradictions of global capitalism. Nor is it standardizing in the way that liberal globalization is. Bergoglio conceives the world in terms of what could be defined as connective pluralism: "Our model," we read in *Evangelii Gaudium*, "is not the sphere, which is no greater than its parts, where every point is equidistant from the center, and there are no differences between them. Instead, it is the polyhedron, which reflects the convergence of all its parts, each of which preserves its distinctiveness."

In this sense, one could say that Bergoglio has "decolonized" the concept of periphery.[6]

In terms of the polyhedron, each "center" needs the point of view of the periphery. Each center must become a periphery in order to carry out its function. This center-periphery model is an antinomic formula, typical of Bergoglio's philosophical thought. This is a particularly important formula for the church, which conceives itself as missionary in nature. In *Evangelii Gaudium*, the pope writes,

5. Pasquale Ferrara, "Papa Francesco e le periferie del mondo," n.d., www.treccani.it.
6. Ferrara, "Papa Francesco e le periferie del mondo."

[a] Church which 'goes forth' is a Church whose doors are open. Going out to others in order to reach the fringes of humanity does not mean rushing out aimlessly into the world. Often it is better simply to slow down, to put aside our eagerness in order to see and listen to others, to stop rushing from one thing to another and to remain with someone who has faltered along the way. At times we have to be like the father of the prodigal son, who always keeps his door open so that when the son returns, he can readily pass through it.[7]

The church that goes forth is a church that moves toward the human peripheries, peripheries that are as social as they are existential. Here we touch on a crucial point of Francis's pontificate, a point that takes him far from the domineering and Western perspective of the neocons. The church that goes forth is one that encounters the existential peripheries. This encounter has been blocked, over the last two decades, by a growing bureaucratization of ecclesial life, of priests and bishops, based on roles and structures, careerism and formalities. For the pope, today's secularization is not only the fruit of an economic model that dissolves all types of social relations by desacralizing everything except goods; it is also the fruit of an *ecclesiastical bureaucratization*, of an infinite distance between bishops and clergy, between clergy and people. It is not only a *Ratio* that is closed to the supernatural, in the reigning positivism, but also a *Fides* that has become ideologized, clericalized.

The disease of contemporary Christianity is *clericalism*. It is no longer the worldliness that arose in the 1970s from the historic-political engagement of a Christianity dominated by Marxist culture. Now there is a new worldliness, that of a new Catholic right that embraces the culture of "waste," the sacrificial logic of ascendant post-1989 neocapitalism. It asks only to compromise on certain values that neocapitalism tends to corrode. Thus a Catholicism of order, perfectly inserted in the power of the world, legitimizes itself through the defense of a moral orthodoxy that the "liquid society" dissolves at every step. This Catholicism comes to resemble an "Indian reservation," in perennial distinction from the world with no points of positive contact, encounter, or exchange. What is lacking in this *moral clericalism* is Christ—Christ as the subject of *encounter*, Christ as one who reaches out toward the "peripheries."

7. Pope Francis, *Evangelii Gaudium*, 46.

The notion of periphery is polyvalent. It indicates both a judgment on the contemporary church and a way forward. In his address to the cardinals of the church just prior to the conclave that elected him pope, Bergoglio said, "Evangelizing calls for apostolic zeal. Evangelizing presupposes for the church the 'parresia' of coming out from itself. The church is called to come out from itself and to go to the peripheries, not only geographical, but existential—those of the mystery of sin, of suffering, of injustice, those of ignorance and of the absence of faith, those of thought, those of every form of misery."[8]

Here he evoked the notion of periphery in relation to a new missionary season of the church. It was not just a socio-political notion; it represented the starting point for a church that is not self-referential but "decentralized." Cardinal Bergoglio was diagnosing the church's problem and at the same time the treatment necessary to heal it. He continued:

> When the church does not come out from itself to evangelize, it becomes self-referential and gets sick (one thinks of the woman hunched over upon herself in the Gospel). The evils that, in the passing of time, afflict the church's institutions are rooted in self-referentiality, in a sort of theological narcissism. In Revelation, Jesus says that he stands at the door and knocks. . . . But at times I think that Jesus may be knocking from the inside, so that we will let him out. The self-referential church presumes to keep Jesus Christ inside and not let him out.
>
> The church, when it is self-referential, thinks, without realizing it, that it provides its own light; it stops being the "mysterium lunae" and gives rise to that evil which is so grave: spiritual worldliness (according to de Lubac, the worst evil into which the church can fall)—living to give glory to one another. To simplify, there are two images of the church: the evangelizing church that goes out from itself; that of the "Dei Verbum religiose audiens et fidenter proclamans," or the worldly church that lives within itself, of itself, for itself. This should illuminate the possible changes and reforms to be realized for the salvation of souls.
>
> Thinking of the next pope: a man who, through the contemplation of Jesus Christ and the adoration of Jesus Christ, may help the church to go out from itself toward the existential peripheries, that may help it to be the fruitful mother who lives "by the sweet and comforting joy of evangelizing."[9]

---

8. Jorge Mario Bergoglio, "Evangelizzare le periferie," in Sandro Magister, "Le ultime parole di Bergoglio prima del conclave," Settimo Cielo blog, *L'Espresso*, March 27, 2013.

9. Bergoglio, "Evangelizzare le periferie."

In that address, one can see the entire program of Francis's pontificate outlined in advance. Christianity must turn, first of all, to sinners, to the distant, to the prodigal child, to those who, having not known Christ, are deprived of the Father's affection, rather than only to the healthy. He has in mind those who are far from the "center," which is not the church as an institution but Christ. The "existential peripheries" means those who, socially and spiritually poor, know the love neither of God nor of humanity. It is the condition of contemporary humanity, in which the contradiction between poverty and wealth is tragically sharpened by an unscrupulous globalization and in which secularization has starved the soul to the point that the center, the heart of the West, has become a single, huge, "existential periphery." The idea arises, for Bergoglio, from his pastoral experience as archbishop of Buenos Aires. As he stated on October 4, 2013, in his address to clergy and consecrated people in Assisi:

> the third aspect is missionary: to proclaim even to the outskirts. I also borrowed this from you, from your pastoral plan. The Bishop spoke recently about it. However, I wish to emphasize it, because it is something I also experienced a great deal when I was in Buenos Aires: the importance of going out to meet the other in the outskirts, which are places, but which are primarily people living in particular situations in life. This was true in my former diocese, that of Buenos Aires. The outskirt which hurt me a great deal was to find children in middle class families who didn't know how to make the Sign of the Cross. But you see, this is an outskirt! And I ask you, here in this diocese, are there children who do not know how to make the Sign of the Cross? Think about it. These are true outskirts of existence where God is absent.[10]

Francis had mentioned the connection between the periphery and children unaware of the sign of the cross the previous week, in his September 27, 2013, address to participants in an international congress on catechesis. The image had become a common reference for Bergoglio in explaining his notion of the periphery, or outskirts. It indicates those far from Christ, the socially and intellectually poor, whether located on the outskirts of the metropolis or at its center. This is a warning for today's church, which is increasingly preoccupied with itself. In a systolic and

---

10. Pope Francis, "Address to Clergy, Consecrated People, and Members of Diocesan Pastoral Councils," October 4, 2013, http://www.vatican.va/content/francesco/en/speeches/2013/october/documents/papa-francesco_20131004_clero-assisi.html.

diastolic movement, the church has passed, over the last half century, from Vatican II's razing the bastions (to borrow the title of Hans Urs von Balthasar's 1952 book) to circling the wagons after the subsequent doctrinal confusion; from the season of the militant Catholicism of John Paul II to the ebb, after 1989, of a Catholicism closed in on itself, satisfied with its certainties, relating to the world only through the dialectic of "nonnegotiable values." And this despite the evangelical impetus suggested by the magisterium of Benedict XVI. With Francis resounds John Paul II's bold call to "open wide the doors to Christ," but *now it is addressed not only to the world but, primarily, to the church.* If the world has become a "periphery," the church has correspondingly conceived itself as a "center." As Pope Francis told the Latin American bishops conference on July 28, 2013: "The Church is an institution, but when she makes herself a 'center,' she becomes merely functional, and slowly but surely turns into a kind of NGO. The Church then claims to have a light of her own, and she stops being that '*mysterium lunae*' of which the Church Fathers spoke. She becomes increasingly self-referential and loses her need to be missionary."[11]

A church of the center—one that is centered on itself—is no longer missionary. This is the message that Francis offered to "his" Jesuits in the 2013 interview with Fr. Spadaro:

> The Society of Jesus is an institution in tension . . . always fundamentally in tension. A Jesuit is a person who is not centered on himself. The Society itself also looks to a center outside itself; its center is Christ and his Church. So if the Society centers itself in Christ and the Church, it has two fundamental points of reference for its balance and for being able to live on the margins, on the frontier. If it looks too much in upon itself, it puts itself at the center as a very solid, very well "armed" structure, but then it runs the risk of feeling safe and self-sufficient.
>
> The Society must always have before itself the *Deus semper maior*, the always-greater God. . . . This tension takes us out of ourselves continuously.[12]

11. Pope Francis, "Address to the Leadership of the Episcopal Conferences of Latin America during the General Coordination Meeting," July 28, 2013, http://www.vatican .va/content/francesco/en/speeches/2013/july/documents/papa-francesco_20130728_gmg -celam-rio.html.

12. Pope Francis, *My Door Is Always Open*, 23.

A de-centered church—one that is turned toward the peripheries—is a missionary church. For this reason, *Evangelii Gaudium*, the programmatic document of Francis's pontificate—which is a restatement for today's context of *Evangelii Nuntiandi*, Pope Paul VI's 1975 apostolic exhortation on evangelization in the modern world—responds to the notion of "existential peripheries." The pontificate of the first Jesuit pontiff can only be a missionary pontificate. Hence his "conciliar," pastoral approach, the primacy accorded to encounter over conflict, in line with Benedict XVI: "Being Christian is not the result of an ethical choice or a lofty idea, but the encounter with an event, a person, which gives life a new horizon and a decisive direction."[13] Hence the conception of authority as paternity, as a shepherd who knows the smell of his sheep, as a merciful father who relates to his prodigal son, to the one who is "far off." The authority, in the church, is the one who seeks the encounter, who opens the doors, who steps out of the doors to meet those who are far off. This is because "the Church is not a tollhouse; it is the house of the Father, where there is a place for everyone, with all their problems."[14]

The church of Francis is *a people's church in a secularized world*. It is a church that does not want to remain in the center of the metropolis, in the residential districts, but goes to where Christ is unknown, on the margins of the city. It wants to renew the "center" starting from the periphery, starting from mercy toward the least ones.

Bergoglio has never looked at reality from the perspective of Plaza de Mayo, seat of the cathedral and the government building, but always and only from the everyday places that represent a sign of the times; it is from there that, according to Father Jorge, Christians must start, especially from that particular place which is the face of the neighbor. To rediscover the thread of mercy, here he developed his idea of the church as a "field hospital," taking the cross to navigate the labyrinth of the city and upending his gaze to see anew its profiles. As bishop he goes to celebrate Mass in the public squares. He knows the neighborhoods, the parishes, the metro lines, and the bus routes. Every year Bergoglio celebrates a Mass for all victims of human trafficking in the Plaza de la Constitución, a few steps from the

13. Pope Benedict XVI, *Deus Caritas Est*, December 25, 2005, 1, https://www.vatican.va/content/benedict-xvi/en/encyclicals/documents/hf_ben-xvi_enc_20051225_deus-caritas-est.html; cited in Pope Francis, *Evangelii Gaudium*, 7.

14. Pope Francis, *Evangelii Gaudium*, 47.

train station where every day thousands of people arrive from the suburbs and then return home late in the evening, often after a poorly paid day of hard work. It is the link between the infinite city and the province. . . . Plaza Constitución is the obligatory gateway for those coming from the south and the southwest. But there are also those who live there. They are *the people of the street*: the homeless, the unemployed, the drug addicts, the migrants waiting to be recruited by a *caporale*. And, above all, prostitutes: a crowd of girls, often minors, sell themselves from early morning to late into the night. It is impossible not to see them. Since 2009, Bergoglio has chosen to celebrate the Mass dedicated to the victims of human trafficking in this emblematic square. The first time, he celebrated the Mass in the Madre de los Emigrantes church, also in the Constitución district; after that, he decided to celebrate them outdoors.[15]

Silvina Pérez is correct to write that "here [Bergoglio] developed his idea of the church as a 'field hospital.'" It is a metaphor that matured through an experience of immersion, of incarnation, of coming face to face with the painfully destitute neighbor, materially and spiritually. It is not a formula derived from a "progressive" ideology, which is an accusation one hears from critics who totally ignore Bergoglio's biography. The cardinal-archbishop of Buenos Aires was truly struck by the pain of the world.

It was precisely here that the Church was born, in the margins of the Cross where so many of the crucified are found. If the Church disowns the poor, she ceases to be the Church of Jesus; she falls back on the old temptation to become a moral or intellectual elite. There is only one word for the Church that becomes a stranger to the poor: "scandal." The road to the geographic and existential margins is the route of the Incarnation: God chose the peripheries as the place to reveal, in Jesus, His saving action in history.[16]

Hence the idea of establishing in the Archdiocese of Buenos Aires, on August 7, 2009, the vicariate for the *villas de emergencia*. As Austen Ivereigh has written,

15. Pérez and Scaraffia, *Francesco*, 71–72.
16. Pope Francis, *Let Us Dream*, 120.

Bergoglio evangelized the city from its margins. "The idea is that the Church is first among the poor and from there reaches out to everyone," says Father Gustavo Carrara, whom Bergoglio put as the head of his slum priests' vicariate. "It's the opposite of what in economics is called the trickle-down effect—only it never does trickle down. It's not about the poor and only the poor. It's *from* them, to the rest." The vicariate, created in August 2009, was a way to incorporate the pastoral slum outreach into the official structure of the diocese. Its first coordinator, Father Pepe Di Paola, says that for Bergoglio "the center of Buenos Aires is not the Plaza de Mayo, where the power resides, but *las periferias*, the outskirts of the city."[17]

The periphery here is not a simple sociological concept, dialectically opposed to the rich and opulent "center" according to the populist or neo-Marxist model. It indicates, first of all, an *anthropological context*, a way of existing that is still marked by a solidarity that is little known elsewhere. In a 2012 interview on the radio station of the Villa 22 community, Bergoglio said two things about the barrios struck him:

> First is a great sense of solidarity. You can be pretty pissed at someone, or whatever, but there's a need and immediately solidarity makes itself felt. It does me good to see solidarity. There's less egotism than in other parts, there's more solidarity. The second thing is the faith that is here, faith in the Virgin, faith in the saints, faith in Jesus. I'm really struck by how, not just this one, but all the [shantytowns] are barrios of faith. . . . These two things have always struck me: solidarity and faith. Put them together, and what do you get? The ability to celebrate. It's great how in these barrios people celebrate, make fiesta—they're joyful. So you have those two things, faith and solidarity, and when we put them together you get joy.[18]

In a surprising way, Bergoglio here linked the notion of periphery to that of solidarity, faith, and joy, all without any naive idealization.

"What convinced Bergoglio to create the new slum priests' vicariate in August 2009," Ivereigh wrote, "was the drug dealers a few months earlier announcing their intention to kill Padre Pepe. The dealers didn't like a declaration by the slum priests in March that year in response to a

---

17. Austen Ivereigh, *The Great Reformer: Francis and the Making of a Radical Pope* (New York: Henry Holt, 2014), 305.

18. Ivereigh, *The Great Reformer*, 306–7.

congress debate on the decriminalization of drugs. The priests said that the drugs were already de facto in the villas, where they were bought and sold with impunity, and wreaked havoc in the lives of fragile people."[19]

The slums are not a paradise. However, in contact with faith, they were able to reveal an unknown humanity, a message of solidarity that is precious also for the "center." Father Pepe Di Paola who "with Bergoglio's support had brought the Virgin of Caacupé to the slum in 1997 was the architect of a thirteen-year parish operation that had given birth to fifteen chapels, a high school, a trade school, a home for the elderly, various soup kitchens, drug prevention programs, a recovery center, two farms where recovering addicts live and work, a day care center for kids, and a community newspaper and radio."[20]

On the part of Father Pepe and his companions, constantly supported by the presence of Bergoglio, it was an extraordinary presence and action of renewal.[21] Evangelization and human development happened together. The barrios, miserable offshoots of the great metropolises, could be reborn to new life and demonstrate to the heart of the city a forgotten measure of solidarity. They were the best example of the fruits of the missionary church.[22]

19. Ivereigh, *The Great Reformer*, 307.

20. Ivereigh, *The Great Reformer*, 307–8.

21. On Fr. Pepe, see the book-length interview, José Maria di Paola, *Dalla fine del mondo: Il mio cammino tra i più poveri* (Rome: Castelvecchi, 2017). See also Ivereigh, *The Great Reformer*, 307–9.

22. As an example of a rebirth in the tragic time of the pandemic, the testimony of Alver Metalli relating to Villa 21 in Buenos Aires, one of the great slums of the Argentine capital, is worth attention. In December 2020, Metalli wrote,

In some provinces of Argentina, people are still dying of Covid, but perhaps the worst is behind us. The dead were incinerated, as ordered by the health authorities. The living are healing the many open wounds: family members, friends, missing neighbors, compromised economic activities, reduced work. Life in the slum, which was already in precarious balance, was disrupted by a seven-month-long tsunami. The fragile economy of the *villas miserias* brought to its knees. Yet there is the sign of a generous, stubborn, contagious solidarity, which fed thousands of people every day, created clinics for isolating of the infected, set up shelters for those at risk, disinfected streets, courtyards, squares, gardens and schools so that the little ones could play with a certain degree of safety. A response that had the inspiring soul and organizational thrust in a group of priests. . . . In order to stand up and face adversities that affect everyone's life without distinction, there must be a sensitivity educated to need, a chain of small and large experiences of help to the needs of others, attention to the precariousness of

"The Church which 'goes forth,'" Francis wrote, "is a community of missionary disciples who take the first step, who are involved and supportive, who bear fruit and rejoice. An evangelizing community knows that the Lord has taken the initiative, he has loved us first (cf. 1 Jn 4:19), and therefore we can move forward, boldly take the initiative, go out to others, seek those who have fallen away, stand at the crossroads and welcome the outcast."[23]

Evangelization and Human Development: The "Great" Paul VI's *Evangelii Nuntiandi* and the End of Christianity

Francis has referred to Pope Paul on many occasions throughout his pontificate, taking him, in some ways, as a model. On two points, in particular, his full harmony with his predecessor is clear. Both points mark Francis's profound distance from the Catholic neoconservative perspective.

The first is the link between evangelization and human development. As we have seen, George Weigel has made clear, in his 2009 comments on Benedict XVI's *Caritas in Veritate*, his fear of Paul VI's *Populorum Progressio*. For the neocons, this was the greatest concern: that papal teaching, following the "turning point" of *Centesimus Annus*, might once again reflect the full tradition of Catholic social teaching inaugurated by Leo XIII. The distance of the neocons from the pope is based on this

---

others, refined by previous gestures of love for one's neighbor, a look of sympathy toward human brothers and sisters extracted from within each and cultivated over time. What happened in the era of the pandemic, the great mobilization that has been seen in action in the slums, has a background of faith—sustained, developed, and translated into works—that belongs to the individual and belongs to the people. A background of popular devotion made of invocation of the saints and imitation of their virtues, of confidence in the Madonna, of rosaries. People who had to isolate themselves at home for health reasons, elderly people, others at risk for diseases prior to the onset of the pandemic, who prayed for all the others who risked their health in the service of others. (Alver Metalli, "Nota per i posteri: nella pandemia splende la formidabile risposta della solidarietà umana," SIR: Agenzia d'informazione, December 2, 2020)

Metalli, the former editor of the magazine *Incontri*, founding editor of the monthly *30 Giorni*, and also a novelist, has shared for years the experience of Fr. Pepe Di Paola in Villa 21. See Metalli, *Quarantena—Cuarentena: Diario dalla "peste" in una bidonville argentina—Diario desde la "peste" en una villa miseria argentina*, preface by Pope Francis (Cinisello Balsamo: Edizioni San Paolo, 2020).

23. Pope Francis, *Evangelii Gaudium*, 24.

hypothetical "return." Francis's proximity to Paul is the crux of the contrast. To his critics, this proximity is suspicious. As with the theme of the "peripheries," so also here, on the terrain of social doctrine, we find ourselves close to the positions of liberation theology, positions consistent in some ways with the social encyclical *Populorum Progressio*. In reality, Francis's similarities to Paul VI go well beyond *Populorum Progressio*, which, nevertheless, remains "a milestone in the conception of justice."[24]

But perhaps the point of greatest contact is *Evangelii Nuntiandi*. Here Bergoglio could find the antinomic and balanced synthesis between the two aspects of the Christian's presence in the world: evangelization and human development. They are two points equally distant from the Catholic neoconservative perspective, for which mission, far from being the proclamation of the kerygma and witness, is above all a militant defense of certain values, and human development means expanding the conveniences of modern society.

Francis canonized Paul on October 14, 2018. In an article marked by his characteristic sharpness, Vatican reporter Piero Schiavazzi wrote: "After the dual canonization of Roncalli and Wojtyla, automatically, on the strength of momentum that rose from below, that of Montini constitutes Bergoglio's first 'political' canonization, desired, guided, and strongly sought from above."[25] The adjective *political* here is probably not the most appropriate. In reality, Francis's interest in Paul is long and deep, and the adjective fails to describe it. By canonizing Montini, Bergoglio wasn't simply shining a spotlight on his predecessor but also indicating him as a model, an inspiration. As Austen Ivereigh observes, "For Francis, as for his generation, the 'great light' was Paul VI."[26] Paul is, for the Argentine pontiff, the pope of the council and of *Evangelii Nuntiandi*.[27] This is perhaps the document of Paul's that Francis most appreciates, the one in which the missionary spirit of Vatican II finds its perfect synthesis.

24. Jorge Mario Bergoglio, "Servizio della fede e promozione della giustizia: Alcune riflessioni sul Decreto IV della XXXII Congregazione Generale della Compagnia di Gesù," *Stromata*, January-June 1988; It. trans. in Jorge Mario Bergoglio–Pope Francis, *Pastorale sociale*, 74.

25. Piero Schiavazzi, "La Chiesa in cerca di un Paolo VII: Bergoglio delinea l'identikit del successore," Huffington Post, October 14, 2018.

26. Ivereigh, *The Great Reformer*, 387.

27. See Pierre de Charentenay, *Paolo VI alle radici del magistero di Francesco: L'attualità di Ecclesiam Suam ed Evangelii Nuntiandi* (Vatican City: Libreria Editrice Vaticana, 2018).

Paul VI is a model for Francis precisely because his vision of the church corresponds to the idea of the symphony of opposites that is the golden thread of Bergoglian thought. Criticized from the right and from the left, Pope Montini was able to ferry the church beyond the post-conciliar storm; he did not fail in the task, led by the Spirit, of keeping the body of Christ united in the drama of the time. This is a task that Francis obviously feels to be his own. Less than two years into the pontificate, journalist Luigi Accattoli observed, "Francis often remembers Montini 'with affection and admiration.' He usually refers to him as 'the great Paul VI.' He has used this expression at least eleven times. . . . Once he called him 'the great protagonist of ecumenical dialogue' (January 25, 2014), and on another occasion "the great helmsman of the council' (October 19, 2014)."[28]

Indeed, Francis has said that *Evangelii Nuntiandi* is "to my mind the greatest pastoral document that has ever been written to this day."[29] This esteem is clear in *Evangelii Gaudium*, the manifesto of the Francis pontificate, even the title of which offers a nod to Paul's apostolic exhortation. Contrary to accusations of critics who depict Francis as interested only in sociological concerns, *Evangelii Gaudium* cites the social documents of Paul VI, such as *Octogesima Adveniens* and *Populorum Progressio*, five times (the former in sections 184 and 190, the latter in sections 181, 190, and 219), while it cites *Evangelii Nuntiandi* eleven times (sections 10, 12, 123, 146, 150, 151, 154, 156, 158, 176, and 181). Further evidence is given if one looks to the concluding document of the major gathering of the Latin American church at Aparecida, led by Cardinal Bergoglio, in 2009; almost every one of its references to Paul VI is a citation of *Evangelii Nuntiandi* (sections 14, 109, 210, 258, 262, 281, 283, 331, 485, and 553). It is a beacon that Bergoglio, as cardinal and as pope, has always looked to as a relevant model for evangelization in the contemporary world.

Again less than two years into the pontificate, Accattoli observed:

Privileged references to *Evangelii Nuntiandi* as a text that "remains relevant" are found in many of Francis's speeches, just as they were in previous

---

28. Luigi Accattoli, "Che prende Bergoglio da Montini?," Il blog di Luigi Accattoli, n.d., http://www.luigiaccattoli.it/blog/collaborazione-a-riviste/che-prende-bergoglio-da-montini/.

29. Pope Francis, "Address to Participants in the Pilgrimage from the Diocese of Brescia," June 22, 2013, http://www.vatican.va/content/francesco/en/speeches/2013/june/documents/papa-francesco_20130622_pellegrinaggio-diocesi-brescia.html.

texts of Cardinal Bergoglio: June 13, 2013 (to the council of the synod of bishops); July 27, 2013 (to the bishops of Brazil); July 26, 2014 (pastoral visit to Caserta, Italy); October 19, 2014 (angelus following the beatification of Paul VI). Francis offered a vivid explanation of this passion for *Evangelii Nuntiandi* at the opening of the ecclesial conference of the diocese of Rome, June 16, 2014: "I was so pleased that you, Fr. Giampiero, mentioned *Evangelii Nuntiandi*. To this day, it is the most important post-conciliar pastoral document, which hasn't been surpassed. We should always go back to it. That apostolic exhortation is a great source of inspiration. And it was the work of the great Paul VI, of his own hand."[30]

Why, it is worth asking, is *Evangelii Nuntiandi* so important to Pope Francis? To answer, it is necessary to understand the significance that the apostolic exhortation had for Bergoglio when it was published in 1975. At that time, he was serving as the young provincial of the Argentine Jesuits at a tragic historical moment in which the church in that nation was largely divided into two extreme wings: that of the pro-revolutionary left and that of the right, supportive of the military dictatorship. The provincial Bergoglio was intent on holding together the Jesuits attracted by the siren calls of either embracing pro-Marxist liberation theology or rejecting it in fear of violent retribution from the military. In this context, *Evangelii Nuntiandi*, with its idea of the church as *coincidentia oppositorum*, as a superior synthesis, beyond progressive or reactionary political theologies, had a liberating value. *Evangelii Nuntiandi* stood beyond the dialectical antithesis between faith and social commitment that divided, on the right and on the left, the troubled Catholic conscience of the 1970s. As Bergoglio stated,

> Our temptations can take on different aspects, but they all boil down to "three temptations" and, more fundamentally, to one: that of establishing a "dichotomy" and from there making us opt for a false "reductionism." Paul VI's *Evangelii Nuntiandi*, the *magna carta* of evangelization in present times, suggests this to us. It notes a series of "dichotomies" and the corresponding ways that the dual terms of the misguided contrasts are reduced to one: between Christ and the church (n. 16), between explicit and implicit

30. Luigi Accattoli, "Che prende Bergoglio da Montini?" The quotation is from Pope Francis, "Address to Participants in Rome's Diocesan Conference Entitled 'A People Who Generates Its Children, Communities, and Families in the Great Stages of Christian Initiation,'" June 16, 2014, https://www.vatican.va/content/francesco/en/speeches/2014/june/documents/papa-francesco_20140616_apertura-convegno-diocesano.html.

proclamation of the Gospel (nn. 21–22), between Gospel and human development (nn. 31–34), between personal conversion and reform of structures (n. 36), between gradual change and rapid change (n. 76), and so on. All these "dichotomies" divide what God has united; the "spirit of the Evil One," as Saint Peter Faber said, is a "spirit of division" and not of union.[31]

Besides the valuable idea of synthesis, *Evangelii Nuntiandi* also contained another element that made it precious in the eyes of Bergoglio: the section of chapter 4 on the topic of popular piety. Pope Paul wrote:

> Popular religiosity, of course, certainly has its limits. . . .
> But if it is well oriented, above all by a pedagogy of evangelization, it is rich in values. It manifests a thirst for God which only the simple and poor can know. It makes people capable of generosity and sacrifice even to the point of heroism, when it is a question of manifesting belief. It involves an acute awareness of profound attributes of God: fatherhood, providence, loving and constant presence. It engenders interior attitudes rarely observed to the same degree elsewhere: patience, the sense of the cross in daily life, detachment, openness to others, devotion. By reason of these aspects, we readily call it "popular piety," that is, religion of the people, rather than religiosity.[32]

Bergoglio quoted the passage in a 1988 article on the intersection of faith and work for justice. As pope, he referred to it several times. In 2016 he said,

> Going on pilgrimage to the shrines is one of the People of God's most eloquent expressions of faith, and it manifests the piety of generations of people who have humbly believed and entrusted themselves to the intercession of the Virgin Mary and the Saints. This popular religiosity is an authentic form of evangelization which always needs to be promoted and enhanced, without minimizing its importance. It is curious that in the

---

31. Jorge Mario Bergoglio–Pope Francis, *Meditaciones para religiosos* (Buenos Aires: Ediciones Diego De Torres, 1982); It. trans. *Nel cuore di ogni padre: Alle radici della mia spiritualità* (Milan: Rizzoli, 2014), 291.

32. Pope Paul VI, *Evangelii Nuntiandi*, December 8, 1975, 48, https://www.vatican.va/content/paul-vi/en/apost_exhortations/documents/hf_p-vi_exh_19751208_evangelii-nuntiandi.html. [Translator's note: The chapter and subsection headings and divisions (referred to by the author in introducing this quotation) that appear in all other language versions of the document are absent from the English translation on the Vatican website.]

Evangelii Nuntiandi, Bl. Paul VI speaks of popular religiosity, but says that it is better to call it "popular piety"; then, in the Aparecida Document, the Latin American Episcopate goes one step further and speaks of "popular spirituality." All three concepts are valid, but in concert.[33]

He repeated the same idea in a November 2018 address: "In many ways, our Shrines are irreplaceable because they keep popular piety alive, enriching it with a catechetical formation that sustains and reinforces the faith and at the same time nurtures the testimony of charity. This is very important: keep popular piety alive and do not forget the jewel that is number 48 of *Evangelii nuntiandi*, where Saint Paul VI changed the name from 'popular religiosity' to 'popular piety.' It is a gem."[34]

Behind this important section of the document was the work of theologian Lucio Gera, one of the originators of the "theology of the people" developed by the Rio de la Plata school in Argentina. Unlike Gustavo Gutiérrez's liberation theology, the theology of the people rejected revolutionary violence and, at the same time, affirmed the right to justice and the preferential option for the poor based on the popular piety of Christian faith. This theology made its presence felt in the final document of the third continent-wide meeting of the Latin American bishops at Puebla in 1979. "At Puebla," Ivereigh wrote, "they took Paul VI's *Evangelii Nuntiandi*—which had itself been influenced by Gera—and applied it to Latin America, citing it ninety-seven times in the concluding statement."[35]

The balanced synthesis between poles—evangelization and human development; faith and justice—and the esteem for popular piety explain the value that *Evangelii Nuntiandi* holds for Bergoglio. It is a value that remains associated, in his memory, with the meeting that, together with 237 delegates from ninety provinces of five continents, he attended in Rome with the pope, between December 1974 and March 1975, on the occasion of the General Congregation of the Society of Jesus. On the occasion of its opening, the assembled Jesuits had an audience with Paul

---

33. Pope Francis, "Address to Those Engaged in Pilgrimage Work and for Rectors of Shrines," January 21, 2016, http://www.vatican.va/content/francesco/en/speeches/2016/january/documents/papa-francesco_20160121_giubileo-operatori-santuari.html.

34. Pope Francis, "Address to participants at the International Convention of the Rectors and Pastoral Workers of Shrines," November 29, 2018, http://www.vatican.va/content/francesco/en/speeches/2018/november/documents/papa-francesco_20181129_convegno-santuari.html.

35. Ivereigh, *The Great Reformer*, 184–85.

VI, who delivered an important address. Bergoglio later described it as "one of the most beautiful addresses ever made to the Society by a pope."[36]

Paul told the gathering, "The originality of Ignatius lies, it seems to us, in having intuited that the times required people who were completely available, capable of detaching themselves from everything and of following any mission indicated by the pope and claimed in his opinion by the good of the Church."[37] Commenting on it, Bergoglio observed, "The availability, inherent in the core of the Ignatian charism, is, therefore, directly related to this openness to peoples, to esteem for peoples, to affection for peoples. The Jesuit's willingness puts him in a tension that is often painful: he must be willing to go to any place and, at the same time, to insert himself in the place where he is, inculturating himself as if he were the only one. This 'creates tension,' it hurts, it is the cross with which the incipient Society wanted to strengthen the peoples in the unity of the Church."[38]

Paul VI's perspective, with its tension between the universality of the church and the particular inculturation of the faith, with its antinomy, gave rise to the "tensioning thought" that, for Bergoglio, constitutes the distinct mark of authentic Christian thought. As he wrote in 1988: "The attitude of inculturation is not 'quiet' but in tension with universality with respect to bipolarity (Paul VI already stated this in *Evangelii Nuntiandi*). It is a tension that is never completely resolved, but which, at every step, is resolved in the antinomy (always on a higher level, while maintaining the virtuality of bipolar tension) of a sort of concrete universal."[39] In the climate of the 1970s and 1980s, this polarity, theorized and experienced, clashed with the rejection of antinomy in favor of dialectics. The polarity between faith and commitment to justice, between evangelization and human development, was resolved by many with the choice of one pole over the other. Social commitment, which had become all-encompassing, dominated the theological moment. The result was a political theology, a theology called upon to bless the politics of the moment.

---

36. Jorge Mario Bergoglio, *Reflexiones espirituales sobra la vida apostólica* (Buenos Aires: Ediciones Diego de Torres, 1987); It. trans. of Part 6, "Che cosa sono i gesuiti?," in Jorge Mario Bergoglio–Pope Francis, *Chi sono i gesuiti: Storia della Compagnia di Gesù* (Bologna: EMI, 2014), 20.

37. Cited in Bergoglio–Pope Francis, *Chi sono i gesuiti*, 31.

38. Bergoglio–Pope Francis, *Chi sono i gesuiti*, 31.

39. Jorge Mario Bergoglio, "Servizio della fede e promozione della giustizia," 86.

This explains the reaction of many of the Jesuit delegates to Paul VI's address on the occasion of the General Congregation of the Society. Some of them, Ivereigh recalls, "were mystified by the address, others distressed that, while they had come to Rome to discuss poverty and justice, the pope seemed obsessed with discipline and doctrine. But for some of those present, including Bergoglio, it struck a chord. He recognized in the pope's analysis an accurate discernment of what had gone wrong in the Argentine province as well as elsewhere. . . . Paul VI's allocution 'in many ways shaped how Bergoglio saw the Society,' says Father Swinnen, novice master at the time."[40] This explains Bergoglio's reserve with regard to Decree Four on social justice that emerged from the work of the Thirty-second Congregation, with a controversial formulation about the place of social justice work in the ministry of Jesuits:

> During his provincial address in 1978, Bergoglio made many references to [the Thirty-second Congregation], but none to Decree Four. What he did quote was Paul VI's historic teaching document on evangelization, *Evangelii Nuntiandi*, issued a few months after the end of [the Thirty-second Congregation] in December 1975. In it Paul VI makes clear—in line with Medellín—that there can be no proclamation of the Gospel without also attending to the liberation of people from 'concrete situations of injustice.' But Paul VI also warns about the Church reducing its mission to a "mere temporal project," leaving it open to "manipulation by ideological systems and political parties." That was the discerning nuance lacking in many of the applications of Decree Four.
>
> *Evangelii Nuntiandi* would be Bergoglio's favorite church document, the one he would cite throughout his time as provincial, rector, and later bishop. Not long after his election, Francis described it as "the greatest pastoral document that has ever been written." Its great purpose was to reconcile eternal Church teaching with the diversity of cultures.[41]

Evangelii Nuntiandi is the synthesis the church needs in order to address current events without falling into the trap of ideologies. Being incarnate in the world and the transcendence of God are the two poles that the Christian, a contemplative in action, must hold firm in their indissoluble tension. The "great Paul VI" indicated the way, the same that

---

40. Ivereigh, *The Great Reformer*, 120.
41. Ivereigh, *The Great Reformer*, 121–22.

would mark the gathering of Latin American bishops in Aparecida under the guidance of Cardinal Bergoglio in 2007 and the same that is found at the center of Francis's *Evangelii Gaudium*, which, with its characteristic relationship between primacy of the kerygma and commitment to justice, constitutes the manifesto of the pontificate in relationship to both the church and the world.

A second point manifests Francis's dependence on Paul VI, who, for him, represents not only the pontiff of polarity, of the church as *coincidentia oppositorum*, but also one who understood the epochal turning point in which the conciliar church lives its life: that of "the end of Christianity." Francis spoke of that turning point in his address to the Roman Curia on December 21, 2019. Here Francis noted that "what we are experiencing is *not simply an epoch of changes, but an epochal change*. We find ourselves living at a time when change is no longer linear, but epochal." Then he continued:

> In big cities, we need other "maps," other paradigms, which can help us reposition our ways of thinking and our attitudes. Brothers and sisters, *Christendom no longer exists!* Today we are no longer the only ones who create culture, nor are we in the forefront or those most listened to. We need a change in our pastoral mindset, which does not mean moving towards a relativistic pastoral care. We are no longer living in a Christian world, because faith—especially in Europe, but also in a large part of the West—is no longer an evident presupposition of social life; indeed, faith is often rejected, derided, marginalized and ridiculed.[42]

The comment highlights the difference between the pope's perspective and that of the Catholic neoconservatives, who, after September 11, 2001, founded their entire ecclesial geopolitics upon the defense of the "Christian West" against the external adversary. From Bergoglio's point of view, similar to that of Guardini in *The End of the Modern World*, Europe has, in the space of two centuries, exhausted its Christian vigor, with secularization decaying its Christian roots. The plant needs to be pruned and, in many cases, to be generated anew. If Christianity is flourishing in many parts of Latin America and the world, the same cannot be said of Europe.

42. Pope Francis, "Christmas Greetings to the Roman Curia," December 21, 2019, http://www.vatican.va/content/francesco/en/speeches/2019/december/documents/papa-francesco_20191221_curia-romana.html#_ftn17.

To mark this awareness, the fundamental fact of *the end of Christianity*, the pope included in the written text of his 2019 address to the Roman Curia a footnote that reminded readers that "an *epochal change* was noted in France by Cardinal Suhard (we can think of his pastoral letter *Essor ou déclin de l'Église*, 1947) and by the then-Archbishop of Milan, Giovanni Battista Montini. The latter also questioned whether Italy was still a Catholic country (cf. *Opening Address at the VIII National Week of Pastoral Updating*, September 22, 1958, in *Discorsi e Scritti milanesi 1954–1963*, vol. II, Brescia-Roma 1997, 2328)."[43] The 1958 Montini text cited here followed a pastoral letter that the archbishop offered to his faithful for Lent 1957 titled "On the Religious Sense."[44] There the archbishop of Milan invited his flock to cultivate—in the face of the changes in mentality and culture and the rise of secularism and atheism—the religious dimension of humanity, recognizing it as a precondition for a living faith and not merely a ritual one. Coming a decade after the well-known pastoral letter of Cardinal Suhard, Montini's pastoral letter had a prophetic value, identifying the challenge for faith posed by the decline of Christianity.

In his 2019 address to his Curia, Francis recalled Montini's 1958 address as a document that was both farsighted and still relevant. And this was not the only time.

In a 2014 address to the participants in the international congress on the pastoral care of large cities, the pope said: "It gives me joy to think that we are following a path together, and that we do so in the footsteps of so many holy pastors who came before us; I am referring only to the example of Blessed Giovanni Battista Montini, who during his episcopate in Milan, managed the great city mission with passionate zeal. In the writings of Blessed Paul VI, when he was Archbishop of Milan, there was a boatload, a boatload of things that could help with this."[45] The reference to Montini's lesson is important, because it is connected, once again, with the idea of the end of Christianity. "We come," Francis said, "from a

43. Pope Francis, "Christmas Greetings to the Roman Curia," n. 17.

44. Giovanni Battista Montini, "Lettera pastorale all'arcidiocesi ambrosiana per la Quaresima 1957 'Sul senso religioso,'" in Montini, *Discorsi e scritti milanesi (1954–1963)* (Brescia: Istituto Paolo VI, 1997), 1212–1235; now also in Giovanni Battista Montini and Luigi Giusani, *Sul senso religioso* (Milan: Rizzoli, 2009), 45–76.

45. Pope Francis, "Address to Participants at the International Pastoral Congress on the World's Big Cities," November 27, 2014, http://www.vatican.va/content/francesco /en/speeches/2014/november/documents/papa-francesco_20141127_pastorale-grandi -citta.html.

centuries-old pastoral practice, in which the Church has been the single point of reference for culture. It's true, it is our legacy. As the authentic Teacher, she felt the responsibility to outline and impose, not only the cultural forms, but also values, and to more profoundly trace the personal and collective imagination, in other words the histories, the cornerstones that people lean on to find the ultimate meanings and answers to their essential questions. *We are no longer in that time. It has past [sic]. We are no longer in Christianity, no more."*[46]

In the West, Christianity can no longer be presupposed, despite the insistence of Catholic neoconservative ideology. It certainly represents a legacy of a great history, but it concerns the present marginally at best. To make the content of faith comprehensible again, it is necessary to start afresh from that "religious sense" that, according to Montini's 1957 pastoral letter, is the vehicle for reaching the human heart in its universality. It is not just a question of a "natural" religiosity but a "historical" one. Christianity has not disappeared; it has permeated the profound sensitivity of peoples, the way they feel and judge. From there, according to the pope, it is necessary to start again.

In his address of November 2014, Francis said:

> God lives in the cities. It is necessary to go and look for Him, and to stop there, where He is at work. I know it is not the same thing on the various continents, but we have to uncover, in the religiosity of our peoples, the authentic religious substratum, which in many cases is Christian and Catholic. Not in all: there are non-Christian religiosities. But it is necessary to go there, to the core. We must neither fail to appreciate nor disregard this experience of God which, while sometimes being dispersed or blended, calls to be discovered and not built. It is there that the *semina Verbi* are sown by the Spirit of the Lord. It is not good to make hasty and general assessments such as: "This is only an expression of natural religiosity." No, this cannot be said! That is where we can begin the dialogue of evangelization, as Jesus did with the Samaritan woman and surely with many others beyond Galilee. A consciousness of one's own Christian identity and also empathy for the other person are necessary for the dialogue of evangelization.[47]

46. Pope Francis, "Address to Participants at the International Pastoral Congress on the World's Big Cities" (emphasis mine).

47. Pope Francis, "Address to Participants at the International Pastoral Congress on the World's Big Cities."

The theme of the "piety of the people," which matured in the Latin American context, is here understood from a European perspective. *It takes on a new meaning after the end of Christianity.* It is not an archaeological, nostalgic, evocative perspective of a past that has faded or is destined to fade. The secularized West is no longer "Christian." Secularization doesn't fully dissolve and transform its "values"; in the depths of its soul it retains traces of a sense that distinguishes it from other civilizations. It is an underground identity, not manifest, an identity that is not brandished like a banner but can be found through actions and words that actualize Christianity again in the present. Historically "Christian" religiosity is the substratum that can be brought to light "empathically," through authentic personal encounters, marked by the consciousness of Christ. This is why mission comes before the moral agenda. In a deeply secularized world, Christian witness is a face in the crowd, an embrace in the midst of solitude, mercy in the desert. Paul VI mapped out the way, first of all with his great insights—the end of Christianity, the Christian approach not starting from values but from the popular religious dimension, the consequent conciliar turning point—and secondly in correctly describing the form of Christian action in the contemporary world, the polar combination between evangelization and human development. These are lessons that Bergoglio made his own and made current again.

The Way of Mercy: The Theology of Tenderness and the Dialectic of the Great and the Small

Francis, the pope of the peripheries, of human development, is also *the pope of mercy.* It's yet another attribute that rankles "Christianists," who are concerned only about truth, reason over the heart, the sword that divides rather than the embrace that unites. The Manichean spirit that dominates the contemporary theological-political scene wants conflict rather than peace. In this viewpoint, Bergoglio's Christianity is feminine, saccharine happy-talk. Catholic neoconservatives, on the other hand, want a "manly" faith. As the American commentator Daniel Pipes has put it, "Americans are from Mars; Europeans from Venus."[48] In this polarization, conservatives misunderstand and distort, again, Bergoglio's

---

48. Daniel Pipes, "Europeans: From Venus?," *New York Post*, July 16, 2002.

authentic thought. This is a point of the utmost importance that requires a clarification.

Although Pope Francis's theology of tenderness has inspired numerous publications—including Cardinal Kasper's book, *Pope Francis' Revolution of Tenderness and Love*[49]—the theological-philosophical foundations behind it still await serious investigation. It is not a question of the Argentine pope's sentimentality, as some suggest, accusing him of dissociating mercy from truth by prioritizing the former. It is, rather, an authentic Gospel approach that presupposes a thought and a spirituality rooted in Ignatian formation.

All of Francis's thought is marked by a philosophy of polarity that seeks to unite intellect and heart, reason and sentiment, against the rationalistic tendencies of modern thought. This is because "the Ignatian choice is never merely theoretical but presupposes a dimension of pathos."[50] Concrete thought is marked by pathos; it bears the impact of being immersed in the flesh, carries the stamp of joy and pain that mark the human condition. This condition is embraced by theology *through a sensitivity to the concreteness of historical time*. This is not historicism but the actualization of the dynamics of the incarnation. For Francis, a theology of tenderness is justified today on the basis of two fundamental reasons.

> Theology and tenderness seem to be two distant words: the first seems to recall the academic context, the second interpersonal relations. In reality our faith links them inextricably. Theology, in fact, can not be abstract—if it were abstract, it would be ideology—as it arises from an existential knowledge, born from the encounter with the Word made flesh! Theology is then called to communicate the concreteness of God's love. And tenderness is a "concrete existential" asset, to translate in our times the affection that the Lord nourishes for us.
>
> Today, in fact, there is less focus on the concept or practice and more on "feeling" than in the past. We may like it or not, but it is a fact: we start from what we feel. Theology can certainly not be reduced to sentiment, but neither can it ignore that in many parts of the world the approach to vital issues no longer begins with the ultimate questions or social demands, but with what the person feels emotionally. Theology is called upon to

---

49. Walter Kasper, *Pope Francis' Revolution of Tenderness and Love: Theological and Pastoral Perspectives* (Mahwah, NJ: Paulist, 2015).

50. Bergoglio, "Servizio della fede e promozione della giustizia," 87.

accompany this existential quest, bringing the light that comes from the Word of God. And a good theology of tenderness can present divine charity in this sense. It is possible, because the love of God is not an abstract general principle, but personal and concrete, that the Holy Spirit communicates intimately. Indeed, He reaches and transforms the feelings and thoughts of man.[51]

Here the pope makes a statement of great importance: "the approach to vital issues no longer begins with the ultimate questions or social demands, but with what the person feels emotionally." The meeting point where Christianity can engage the world is no longer philosophy, as was the case during the 1950s, with a culture marked by existentialism; nor is it political, as during the 1970s, with a culture marked by the militant and ideological commitment of Marxism. The new opportunity is in the sensibility that characterizes the present hour. This is a historical judgment that motivates the insistence with which Francis speaks of God's tenderness. Humanity today is, in its frailty, particularly receptive to the affective dimension. In the "world without ties," in liquid society, people do not reach an understanding of the meaning of their lives through logical reasoning, but through the discovery of being loved.

Pope Benedict XVI understood this perfectly. This is clear in a 2016 interview—three years into the Francis pontificate—with Fr. Jacques Servais, in which the pope emeritus said:

> I believe it is a 'sign of the times' that the idea of God's mercy is becoming increasingly central and dominant. . . .
>
> Pope John Paul II felt this impulse very strongly even though this was not always immediately apparent. But it is certainly no coincidence that his last book, which was published just before his death, talks about God's mercy. . . .
>
> Pope Francis fully shares this line. His pastoral practice finds expression in his continuous references to God's mercy. It is mercy that steers us toward God, while justice makes us fearful in his presence. I believe this shows that beneath the veneer of self-confidence and self-righteousness,

---

51. Pope Francis, "Address to Participants at the Conference on the Theme 'The Theology of Tenderness of Pope Francis,'" September 13, 2018, https://www.vatican.va /content/francesco/en/speeches/2018/september/documents/papa-francesco_20180913 _convegno-tenerezza.html.

today's mankind conceals a profound knowledge of its wounds and un-worthiness before God. It awaits mercy. It is certainly no coincidence that people today find the parable of the Good Samaritan particularly attractive. And not just because it strongly highlights the social aspect of human existence, nor just because in it the Samaritan, a non-religious man, seems to act according to God's will toward religious representatives, while official religious representatives have become immune, so to speak, to God.

Clearly the people of today like this. But I also find it equally important that deep down, humans expect the Samaritan to come to their rescue that he will bend down and poor oil on their wounds, take care of them and bring them to safety. Essentially, they know they need God's mercy and gentleness. In today's tough and technified world where feelings no longer count for anything, expectations are growing for a redeeming love that is given freely. It seems to me that in divine mercy, the meaning of justifying faith is expressed in a new way. Through God's mercy—which everyone seeks—it is possible even today to interpret the crux of the doctrine of justification, fully ensuring its relevance.[52]

Benedict is in total harmony with Francis here. His words highlight the golden thread that, beyond the diversity of accents and style, unites the two pontificates.[53] As Francis says in his book-length conversation with Andrea Tornielli, *The Name of God Is Mercy*:

52. English translation of an excerpt from an interview in Daniele Libanori, ed., *Per mezzo della fede: Dottrina della giustificazione ed esperienza di Dio nella predicazione della Chiesa e negli Esercizi Spirituali* (Rome: San Paolo, 2016), in Andrea Tornielli, "Benedict XVI: 'It's mercy that steers us towards God,'" Vatican Insider blog, *La Stampa*, March 16, 2016, https://www.lastampa.it/vatican-insider/en/2016/03/16/news/benedict-xvi-it-s -mercy-that-br-steers-us-towards-god-br-1.36577840.

53. Gian Enrico Rusconi recognizes this when he writes, "Pope Francis is located and legitimized [by Benedict XVI] in line with his predecessors, in particular with John Paul II" (*La teologia narrativa di papa Francesco* [Rome: Laterza, 2017], 57). This is a significant recognition, because Rusconi structures his volume starting from the thesis of an antinomy, in Francis, between his clear fidelity to tradition and the primacy of mercy that would lead to lessening the importance of divine punishment, consequent to original sin. It is an antinomy that does not, however, differentiate Francis from Benedict, as the Catholics critical of Pope Bergoglio would like. For Rusconi,

Ratzinger does not directly call into question, except by allusion, original sin as the cause of evil, and therefore he eludes (like Bergoglio) the aporia of why God did not immediately manifest his mercy toward the ancestors. Furthermore, Ratzinger goes so far as to criticize the position of Anselm of Canterbury, who with an irreproachable

Yes, I believe that this is the time of mercy. The Church is showing her
maternal side, her motherly face, to a humanity that is wounded. She does
not wait for the wounded to knock on her doors, she looks for them on
the streets, she gathers them in, she embraces them, she takes care of them,
she makes them feel loved. And so, as I said [in July 2013, during the return
trip from Rio de Janeiro], and I am ever more convinced of it, this is a
kairós, our era is a *kairós* of mercy, an opportune time.[54]

It is this judgment about the existential condition of our time that explains the pope's insistence on the tenderness of God as a way of encountering humanity of today, the sinner of today. This is not the pope adopting
the sentimental reductionism that marks so much contemporary Christianity, characterized by a spiritualism that replaces Christ with love, an
approach that, echoing Feuerbach, says not that God is love but that love
is God. Francis's perspective is evangelical and, as such, it is historical. It
proposes Christianity not, first of all, as a doctrine or a moral law but emi-
nently as a reflection of the attitude with which Christ relates to the world.
This is what emerges from Francis's 2015 address to the representatives of
the Italian church. On that occasion, in Florence, the pope said: "I do not
want to design here a '*new humanism*' in the abstract, a certain idea of man,
but to present in a simple way some of the traits of Christian humanism
which is the humanism of the 'mind of Christ Jesus' (Phil 2:5)."[55]

Christian humanism is, in a theologically surprising way, not primarily a doctrine or an ethical choice but the "mind of Christ Jesus." An
"affective" element marks the *novum* of Christian humanity in history.
The world of *eros* and *techne* desperately needs this element. As Francis
said in unscripted comments to leaders of Caritas Internationalis in November 2016, "the greatest illness of today is 'cardiosclerosis.'"[56] This is

logic justifies the terrible punishment inflicted on the ancestors as the only adequate
response to the offense done to the infinite nature of God. . . . Ratzinger reiterates that
Anselm's conceptuality has become incomprehensible to us and therefore invites us to
understand "in a new way the truth that is hidden in this manner of expression." (58–59)

54. Pope Francis, *The Name of God Is Mercy*, trans. Oonagh Stransky (New York:
Random House, 2016), 6.

55. Pope Francis, "Address to the Participants in the Fifth Convention of the Italian
Church," November 10, 2015, http://www.vatican.va/content/francesco/en/speeches/2015
/november/documents/papa-francesco_20151110_firenze-convegno-chiesa-italiana.html.

56. Dominic Agasso, Jr., "We are suffering from 'cardiosclerosis,' we need a revolution
of tenderness," Vatican Insider blog, *La Stampa*, November 17, 2016, https://www.lastampa

why "a revolution of tenderness is needed today, in a world dominated by a throwaway culture. If I throw away, then I don't know what tenderness is."[57] Tenderness "is revolutionary, tenderness is closeness, it is the great gesture of the Father towards us: the closeness of his son, who showed His closeness to us, He became one of us, this is the Father's docility."[58] The pope continued by noting that he had read that day "the passage of the Gospel in which God weeps, He weeps because he remembers the love He feels for His people and which the people do not recognise and do not wish to reciprocate. This moment of tenderness is not an idea, it is the essence, our God is Father as well as mother and 'just as a mother never forgets her children, so I never forget about you.' A mother's love is the greatest love there is."[59]

Connected to this historical judgment is the second element which, starting from Ignatian thought marked by *pathos*, helps to outline the theology of tenderness. It is founded upon the implications of the theology of the incarnation. Here the Christian offers a witness that "is hidden, full of tenderness, in those small gestures, gestures of proximity, where all the word becomes flesh: flesh that approaches and embraces, hands that touch and bandage, that anoint with oil and soothe wounds with wine; meat that approaches and accompanies, that listens; hands that break bread."[60] As Francis said in his conversation with Fr. Spadaro,

> The image that comes to my mind is that of a nurse in a hospital who heals our wounds, one at a time. Just like God, who gets involved and meddles in our miseries, He gets close to our wounds and heals them with His hands. And to actually have hands, He became man. It is a personal work of Jesus. A man made sin, a man comes to cure it. Closeness. God doesn't save just because of a decree, a law; he saves us with tenderness, he saves us with caresses, he saves us with his life, for us.[61]

.it/vatican-insider/en/2016/11/17/news/we-are-suffering-from-cardiosclerosis-we-need-a-revolution-of-tenderness-1.34772427.

57. Agasso, "We are suffering from 'cardiosclerosis.'"

58. Agasso, "We are suffering from 'cardiosclerosis.'"

59. Agasso, "We are suffering from 'cardiosclerosis.'"

60. Jorge Mario Bergoglio, "Omelia pronunciata durante la messa di chiusura del Congresso nazionale di dottrina sociale della Chiesa," in Jorge Mario Bergoglio–Pope Francis, *Pastorale sociale*, 151.

61. Pope Francis, *My Door Is Always Open*, 71–72.

God "saves us with tenderness"—this is the heart of the Gospel message according to Bergoglio. This means that God does not save us "from afar," from above. The method is that of proximity. *God became human in order to have hands.* This image makes clear Bergoglio's conception of witness as immersion in reality. Hands suggest contact, touch, embrace, caress, work. Christianity appears here as a physical fact, an incarnation from beginning to end. "What is fundamental for me is the closeness of the Church. The Church is a mother, and mothers don't communicate 'by correspondence.' A mother gives affection, touch, kisses, love. When the Church, busy with a thousand things, neglects closeness, it forgets about it and only communicates in written documents, it's like a mother communicating with her son by letter."[62]

Bergoglio's *Christian empiricism*, deeply rooted in the fabric of the Spiritual Exercises of St. Ignatius, does not like mediations, the intermediaries that dominate in a bureaucratized church in which people are defined by "roles." A mother "gives affection, touch, kisses, love." The maternal image of the church confirms the priority of the *aesthetic*, tactile factor; it explains the closeness of Bergoglio, since the beginning of the twenty-first century, to the theological aesthetics of Hans Urs von Balthasar. This is not just a question of a concession to Baroque spirituality, typical of Latin American Catholicism. Francis understands his theology of tenderness within the context of a contemporary world that no longer knows the gratuitousness of true love, divided as it is between coldness and eros. It is a world characterized by a kind of *spiritual orphanhood.*

> This attitude of spiritual orphanhood is a cancer that silently eats away at and debases the soul. . . . The loss of the ties that bind us, so typical of our fragmented and divided culture, increases this sense of orphanhood and, as a result, of great emptiness and loneliness. The lack of physical (and not virtual) contact is cauterizing our hearts (cf. *Laudato Si'*, 49) and making us lose the capacity for tenderness and wonder, for pity and compassion. Spiritual orphanhood makes us forget what it means to be children, grandchildren, parents, grandparents, friends and believers. It makes us forget the importance of playing, of singing, of a smile, of rest, of gratitude.[63]

---

62. Pope Francis, *My Door Is Always Open*, 68–69.

63. Pope Francis, "Homily on the Solemnity of Mary the Holy Mother of God and the World Day of Peace," January 1, 2017, http://www.vatican.va/content/francesco/en/homilies /2017/documents/papa-francesco_20170101_omelia-giornata-mondiale-pace.html.

Faced with this "orphanhood," a world without a father or a mother, *God can return to being Father only if the church presents itself as mother.* In this maternity resides the "merciful" face of the church, the response to the present emptiness of the world. For the pope, "Tenderness is closeness and closeness means touching, embracing, consoling, not being afraid of the flesh because God took human flesh and Christ's flesh today are the discarded, the displaced, the victims of war." For this reason, "the proposals of spirituality are too theoretical, they are new forms of Gnosticism." Today, "in this throwaway culture, which follows the ideology of the money god, I believe the greatest illness of today is cardiosclerosis."[64]

The theology of tenderness presupposes, as is evident, a theology of the incarnation, a direct critique of Gnosticism that, together with Pelagianism, constitutes for Francis a source of profound corruption of the faith. Tenderness requires a physical, direct relationship with the flesh of the other, with their wounds, their fragility, with that corporeality that every spiritualism, every Gnosticism, tends to despise and to shy away from. As Francis said in his speech to healthcare workers in 2018:

> Being with the sick and practicing your profession, you personally touch the sick, and more than anything else, you take care of their bodies. When you do so, remember how Jesus touched the leper: not in a distracted, indifferent or annoyed manner, but attentive and loving, so it makes him or her feel respected and taken care of. In doing so, the contact that you establish with patients accompanies them as an echo of God the Father's closeness, of his tenderness for each one of his children. Precisely *tenderness*: tenderness is the "key" to understanding the sick. The sick cannot be understood with harshness. Tenderness is the key to understanding them, and is also a precious medicine for their healing. And tenderness passes from the heart to the hands; it passes, with full respect and love, through the "touching" of wounds.[65]

Tenderness passes from the heart to the hands; Bergoglio's anthropology unites the mind, the heart, the hands. Tenderness is more than a look; it becomes an embrace, support, caress. At its base, there is an integral vision of humanity.

64. Agasso, "We are suffering from 'cardiosclerosis.'"

65. Pope Francis, "Address to Members of the Italian Federation of the Boards of Nursing Professions (FNOPI)," March 3, 2018, http://www.vatican.va/content/francesco/en/speeches/2018/march/documents/papa-francesco_20180303_ipasvi.html.

Bergoglio's theology of tenderness depends, at its root, on a precise Ignatian conception of the relationship between humanity and God. This is a little-studied aspect of the pope's spirituality. It came to light in a particularly evident way in his weekday Mass homily on December 14, 2017, in the chapel of Casa Santa Marta. On that occasion, referring to the approaching feast of Christmas, the pope said that the annual feast brings Christians face to face with "one of the greatest mysteries, it is one of the most beautiful things: our God has this tenderness that draws us closer and saves us with this tenderness." He said that God "chastises us sometimes, but he caresses us." This is "the tenderness of God," who says to us, "Do not be afraid, I come to your aid, your redeemer is the holy one of Israel." And so, "it is the great God who makes himself small, and in his littleness he never ceases to be great and *in this great dialectic he is small: there is the tenderness of God, the great one who makes himself small and the small one who is great.*"[66]

The pope continued, "Christmas helps us to understand this: in that manger, the little God. . . . A phrase of St. Thomas comes to mind, in the first part of the *Summa.* Wanting to describe 'what is divine? what is the most divine thing?' he says: *Non coerceri a maximo contineri tamen a minimo divinum est.*" Here the pope was referring to the so-called epitaph of St. Ignatius, composed by an unknown Jesuit in the seventeenth century in honor of the saint. It might literally be translated: "Not to be confined to what is greater, but to be concerned with what is smaller: this is divine." Essentially, the pontiff continued in his homily, the axiom is an invitation "not to be frightened by big things, but to take small things into account. This is divine—both together." And the Jesuits know this expression well, he said, because "it was included on one of the tombstones of St. Ignatius, as if to describe the strength of St. Ignatius and also his tenderness."[67]

These comments of Francis are especially important because the expression he refers to here, the epitaph of St. Ignatius, played a decisive role in his own early intellectual and spiritual formation. As a young man,

66. Pope Francis, "Tenere conto delle piccole cose" (morning meditation in the chapel of the Domus Sanctae Marthae), December 14, 2017, http://www.vatican.va/content/francesco/it/cotidie/2017/documents/papa-francesco-cotidie_20171214_tenere-conto-piccole-cose.html.

67. Pope Francis, "Tenere conto delle piccole cose."

Bergoglio encountered a long analysis of the motto in the final part of a 1956 book by the French philosopher-theologian Gaston Fessard, *La dialectique des Exercices spirituels de Saint Ignace de Loyola*.[68] As I have shown in my earlier book, *The Mind of Pope Francis: Jorge Mario Bergoglio's Intellectual Journey*, Fessard, one of the most significant Jesuit intellectuals of the second half of the twentieth century, is a key figure in Bergoglio's formation.[69] The latter's polar, dialectical thinking draws its nourishment from the reflection gained in reading in Fessard's 1956 work. As the pope acknowledged: "The—in quotes—'Hegelian' writer, but he is not Hegelian, though it may seem like he is—who had a big influence on me was Gaston Fessard. I've read *La dialectique des Exercices spirituels de saint Ignace de Loyola*, and other things by him, several times. That work gave me so many elements that later became mixed in [to my thinking]."[70]

Bergoglio seems to have become aware of the analytical commentary on the Ignatian epitaph in the latter part of Fessard's book through Miguel Angel Fiorito, his philosophy professor at the Colegio Máximo San José in the city of San Miguel, Argentina. In a 1981 article, Bergoglio cites two articles by Fiorito—one from 1956, "La opción personal de S. Ignacio," and one from 1957, "Teoría y práctica de G. Fessard."[71] The latter article was a commentary on the so-called Ignatian epitaph. Fiorito, an interpreter of the *Spiritual Exercises*, made reference to Fessard's analysis of the epitaph and offered an interpretation in light of the dialectical model offered by Fessard. Fiorito wrote, "The (so-called) epitaph of St. Ignatius contains two complementary sentences. . . . The first sentence (*non coerceri a maximo, contineri tamen a minimo, divinum est*) highlights a fundamental characteristic of Ignatian spirituality . . . because it expresses dialectically—that is, by the opposition of contraries—the

68. Gaston Fessard, *La dialectique des Exercices spirituels de Saint Ignace de Loyola* (Paris: Aubier, 1956), 307–41.

69. Borghesi, *The Mind of Pope Francis*, 1–19.

70. Pope Francis, audio recording of January 3, 2017, in Borghesi, *The Mind of Pope Francis*, 6.

71. Miguel Angel Fiorito, "La opción personal de San Ignacio: Cristo o Satanás," *Ciencia y Fe* 12 (1956), 23–56 (now in Fiorito, *Escritos 1952–1959*, J. L. Narvaja, ed. [Vatican City: La Civiltà Cattolica, 2019], 162–83); Fiorito, "Teoría y práctica de los Ejercicios Espirituales según G. Fessard," *Ciencia y Fe* 13 (1957) (now in *Escritos 1952–1959*, 233–50). Both articles are cited in Jorge Mario Bergoglio, "Responsabilidad como Provincia frente a las futuras vocaciones," *Boletín de Espiritualidad* 12 (1981), 20–27, n. 71.

fundamental dynamism of the holy soul of Ignatius, who points always to the highest ideal, God, but is at the same time attentive to the smallest details of the divine plan."[72]

Having encountered the motto in Fessard's book by way of the Fiorito article, it became for Bergoglio the ideal expression of the polar tension that animates the spirituality of St. Ignatius. Explaining its meaning in 1981, Bergoglio wrote, "We could translate it this way: without turning away from that which is higher, we must bend down to pick up what is apparently small in the service of God; or, while remaining attentive to what is farther away, we must worry about what is closer. It is applied to religious discipline . . . *and is useful for characterizing Ignatian spirituality dialectically (in the sense adopted by Fessard).*"[73]

The insight of the St. Ignatius epitaph has remained with Bergoglio throughout his life. More than half a century after first encountering it, he said, as pope,

> I was always struck by a saying that describes the vision of Ignatius: *non coerceri a maximo, sed contineri a minimo divinum est* ("not to be limited by the greatest and yet to be contained in the tiniest—this is the divine"). I thought a lot about this phrase in connection with the issue of different roles in the government of the Church, about becoming the superior of somebody else: it is important not to be restricted by a larger space, and it is important to be able to stay in restricted spaces. This virtue of the large and small is magnanimity. Thanks to magnanimity, we can always look at the horizon from the position where we are. That means being able to do the little things of every day with a big heart open to God and to others. That means being able to appreciate the small things inside large horizons, those of the Kingdom of God.[74]

72. Miguel Angel Fiorito, "Teoría y práctica de los Ejercicios Espirituales según G. Fessard," 350–51.

73. Jorge Mario Bergoglio–Pope Francis, *Nel cuore di ogni padre*, 282n4. Emphasis mine.

74. Pope Francis, *My Door Is Always Open*, 21. On the St. Ignatius epitaph, see Jorge Mario Bergoglio, "Condurre nelle grandi e nelle piccole circostanze," *Boletín de Espiritualidad* 73 (October 1981). In a "Letter on Inculturation to the Whole Society" of May 14, 1978, Father General Pedro Arrupe recalls the Ignatian maxim: "The ignatian spirit was once summed up in this sentence: 'Non cohiberi a maximo, contineri tamen a minimo, divinum est.' In our context, this maxim challenges us to hold on to the concrete and the particular, even to the last cultural detail, but without renouncing the breadth and uni-

The dialectic of the great and the small, this tension that characterizes Ignatius's faith and spirituality, became a fixed point of Bergoglio's vision. In fact, through Fiorito, the "dialectic" of Fessard's explanation of the *Spiritual Exercises* became, for the young student, a lasting point of reference. It led him to further reading that was decisive for his formation. Fiorito and Fessard had helped him understand the "polarity," *the opposition of contraries*, that guides the Ignatian soul. From this intuition, the rest flows— including, it is essential to note, his theology of tenderness. This theology combines the Ignatian idea of "God ever greater" with St. Paul's idea, in Philippians 6:2-11, of the Lord who takes the condition of a slave. The theology of tenderness is a theology of the abasement of the Lord who makes himself a servant, that is, who makes himself small *in order to be able to communicate with the small*. Salvation thus comes to humanity not through strength and power, which are also attributes of God, but through the weakness of the Son. *God chooses tenderness as the method of salvation.* Tenderness comes from the dialectic of the great and the small, of the great that becomes small and of the small that becomes great. Only in the logic of the incarnation, of the abasement of God into the condition of slave as the supreme sign of love for humanity, does the logic of tenderness become comprehensible. Bergoglio's theology arises from reflection upon the Ignatian epitaph. There, the paradoxical relationship between God and humanity that develops in Christian logic finds its explanation.

The dialectic of the great and the small as a reference point of the theology of tenderness finds its expression, according to Francis, in the mystery of Christmas. In the birth of the child God,

> the 'sign' is in fact the humility of God, the humility of God taken to the extreme; it is the love with which, that night, he assumed our frailty, our suffering, our anxieties, our desires and our limitations. The message that everyone was expecting, that everyone was searching for in the depths of their souls, was none other than the tenderness of God: God who looks

---

versality of those human values which no culture, not the totality of them all, can assimilate and incarnate in [a] perfect and exhaustive way." Pedro Arrupe, "Letter on Inculturation to the Whole Society," in Arrupe, *Other Apostolates Today, Selected Letters and Addresses*, vol. 3, ed. Jerome Aixala, SJ (St. Louis: Institute of Jesuit Sources, 1981), 171–81 at 176. The maxim was also studied by Hugo Rahner, "Die Grabschrift des Loyola," *Stimmen der Zeit*, February 1947, 321–39.

upon us with eyes full of love, who accepts our poverty, God who is in love with our smallness. . . .

How much the world needs tenderness today! The patience of God, the closeness of God, the tenderness of God.

The Christian response cannot be different from God's response to our smallness. Life must be met with goodness, with meekness. When we realize that God is in love with our smallness, that he made himself small in order to better encounter us, we cannot help but open our hearts to him, and beseech him: "Lord, help me to be like you, give me the grace of tenderness in the most difficult circumstances of life, give me the grace of closeness in the face of every need, of meekness in every conflict."[75]

The pope has spoken of this tenderness on several occasions when commenting on some of the parables, such as that of the Prodigal Son and that of the Good Samaritan. The father in the former tale is a father of tenderness. In 2016 the pope recalled, "After serving for several years as the Bishop of Vittorio Veneto, Albino Luciani held some training exercises for parish priests, and when commenting on the parable of the Prodigal Son once said this about the father: He waits. Always. And it is never too late. That's what he's like, that's how he is . . . he's a father. A father waiting at the doorway, who sees us when we are still far off, who is moved, and who comes running toward us, embraces us, and kisses us tenderly."[76]

And at a general audience the same year:

The reception of the prodigal son is described in a moving way: "while he was yet at a distance, his father saw him and had compassion, and ran and embraced him and kissed him" (v. 20).

What tenderness! He sees him at a distance: what does this mean? That the father had constantly gone to the balcony to look at the road to see if his son would return; that son who had misbehaved in many ways found the father there waiting for him. How beautiful is the father's tenderness! The father's mercy is overflowing, unconditional, and shows itself even before the son speaks. Certainly, the son knows he erred and acknowledges it: "I have sinned . . . treat me as one of your hired servants" (vv. 18-19). These words crumble before the father's forgiveness. The embrace and the

75. Pope Francis, "Homily for the Solemnity of the Nativity of the Lord," December 24, 2014, http://www.vatican.va/content/francesco/en/homilies/2014/documents/papa-francesco_20141224_omelia-natale.html.

76. Pope Francis, *The Name of God Is Mercy*, 51–52.

kiss of his father makes him understand that he was always considered a son, in spite of everything.[77]

Here Francis brings together mercy, compassion, and tenderness. "Mercy," he says, "is divine and has to do with the judgment of sin."[78] He explains the reason in *Evangelii Gaudium*, by quoting St. Thomas Aquinas: "In itself mercy is the greatest of the virtues, since all the others revolve around it and, more than this, it makes up for their deficiencies. This is particular to the superior virtue, and as such it is proper to God to have mercy, through which his omnipotence is manifested to the greatest degree."[79] If mercy is the divine expression of love, the human expression of it is compassion.

> Compassion has a more human face. It means to suffer with, to suffer together, not to remain indifferent to the pain and the suffering of others. It is what Jesus felt when he saw the crowds who followed him. . . . Let us reflect on the beautiful pages that describe the resurrection of the son of the widow from Nain: When Jesus arrived in this village on the Galilee, he was moved by the tears of the widow, who was devastated by the loss of her only son. He says to her, "Woman, do not weep." As Luke writes in the Gospel: "When the Lord saw her, he was moved with pity for her" (7:13). God Incarnate let himself be moved by human wretchedness, by our need, by our suffering. The Greek verb that indicates this compassion is σπλαγχνίζομαι [*splanchnízomai*, ed.], which derives from the word that indicates internal organs or the mother's womb. It is similar to the love of a father and mother who are profoundly moved by their own son; it is a visceral love. God loves us in this way, with compassion and mercy.[80]

He loves us according to the double divine-human polarity in accord with his dual nature. Here again, the idea of the great that becomes small and of the small that becomes great. The encounter between divine mercy and human compassion is tenderness, the gaze of a God who is merciful

---

77. Pope Francis, "General Audience," May 11, 2016, http://www.vatican.va/content /francesco/en/audiences/2016/documents/papa-francesco_20160511_udienza-generale .html.

78. Pope Francis, *The Name of God Is Mercy*, 91.

79. St. Thomas Aquinas, *Summa Theologiae*, II-II, q. 30, a. 4, in Pope Francis, *Evangelii Gaudium*, 37.

80. Pope Francis, *The Name of God Is Mercy*, 91–92.

and compassionate at the same time. This is not a theological sentimen-tality, a dissociation of mercy and truth; it describes the way God can existentially raise the sinner crushed by sin. Today, says Francis,

> humanity is wounded, deeply wounded. Either it does not know how to cure its wounds or it believes that it's not possible to cure them. And it's not just a question of social ills or people wounded by poverty, social exclusion, or one of the many slaveries of the third millennium. Relativism wounds people too: all things seem equal, all things appear the same. Humanity needs mercy and compassion. Pius XII, more than half a century ago, said that the tragedy of our age was that it had lost its sense of sin, the awareness of sin. Today we add further to the tragedy by considering our illness, our sins, to be incurable, things that cannot be healed or forgiven. We lack the actual concrete experience of mercy. The fragility of our era is this, too: we don't believe that there is a chance for redemption; for a hand to raise you up; for an embrace to save you, forgive you, pick you up, flood you with infinite, patient, indulgent love; to put you back on your feet.[81]

God's tenderness relates to the fragility of the world. The Father does not break the bruised reed, does not utter recriminations over the violated law, welcomes the returning sinner, embraces the humiliated son. Before humanity of today, Francis said in an address to the bishops of Mexico, "*La Virgen Morenita* teaches us that the only power capable of conquer-ing the hearts of men and women is the tenderness of God. That which delights and attracts, that which humbles and overcomes, that which opens and unleashes, is not the power of instruments or the force of law, but rather the omnipotent weakness of divine love, which is the irresist-ible force of its gentleness and the irrevocable pledge of its mercy."[82]

These words take us to the heart of Francis's theology. The tenderness of God relates to the humanity of today, bent by sin, deprived of hope of getting up again. For this reason, one of the pope's favorite metaphors is that of the church as a field hospital: "I see clearly what the Church needs most today, and it is the ability to heal wounds and to warm the hearts of the faithful, together with closeness, and proximity. I see the Church as a field hospital after battle. It is useless to ask a seriously injured person

---

81. Pope Francis, *The Name of God Is Mercy*, 15–16.

82. Pope Francis, "Address to the Bishops of Mexico," February 13, 2016, http://www.vatican.va/content/francesco/en/speeches/2016/february/documents/papa-francesco_20160213_messico-vescovi.html.

if he has high cholesterol and about the level of his blood sugars! You have to heal his wounds. Then we can talk about everything else."[83] He continues, "I dream of a Church that is both Mother and Shepherdess. The Church's ministers must be merciful, take responsibility for the people and accompany them like the Good Samaritan, who washes, cleans and raises up his neighbor. This is pure Gospel. God is greater than sin."[84]

The Good Samaritan becomes the image of the church dreamed of by Francis, in an extraordinary similarity with the *other* Francis, the one from Assisi. As Bergoglio said to health care workers and patients at Rio de Janiero's St. Francis of Assisi of the Providence of God Hospital, "To embrace, to embrace—we all have to learn to embrace the one in need, as Saint Francis did."[85] Reflecting on this comment, Fr. Antonio Spadaro wrote:

> To knock at the door of the heart you therefore need to have 'bare' hands, to have no filters, to touch the flesh. For Pope Francis this physical dimension is not an accessory, a mere question of "style," but part of the communication of the strong message of the Incarnation.
>
> The paradigm for this ability to communicate is the parable of the Good Samaritan (Lk 10:29-35), and the reference to the "Samaritan Church" is already present in the foundational document of Aparecida, produced by the Fifth Episcopal Conference of Latin America held in the Brazilian city in 2007, in which Cardinal Bergoglio played a central role.[86]

Francis confirmed Spadaro's words in his weekday Mass homily of December 14, 2017, already mentioned above, posing a question, "Someone might ask: what is the theological reference for God's tenderness? Where can God's tenderness be found clearly? Where is God's tenderness best manifested?" The pope then provided the answer: "The wound. My wounds, your wounds, when my wound meets his wound." Then he continued,

> When I think about what happened to that poor man who fell into the hands of the robbers on the way from Jerusalem to Jericho, I like to think

83. Pope Francis, *My Door Is Always Open*, 54.

84. Pope Francis, *My Door Is Always Open*, 54–55.

85. Pope Francis, "Address at St. Francis of Assisi of the Providence of God Hospital," July 24, 2013, http://www.vatican.va/content/francesco/en/speeches/2013/july/documents /papa-francesco_20130724_gmg-ospedale-rio.html.

86. Pope Francis, *My Door Is Always Open*, 70 (English translation slightly corrected).

about what happened when he regained consciousness and lay on the bed. He certainly asked the innkeeper, "What happened?"

The innkeeper told him, "You were beaten. You lost consciousness."

"But why am I here?"

"Because someone came and cleaned your wounds. He took care of you, brought you here, paid your fee, and said he will come back to settle the accounts if there is anything more to pay."

This is the theological reference for God's tenderness: our wounds.[87]

The Father, like the father in the parable of the Prodigal Son or the helpful man in that of the Good Samaritan, is the one who bends over the wounds of the world with *tenderness*. "In this sense, tenderness refers to the Passion. The Cross is in fact the seal of divine tenderness, which is drawn from the wounds of the Lord. His visible wounds are the windows that open onto His invisible love. His Passion invites us to transform our heart of stone into a heart of flesh, to become passionate about God. And about man, for the love of God."[88] Tenderness arises from the Lord who makes himself small, who renounces strength and power. The epitaph of St. Ignatius—*non coerceri a maximo, contineri tamen a minimo, divinum est*—lies at the heart of Francis's theology of tenderness.

87. Pope Francis, "Tenere conto delle piccole cose."

88. Pope Francis, "Address to Participants at the Conference on the Theme 'The Theology of Tenderness of Pope Francis.'"

Conclusion

Theo-populism, the United States, and the Future of the Church

On January 20, 2021, President Donald Trump, accompanied by his wife, Melania, walked across the green lawn of the White House for the last time. The images of the farewell showed very few people present, and not only because of COVID-19 concerns. The dismissal of the man who for four years represented the symbol of world populism, the new Constantine who had to protect the faith from the corruption at the hands of the "South American" pope, took place following the political and human disaster of the assault of Capitol Hill by his loyalists. The image of the apparently "alone" pope in St. Peter's Square on March 27, 2020, with which we opened this book, a pope seemingly destined for his own sunset precisely because of the anticipated reelection of the American president, thus corresponds to that of Trump, really alone, abandoned even by his closest collaborators. Theo-populism had suffered a defeat.

As Massimo Faggioli wrote following Trump's electoral defeat:

Over the past four years the White House (through officials like Steve Bannon and Pompeo) has directed a political attempt to divide the Church in two—for and against Pope Francis.

A handful of American bishops and a number of high-profile lay Catholics have given their blessing to this attempt. But the effort at division has failed.

Nonetheless, the *ecclesial* attempt remains, in a Church in the United States that is divided in two like never before. The "culture wars" have taken the form of intra-ecclesial theological wars and have exposed American Catholicism to the risk of a soft schism. . . .

Officials close to the Trump White House—like Pompeo, Bannon and Newt Gingrich, whose third wife is currently the US ambassador to the Holy See—have tried to find sympathetic forces in the Vatican, Italy, and Europe to create a bridgehead of a neo-nationalist Catholicism allied with the European right-wingers.

They have failed.[1]

Opposed by the liberal world, Trump defended the US economy from the threat of China and understood the discontent and frustration of Americans long ignored by the progressive elite. However, he also indulged their worst instincts: white supremacism, isolationism and disinterest in international alliances and balances, unrestrained capitalism in financial markets at the expense of the environment, weakening of the civil rights of African Americans. With his opposition to abortion, he managed to charm evangelical Christians and a segment of American Catholicism, including some of its bishops. Coming after Obama and his libertarianism on abortion, it was easy for Trump to garner a significant part of the ecclesial consensus. And so the anti-Obama Trump became, in the eyes of a Catholic opinion increasingly pushed to the right by the individualistic ethics of the Democratic Party, the anti-Francis Trump, the *kathèkon*, the *salvator mundi* longed for by the delusional Archbishop Viganò.

The sacralization of the figure of Trump is a mirror image of the metamorphosis of populism becoming theo-populism. Like the neocons who, after September 11, 2001, became the movement that has at times been called "theocon," the populist movement underwent a similar process. In its opposition to the liberal, agnostic-relativist-modernist left, the right took on fundamentalist and religious elements. Concerns about political correctness became an embrace of anything politically incorrect. Right and left twisted into a spiral, in a contrast that, becoming anthropological and religious, took on the Manichean form of the struggle of good against evil. In recent years, the pendulum has seemed to swing to the right.

From January 20, 2017, until 2020, theo-populism followed the pontificate of Francis like a hostile shadow. It has hindered his reform plan

---

1. Massimo Faggioli, "The End of the Trumpian Captivity of the American Church," *La Croix International*, November 12, 2020, https://international.la-croix.com/news /signs-of-the-times/the-end-of-the-trumpian-captivity-of-the-american-church/13324.

in every possible way by deforming its image in the Catholic media, presenting it as a dangerous subversion of tradition and a social revolution. The "socialist" pope has been portrayed as the opponent of the West, its traditions, its values. Adding to the criticisms of the Catholic neoconservatives, those of theo-populists have converged into the image of an Obama-like pope—ecumenical, relativist, pacifist, open to dialogue with the Islamic world. They do diverge on one point, though. Where the Catholic neoconservatives, or theocons, see the populist-Peronist in the Latin American pontiff, the theo-populists, on the contrary, see the instrument of the universalist and Masonic Deep State aimed at breaking down the borders and traditions of peoples. It is a divergence of no small importance that should prompt anyone to seek a more accurate interpretation of the authentic thought of Francis.

But ideologies, we know, are hard to correct. The religious emphasis that sustains them prevents their adherents from adopting a critical perspective. A transformation of judgment requires a collision, an impact with reality. What the pope's critics could not foresee was the "event," the factor that upset the linearity of historical processes: the tragic, invisible power of the COVID-19 pandemic. The intangible virus, a source of suffering and death, of serious economic crises and new inroads of poverty, has marked the crisis of populist ideology that has dominated the scene of the past decade.

On the one hand, it brought about the political failure of the American president, who had previously been anticipated to win the 2020 election, precisely because of his poor management of the pandemic, which he underestimated in every possible way. On the other hand, it has prompted a drifting Europe, marked by nationalistic selfishness and by British Brexit, to rediscover the soul lost in the years of globalization, a sense of solidarity that had previously seemed impossible, capable of supporting the economies threatened by the virus and planning a common reaction to the epidemic. In this way the anti-European polemic of the populist movement appears to be deprived of strength and foundation.

The year 2020 will thus be remembered not only as the very sad year of the global plague but also as that of the interruption of the process of disintegration of the world symbolized by populist ideologies. It is a process that has ecclesial repercussions. A fragmented world, divided by grudges and resentments, is not only a dangerous world, a harbinger of tragic conflicts; it is also "caged," hemmed inside steel fencing composed of national, ethnic, and religious cables. Such a world constitutes an obstacle to peace and a serious limitation for the missionary activity of a church that transcends borders. *It is a limitation that has repercussions within the church by dividing it, internally, in an incessant struggle between factions and battle groups, preventing its opening to the outside.*

From an ideological point of view, we are facing the revival of a national-popular romanticism, against the enlightenment of the era of globalization. The situation seems simple: localism versus universalism, roots versus intermixing, frontiers versus unification, right versus left. This is an understandable reaction given the abstract model of post-1989 globalization marked by the mythology of an unbridled neocapitalism, but, like any reaction, it is unhelpful. *The cure for the "liquid society" cannot be found in a political-religious traditionalism*, but the idea that it can is the illusion that, at the moment, pervades the part of the church that is opposed to the pope. Although the critics purport to embrace Benedict XVI in opposition to Francis, this is a radically different position from Ratzinger's. The cultural model that has always guided the German theologian who became pope is based, in fact, on the dialogue between Christianity and modern Enlightenment, exactly what the theo-populists, starting with Archbishop Viganò, abhor, preferring instead a preconciliar, premodern, fundamentalist church.

> As a religion of the persecuted, and as a universal religion that was wider than any one state or people, [Christianity] denied the government the right to consider religion as part of the order of the state, thus stating the principle of the liberty of faith. It has always defined men—all men without distinction—as creatures of God, made in his image, proclaiming the principle that they are equal in dignity, though of course within the given limits of societal order. In this sense, the Enlightenment has a Christian origin, and it is not by chance that it was born specifically and exclusively within the sphere of the Christian faith, in places where Christianity, contrary to its own nature, had unfortunately become mere tradition and the religion of the state. . . . It was and remains the merit of the Enlightenment to have drawn attention afresh to these original Christian values and to have given reason back its own voice. In its Constitution on the Church in the Modern World, the Second Vatican Council restated this profound harmony between Christianity and the Enlightenment, seeking to achieve a genuine reconciliation between the Church and modernity.[2]

2. Ratzinger, *Christianity and the Crisis of Cultures*, 47–49.

Both Benedict XVI and Francis are sons of the Second Vatican Council, whose call for a profound dialogue between the church and modernity is rejected by the new Catholic right. Such a dialogue takes into account truth and freedom, universal and particular, reason and revelation. These are hallmarks of the teaching documents of Pope Francis, from *Evangelii Gaudium* to *Fratelli Tutti*, which outline his response to the globalization-localism antithesis that has torn apart the political and ecclesial conscience of recent decades.

It is a perspective not unlike that expressed by Joe Biden, the second Catholic president of the United States, in his inaugural address on January 20, 2021. Coming after Trump, Biden does not present himself as the Democrat messiah. He is not even the heir of the Clintons or Obama. He is the elderly heir to the Kennedy season of the 1960s, that of John and his brother Robert. He is an admirer of Martin Luther King, whose bust he displays in the Oval Office. He is a social Catholic whose intellectual formation precedes the embrace of the libertarian progressivism that would come to mark the Democratic Party beginning in the 1970s. It is a mindset that, if maintained, would help to dissolve the divisions with Republicans disappointed by Trump and to weave a fruitful dialogue with the Catholic world.

Certainly the stumbling block of abortion remains, a point about which Biden, beyond his personal convictions, will probably be able to do very little, since in recent years the Democratic Party has moved into increasingly radical positions, including that access to any abortion is a constitutional right. The problem is not a small one, because it constitutes the divisive factor par excellence. As Sandro Magister wrote:

> Kennedy's problem was to assure all citizens that his Catholic faith would never affect his loyalty to America. Biden's is instead to bring back together a nation deeply divided, in which the Catholic Church itself is split in half, at all levels: in the hierarchy, among the faithful, among voters, among those elected to Congress. . . .
>
> Biden is undoubtedly a sincere Catholic. Believing and practicing, at Mass every Sunday. In the painful moments of his life as husband and father, the faith has had a strong and visible bearing on him. And also in his public life, he has never made a secret of drawing inspiration from it. Those who criticize him can only blame him, if anything, for not being consistent with his faith in everything, especially in supporting abortion as a constitutional right.

In the United States, much more than in Europe, Italy, and Rome, this is a "*vexata quaestio.*" It never came up with Kennedy, but since the 1973 ruling of the US Supreme Court that legalized abortion, it has loomed ever larger.

The biggest collision came in 2004, when the Democratic candidate in the presidential election, ultimately defeated by George W. Bush, was John Kerry, also Catholic and "pro-choice." Some bishops took this as grounds for denying him Communion. But the contrary view was held by the president of the United States episcopal conference at the time, Wilton Gregory, and the then-Archbishop of Washington and Cardinal Theodore McCarrick, who was also president of the US bishops' committee on domestic policy.

From Rome, then-prefect of the Congregation for the Doctrine of the Faith Cardinal Joseph Ratzinger sent these two a memo on the "general principles" that would lead to the denial of Communion for Catholic politicians who systematically campaign for abortion.

Gregory and McCarrick kept a lid on the memo from Ratzinger, who in a subsequent letter acknowledged that the principles he had offered still left room for "prudential judgment" on whether or not to give Communion, as also admitted by authoritative "neoconservative" cardinals such as Avery Dulles and Francis George.[3]

According to Magister, "it is likely that room will again be made for 'prudential judgments.'" It is certainly desirable, not only for society but also for the church, which otherwise risks forgetting the wisdom of realism that has always marked its relationship with political power. The demonization of power suggests the sort of "state of exception" that Carl Schmitt proposed justifies putting aside the rule of law for the common good. No government, party, or politician is wholly good or wholly bad. Political-religious Manichaeism is a trap, an ideological deviation that, at present, contaminates the world and the church.

Aware of this problem, Biden demonstrated in his inaugural address the great wisdom that is generally lacking in that segment of American Catholicism dominated by a culture war mentality, which he explicitly

---

3. Sandro Magister, "Biden in the White House: Is It the Moment of Truth for American Catholics?," Settimo Cielo blog, *La Stampa*, January 18, 2021, http://magister.blog autore.espresso.repubblica.it/2021/01/18/biden-in-the-white-house-is-it-the-moment -of-truth-for-american-catholics/. (English corrected slightly.)

repudiated in a speech aimed at mending a deeply torn nation. The inaugural address was characterized not by basking in his victory or criticizing his opponent or the opposing party, but by a plea for unity among an American people divided by opposing ideologies.

> Today, on this January day, my whole soul is in this: Bringing America together. Uniting our people. And uniting our nation. I ask every American to join me in this cause. Uniting to fight the common foes we face: Anger, resentment, hatred. Extremism, lawlessness, violence. Disease, joblessness, hopelessness.
>
> With unity we can do great things. Important things. We can right wrongs. We can put people to work in good jobs. We can teach our children in safe schools. We can overcome this deadly virus. We can reward work, rebuild the middle class and make health care secure for all. We can deliver racial justice.
>
> We can make America, once again, the leading force for good in the world. I know speaking of unity can sound to some like a foolish fantasy. I know the forces that divide us are deep and they are real. But I also know they are not new. Our history has been a constant struggle between the American ideal that we are all created equal and the harsh, ugly reality that racism, nativism, fear and demonization have long torn us apart. The battle is perennial. Victory is never assured.
>
> Through the Civil War, the Great Depression, World War, 9/11, through struggle, sacrifice, and setbacks, our "better angels" have always prevailed. In each of these moments, enough of us came together to carry all of us forward. And, we can do so now. History, faith and reason show the way, the way of unity.
>
> We can see each other not as adversaries but as neighbors.
>
> We can treat each other with dignity and respect. We can join forces, stop the shouting and lower the temperature.
>
> For without unity, there is no peace, only bitterness and fury. No progress, only exhausting outrage. No nation, only a state of chaos. This is our historic moment of crisis and challenge, and unity is the path forward. And, we must meet this moment as the United States of America. If we do that, I guarantee you, we will not fail.
>
> We have never, ever, ever failed in America when we have acted together. And so today, at this time and in this place, let us start afresh. All of us. Let us listen to one another. Hear one another. See one another. Show respect to one another.
>
> Politics need not be a raging fire destroying everything in its path. Every disagreement doesn't have to be a cause for total war.

And, we must reject a culture in which facts themselves are manipulated and even manufactured.

My fellow Americans, we have to be different than this. America has to be better than this. And, I believe America is better than this.[4]

The focus of the address was the overcoming of the political theology that dominated the scene after September 11, 2001, the same one that Francis deplores in *Fratelli Tutti* because of its false polarizations. It is the political theology of Carl Schmitt, with its impermeable friend-enemy dialectic so dear to the political-religious right.[5] Biden's address included a passage from St. Augustine:

> I pledge this to you: I will be a president for all Americans. I will fight as hard for those who did not support me as for those who did.
>
> Many centuries ago, Saint Augustine, a saint of my church, wrote that a people was a multitude defined by the common objects of their love. What are the common objects we love that define us as Americans? I think I know. Opportunity. Security. Liberty. Dignity. Respect. Honor. And, yes, the truth.[6]

The quotation from Augustine, from *The City of God* (book 19, chapter 24)—"A people is an assemblage of reasonable beings bound together by a common agreement as to the objects of their love"—is interesting and certainly unusual in a presidential inauguration speech. Interesting for at least two reasons. The first is that we find the same quote in the message that Cardinal Bergoglio addressed to the educational communities of Buenos Aires on April 27, 2006:

> In our effort to find the dimensions that denote the existence of a people and strengthen the bond that constitutes it, we can recall the definition of Saint Augustine: "A people is the ensemble of rational beings associated in the harmonious communion of the things that they love" (Saint Augustine, *De civitate Dei*, 19, 24). And this "harmonious communion" is being shaped, as we have already pointed out, in common actions (values, sym-

4. "President Biden's Full Inauguration Speech, Annotated," *New York Times*, January 20, 2021, https://www.nytimes.com/2021/01/20/us/politics/biden-inauguration-speech-transcript.html.

5. On the political theology of Carl Schmitt, see Borghesi, *Critica della teologia politica*, 165–202.

6. "President Biden's Full Inauguration Speech, Annotated."

bols, fundamental attitudes in the face of life) which, from generation to generation, are acquiring a special profile proper to the community. But speaking of "harmonious communion" or "common destiny" implies, in addition to a series of customs, the firm will to walk in that direction, without which everything collapses irremediably. It implies a humble and contemplative openness to the mystery of the other, which becomes respect, full acceptance starting not from a mere "tolerant indifference," but from the committed practice of love that affirms and promotes the freedom of every human being and makes it possible to build a lasting and living bond together.[7]

In both cases, in Biden's text as in Bergoglio's, the reference to Augustine serves to confirm a certain image of the people, certainly very different from that fostered by populist ideology, thus revealing a harmony in Catholic sentiment.

The second reason for interest in Biden's Augustinian quotation lies in the fact that Augustine appears in Joseph Ratzinger as the critic of political theology, both the one from the left, personified by Origen, and that from the right, represented by the bishop of Constantine, Eusebius of Caesarea.[8] In this Ratzinger followed Erik Peterson who, in his 1935 anti-Nazi essay "Monotheism as a Political Problem," used the authority of St. Augustine to criticize Carl Schmitt's Christian-imperial theology used to justify the support of German Catholics for the new "savior," Adolf Hitler.[9]

Much Catholic thought today moves between *identification* with the world and utter *opposition* to it, between secularization and Manichaeism. Both approaches forget what constitutes, according to Erich Przywara— an author dear to Bergoglio—the nucleus of "Catholic" thought: the *analogia entis*.[10] It is present in the model of polarity that is at the center

---

7. Jorge Mario Bergoglio, "Siamo un popolo con vocazione di grandezza," April 27, 2006; It. trans. in Jorge Mario Bergoglio–Pope Francis, *Nei tuoi occhi è la mia parola*, 437–38.

8. Joseph Ratzinger, *The Unity of the Nations: A Vision of the Church Fathers*, trans. Boniface Ramsey (Washington, DC: The Catholic University of America Press, 2015).

9. Erik Peterson, "Monotheism as a Political Problem: A Contribution to the History of Political Theology in the Roman Empire," in *Theological Tractates*, trans. Michael J. Hollerich (Stanford, CA: Stanford University Press, 2011).

10. Erich Przywara, *Analogia Entis: Metaphysics: Original Structure and Universal Rhythm*, trans. John R. Betz (Grand Rapids, MI: Eerdmans, 2014).

of the thought of Romano Guardini, a central figure in the pope's intellectual formation. "Analogical" thought rejects both monism and Manichaeism. It allows for reconciliation and unity in difference. It prevents polarizations from turning into "contradictions." If Biden is faithful to what he said in his inaugural address, then it can be hoped that the profound conflict that tears apart contemporary society and history will dissolve. Francis would no longer find in the United States an opponent but a fruitful shore. Otherwise we are facing a missed opportunity, serious in its consequences.

The church must, however, rediscover the Catholic sense of the *complexio oppositorum*, leaving behind the current season of Catholic neo-conservatism and theo-populism. It can thus rediscover its originality, the awareness of its eschatological difference, and at the same time offer a decisive contribution for the care of souls and social justice. As the Italian jurist and scholar Marta Cartabia writes:

> The presence of believers in political life runs along the taut line of a polarity that must remain in suspension. On the one hand, they are called, always, to work to change the world in concrete ways, realistically, patiently, humanely. On the other hand, they must remember that the salvation of the world ultimately does not come from its transformation, from a deified politics. Believers participate in the drama and "beauty of the contradictory nature of the world" that Erich Przywara identifies as Augustine's supreme concept.
>
> A primary contribution that the believer can offer to politics is, paradoxically, precisely to free it from any Schmitt-like political theology, from the irrationality of political myths, and from the salvific claim of worldly things. Politics is not enough in itself, and awareness of this is the first and most radical contribution that the church can make to political life. The absolutization of the politician brings with it a lacerating Manichaeism that damages social coexistence. Not surprisingly, Carl Schmitt's political theology has its pivot in the *amicus-hostis* [friend-enemy] logic. The other is the enemy, the one who hinders the realization of the ultimate project. The identification of an enemy, the opposition to and destruction of all its ideas, and, finally, war are the recurring characteristics in the history of every political movement that becomes absolute, claiming to bring heaven to earth.
>
> The thought of Pope Francis is antithetical. He values the polarities of reality in an open dialectic that does not seek synthesis that ends up eliminating one of the two tension poles, but knows how to welcome that

paradoxical coincidence of opposites and that polyphonic harmony of differences upon which all his thought is nourished. His thought is one of reconciliation. Not "irenic," optimistic, or naively progressive, but, on the contrary, dramatic and in tension. Pope Francis's regard upon reality is nourished by dialectical thought of Catholic origin, based on a polar model that presupposes the idea of the other in the self, in complementarity, not in mutual exclusion.[11]

The world, the church, and the United States are in urgent need of a way of thinking marked by reconciliation. After the neoconservative season, which permeated Catholic consciousness in the period following the fall of Communism, the theo-populist wind monopolized the scene. Its setback may be momentary, or it may be lasting. The forces that support it are not dormant; they are smoldering and ready to reemerge stronger than ever. The causes behind it—social, intellectual, and spiritual—need to be understood and overcome. It is not an easy task, neither for the church nor for any others who seek to oppose it. Society and democracy, as Jürgen Habermas understood well after the tragedy of September 11, need a religious openness that the relativistic ideology that accompanies globalization is unable to offer. And this is not to open up new theaters of war, as the neocons think, or to establish a network of fortress communities, as the populists wish, but to build bridges and heal wounds.

The church does not need enemies in order to live. It inevitably encounters them along its path but always wishes, in its heart, to transform them into friends. The church's purpose is to communicate the gentle, divine humanity of the Redeemer to near and far. Every ideology, every political theology that divides humanity into good and bad, right and left, is a stumbling block. They are barriers that exist and have their own meaning; the church must be able to move beyond them without being conditioned by them. If not, its destiny in the secular world is to conceive of itself as a besieged fortress rather than what it is: a "field hospital" serving the wounded on the battlefield of history.

11. Maria Cartabia, Preface to Francesco Occhetta, *Ricostruiamo la politica: Orientarsi nel tempo dei populismi* (Cinisello Balsama: Edizioni San Paolo, 2019), 13–15.

Index of Names

Ferrara, Pasquale, 215–16
Ferretti, Giovanni Lindo, 118n161
Fessard, Gaston, 29, 245–47
Feuerbach, Ludwig, 26, 240
Figueroa, Marcelo, 13, 14n30, 22–23
Fini, Gianfranco, 120
Fiorito, Miguel Ángel, 245–47
Fontana, Stefano, 150n34
Foucauld, Blessed Charles de, 176, 209
Frachon, Alain, 60n45
Francis, Pope, 1–15, 20–23, 26, 28–35, 37–38, 43n, 44, 58, 117–18, 131–34, 135nn, 136–40, 142–43n20, 143–65, 167–211, 213–21, 225–30, 232–52, 253–57, 260, 262–63
Franco, Massimo, 4, 195–96, 200
Frank, Andre Gunder, 215
Franklin, Benjamin, 76
Friedman, Milton, 72
Fukuyama, Francis, 193

Gagliarducci, Andrea, 203n168
Galeazzi, Giacomo, 140n16
Galeotti, Giulia, 209, 210n183
Galli della Loggia, Ernesto, 110–11, 113, 116, 124, 125–26, 127–28, 148–49, 150n34, 151
Gandhi, Mohandas, 176, 207, 209
Garello, Jacques, 72
Gawronski, Jas, 67
Gayte, Marie, 55n35
Gentile, Emilio, 25, 101n129
George, Francis, 258
George, Robert P., 26
Gera, Lucio, 38, 230
Gerl-Falkovitz, Hanna-Barbara, 30n59
Gerson, Mark, 60n45
Gilder, George, 72

Gilson, Étienne, 21
Gingrich, Newt, 254
Giovagnoli, Agostino, 56, 57n38, 58
Giscard d'Estaing, Valéry, 19
Gisotti, Alessandro, 27n53
Giussani, Luigi, 122, 123n166
Gonnet, Dominique, 83n90
González, Blessed Roque, 207
Gotti Tedeschi, Ettore, 152–53, 175–76, 178
Grassi, Piergiorgio, 83n90
Green, Steven K., 83n90
Gregg, Samuel, 14n30, 158–60
Gregory the Great, Pope St., 18
Gregory, Wilton, 258
Gronbacher, Gregory, 72
Guardini, Romano, 20, 29–32, 159, 165–68, 169n87, 174, 183–84, 233, 262
Guerra López, Rodrigo, 30n60
Guinness, Os, 82n90
Guitton, Jean, 30n59
Gutiérrez, Gustavo, 38, 230

Habermas, Jürgen, 263
Harrington, Michael, 60
Harris, Pamela Beth, 83n90
Hauerwas, Stanley, 101n129
Hayek, Friedrich August von, 61, 72, 93, 125n173, 153n41
Hegel, Georg Wilhelm Friedrich, 42, 54, 58, 207, 214
Heidegger, Martin, 165
Herberg, Will, 86n101
Hitler, Adolf, 122n, 261
Hoeveler, J. David, 45n
Hooker, Thomas, 75
Hooper, J. Leon, 82n90, 83n90
Horkheimer, Max, 172
Hudock, Barry, 29n58, 83n90
Hudson, Deal, 205n173